PRAISE FOR

FROM MALTHUS TO MARS

"A compact, insightful, and practical guide for leaders and managers to flourish in our coming Exponential Age."

—**Azeem Azhar**, founder, Exponential View

"Learning to contribute to—and thrive in—new unfolding futures requires insight, reflection, and determination. Tvede and Nielsen provide these needed insights and a wealth of ideas for readers to reflect upon."

—**Patricia Lustig**, CEO of LASA Insights, board member at Association of Professional Futurists, APF, and author of the award-winning *Strategic Foresight*

"While there are many books on the future, few provide the specificity and clarity as *From Malthus to Mars*. Invaluable reading for those who need to understand what the future is bringing and shape their next steps."

—**Shermon Cruz**, chair, Association of Professional Futurists

"*From Malthus to Mars* deftly blends the essential duality of heart and hand to provide practical tools that preemptively identify trends, surmount challenges, and thrust us forward to an inclusively impactful world."

—**Bing Chen**, CEO and founder, AU Holdings

"I thoroughly enjoyed this book. It is a thought-provoking read about futures that don't yet exist and is a great way to get you out of an incremental mindset and practice adaptability in real life. A must-read for leaders who want to be prepared for and shape the future."

—**Michiel Kruyt**, CEO, IMAGINE and author of *Deliberate Calm*

"This book offers a great tutorial, anchored in observable trends and trajectories, into how to become Future Fit, whether you are an individual or an organisation."

—**Daria Krivonos**, CEO, Copenhagen Institute for Futures Studies

"I see almost daily how leaders grapple with increasing complexity, speed, and personal demands. Navigating this reality requires new awareness and deliberate choices. This book provides an impressive sweep of insights to help you navigate this reality effectively. Highly recommended."

—**Nick Chatrath**, author of *The Threshold: Leading in the Age of AI*

"Ambitious and with an original perspective on supertrends and what they mean for organizations and individuals. This book will spark your curiosity while simultaneously prompting reflections on the role you play in orchestrating the future. Most importantly, it will give you the tools and frameworks you need along the way. Prepare to be inspired."

—**Liselotte Lyngsø**, CEO, Future Navigator

"An essential guide to navigating change and creating more ambitious futures, both personally and professionally. I can highly recommend this book to anyone who recognises the challenges that a rapidly evolving future presents and wants to capitalise on its opportunities."

—**Dr. Graham Norris**, organizational psychologist, futurist, and entrepreneur

"Lars and Nicolai invite readers on a comprehensive prance through the past, present, and future, most importantly coming back to today to offer ways to leverage their many insights and recommendations. It is a delightful read for novices and experienced practitioners alike."

—**Jim Burke**, founder of DeepDive Foresight and former regional president at the World Future Society

FROM MALTHUS TO MARS

How to Live, Lead, and Learn in an Exponential World

NICOLAI CHEN NIELSEN AND LARS TVEDE

FC

FAST COMPANY
Press

Fast Company Press
New York, New York
www.fastcompanypress.com

This work is being published under the Fast Company Press imprint by an exclusive arrangement with Fast Company. Fast Company and the Fast Company logo are registered trademarks of Mansueto Ventures, LLC. The Fast Company Press logo is a wholly owned trademark of Mansueto Ventures, LLC.

Distributed by River Grove Books

Design and composition by Greenleaf Book Group and Mimi Bark
Cover design by Greenleaf Book Group and Mimi Bark
Cover image used under license from ©Shutterstock.com/Phonlamai Photo

Publisher's Cataloging-in-Publication data is available.

Paperback ISBN: 978-1-63908-049-6

Hardcover ISBN: 978-1-63908-051-9

eBook ISBN: 978-1-63908-050-2

Audiobook ISBN: 978-1-63908-052-6

First Edition

CONTENTS

INTRODUCTION

We all understand that as the world changes, we need to change with it. The problem is that the pace of change is constantly increasing, and the risk of making wrong turns or falling behind keeps growing. The good news is that you can adapt to these accelerating changes by becoming *Future Fit*.

Future Fitness is the ability to skillfully and efficiently navigate future trends and take action toward your most desired future. Achieving Future Fitness requires efficiency in how you gather data, having appropriate reference models for interpreting the meaning of what you observe, and developing personal habits and mindsets that can help you navigate turbulence. This book guides you through each of these while providing you with additional tools to make you or your organizations more Future Fit.

We have advised more than 200 organizations on organizational changes, management strategies, and the future, including more than thirty Fortune 500 companies. We have also founded or cofounded thirteen companies. Among our start-ups and knowledge platforms, our future-tracking service Supertrends has been particularly important as a source and inspiration for this book.

Supertrends uses artificial intelligence, crowdsourcing, big data, text mining, advanced data visualization, and digital gamification to spot the world's innovations, track their development, and interpret technology-driven market trends. At the time of writing, Supertrends has mapped over 12,000 key innovations, ranging from the first pre-human use of stone tools some 3.3 million years ago to thousands of predicted breakthroughs over the coming years.

Supertrends has developed a comprehensive system for real-time monitoring of global innovation within any sector or technology, as well as a digital simulation tool for creating business strategies that incorporate the expected changes in future technologies. It focuses on how to navigate, make sense of, strategize, and mobilize across business activities. At the time of writing, the company has some 160 associated partners and specialists, including ourselves, who are all either entrepreneurs, scientists, futurists, leadership coaches, or management consultants from around the world. Throughout this book, these are referred to as "Supertrends experts."

Our goal with Supertrends is to provide futurism-as-a-service, supporting clients in every step of their journey to become Future Fit. The tools we describe in this book are the same that Supertrends uses with its clients. This book includes a number of snapshots from the Supertrends timeline—our crowdsourced attempt to determine when major technology breakthroughs are likely to arrive. It should be noted that these predictions are only qualified guesses, albeit each submitted by some of the world's leading experts working on the relevant technologies. These experts revise their predictions from time to time—especially their assessment of when technology breakthroughs will happen. However, in this book, we also draw on numerous scientific studies and other sources, which can be accessed at www.supertrends.com and www.FromMalthusToMars.com.

So, what are *supertrends* (not the company, but the things)? Generally speaking, supertrends are broad trends that change how societies work in important ways. They can be seen in wealth, health, lifestyles, demographics, and more, but their ultimate underlying causes are predominantly social and technological innovation. Building your Future Fitness hinges first of all on understanding how innovation and the resulting super-trends have unfolded in the past so that you may be better able to predict, take advantage of, and influence how they will unfold in the future.

Part 1 of this book maps a brief history of innovation and super-trends, and it charts their likely trajectories through the next decade and beyond. In part 2, we discuss what this means for you as an individual and offer a number of mental hacks and mindsets to build your Future Fitness. In the third and final part of the book, we use a future-backed approach to outline what these trends mean for organizations and their employees in the future world of work.

Building Future Fitness at an individual and an organizational level is relevant for leaders and non-leaders alike. As the pace of change continues to increase and leadership becomes more and more distributed, it is our responsibility to understand what's going on around us, navigate the trends, and adapt the way we work and live in a deliberate way. We can't slow the pace of change, but we know from theory and practice that it is indeed possible to speed up and clarify our own thinking to get ahead—and stay ahead—of the impending changes.

We encourage you to read this book from cover to cover, as each part builds on the previous one. However, each chapter is also relatively self-contained and provides practical tips and checklists that can be regularly referred back to.

We hope that you will enjoy this book and connect with us on social media.

Lars and Nicolai

Future Fitness is the ability to skillfully and efficiently navigate future trends and take action toward your most desired future.

PART 1

INTO THE BLUR
AT ROCKET SPEED

THE WORLD IS UNDERGOING enormous technological changes that directly impact our lifestyles, business models, cultures, economies, and more. These changes are not just random dots popping up on the map. In fact, they are largely trends that follow somewhat deterministic patterns. This is because each new innovation is a recombination of previous innovations. You can't put a roof on a house before putting up the walls, and you can't put up the walls before you dig the foundation. Likewise, the technology universe inevitably unfolds in a certain sequence. Predicting this pattern is complex, but it is not impossible to get some idea of the likely sequence or to get some sense of the likely timing. This is because many trends follow rather reliable paths, whether they are linear, exponential, or, occasionally, hyper-exponential. The most famous predicted path is probably Moore's law for the performance of computer chips, which has correctly predicted almost sixty years of digital development, but there are countless other regularities, as you will see.

We also find that development in some trends at given inflection points tend to trigger the onset of other events or trends. For instance, increasing wealth makes average people want fewer children, while it also makes them more enthusiastic for environmental protection. Many such phenomena apply around the world and across hundreds of cultures, and some of them are remarkably predictable.

There are also patterns in human perception of these phenomena. One is that many—and perhaps most—people systematically underestimate progress and overestimate threats.

There even seem to be specific preconditions that typically inspire bursts of creativity and innovation. When studying the structure of communities—including nations—we can with some conviction predict how innovative they are likely to become. This is a subject of this first part of the book, and it is, in fact, where our tale will start.

Chapter 1

THE END OF MONOTONY

In 2019, the brilliant quantum physicist David Deutsch gave a fascinating TED Talk about what he calls "the great monotony," wherein he posits that the universe itself is actually quite monotonous.

While some astronomers may take issue with that characterization, his point stands that at the time of the big bang some 13.7 billion years ago, a whole lot of new and exciting things started happening, including the development of atoms, molecules, the first planets, stars, meteors, and galaxies. However, most of that novelty was spent as early as 12 or 13 billion years ago. Indeed, quite a lot of it was completed within the first three minutes of the universe's life span.

Since then, as Deutsch describes it, the universe as we know it has largely delivered billions of years of pretty much the same phenomena: stars, comets, barren globes, black holes, and so on.

Of course, an exploding star is very dramatic, but in almost all places, at almost all times, if you placed a webcam on a given object in space, you would notice nothing interesting for ages. And thus, while the idea of traveling to Mars may seem very exciting, for instance, the reality is that once you arrived on a planet with no people or other forms of organic life, there would be very little to see or do. There is probably a lot more action on one square meter of a forest in Brazil than on the entire surface of Mars.

Celestial bodies are always in relative motion, but this is typically in such monotonous ways that today, one can with reasonable certainty predict their fate millions or even billions of years into the future—and also retro-cast their prehistory millions or billions of years back. Out there, it is indeed largely the "great monotony," as Deutsch calls it. And this monotony is not only about lack of action. So far, we've only detected a few hundred distinct chemicals that exist outside of our planet. By contrast, any single animal on Earth can contain billions of different molecules.

A major reason for the great monotony in space is what Deutsch calls "the hierarchy rule." In the universe, large things are unaffected by small things, but small things may be transformed or destroyed by large things. When a comet hits a star, the star is marginally magnified, and the comet is annihilated. Two different things are molded into one and diversity gives way to monotony.

BREAKING THE HIERARCHY RULE

But, as Deutsch points out, there is actually one remarkable known exception to this rule: Earth. Here, on our lovely planet, the great monotony is broken in billions of ways, from the subtle to the dramatic. You can place webcams or microscopes almost anywhere on Earth and witness constant action, surprises, drama, and so on. This is due to the miracle of DNA, which has enabled millions of different life-forms and billions of different chemical substances.

Therefore, in our biological world, the hierarchy rule does not apply. On the contrary, when two DNA molecules meet in a conception, something *new* always emerges—every single time! For instance, every single child on the planet is unique. Even "identical" twins are quite different. Likewise, in contrast to the hierarchy rule, the small entities, namely DNA, actually control the large ones, which are the rest of the biomass. For example, the DNA in the human body constitutes 0.1

percent of our weight, yet it totally controls the remaining 99.9 percent. This is a gross violation of the hierarchy rule. It is rather the opposite, a rule of spontaneous innovation.

It gets even better, because DNA has created and controlled far more than just the biomass that exists at any given time. Before the origin of life, the sky and seas on Earth were brown and red like Mars. This was until DNA enabled photosynthesis in plants, which then colored much of the land green. Then the plants created oxygen, which colored lakes, seas, and the atmosphere blue. DNA also created shellfish, which in turn created the white limestone of the subsoil.

So, DNA—molecules so small that we need an electron microscope to see them—have completely reshaped the entire planet. So much so in fact that one must dig very deep into the ground to find a handful of soil, clay, sand, or rock that is not clearly affected by DNA. In this way, as Deutsch points out, DNA—those tiny things—have had an overall effect that is 10^{40} times greater than themselves. So, no hierarchy rule here, and no great monotony.

RECURSIVE INTELLIGENCE

Of course, a part of that story is that some 300,000 years ago, DNA created humans and made us the only species with the ability to develop exploratory knowledge (i.e., to interpret and develop hypotheses about the world) and to translate these hypotheses into creative innovation. By granting us this ability, microscopic DNA set in motion an ever-accelerating process of not only spontaneous innovation but also recursive intelligence, the phenomenon in which some form of intelligence creates more intelligence, which then continues in a positive feedback loop to produce cascading innovation. So, in essence, not only did DNA transform the planet, but it also turned Earth into a runaway computer.

Yes, DNA did that. These tiny molecules that we cannot even see. And in this book, we examine how this runaway computer continues to accelerate.

When you break away from the laws of monotony and hierarchy,
you get spontaneous innovation and recursive intelligence.
In fact, you get a runaway, spontaneous computer.

WAKING UP THE UNIVERSE

So DNA created humans with brains, who later developed the ability
to communicate and think critically, rationally, and creatively. This in
turn led to the exchange of new ideas, which were continuously tested
and improved upon. This led to the anything-but-monotonous world
we live in today. And because of our ability to continuously build on
existing knowledge, the future will be even more diverse than it is today.
David Deutsch has posited that we might one day even control the
entire universe, in essence causing it to "wake up" by constantly replacing monotony with innovation. The trajectory of this process from the
past into the future is truly fascinating. But interestingly, it hasn't always
been like that.

Chapter 2

HOW WE ESCAPED THE MALTHUSIAN TRAP

According to the World Bank, the trend growth in global GDP (Gross Domestic Product) per capita grew on average 1.93 percent per year from 1960 to 2020.[1] Add just under 1 percent annual population growth, and we reach an annual trend growth in total GDP of a bit below 3 percent.

Of course, "trend growth" means the long-term, or average, tendency; there are business cycles and random events that create temporary deviations around that trend. Anyway, just under 2 percent annual growth per capita per year adds up. In fact, over a period of ten years, it typically increases the average standard of living on the planet by some 20 percent.

That's a lot. In fact, it's almost insane, if you really think about it. Ten years from now, the world population will probably be 20 percent more affluent! And if you compound that for a hundred years, GDP per capita—adjusted for inflation—will be six to seven times higher, which means a whole different world. Just think of all your own friends and family and imagine that they all earned—and owned—approximately six times as much as they own now, starting next Monday. That's the world we'll live in a hundred years from now.

BLUR STRAIGHT AHEAD

So yes, we are jointly racing into a future that will be vastly different, and if that future is blurry—well, that won't slow us down at all. We will get to that blur no matter what, at a blistering speed, like a Formula One car blasting into heavy fog.

And that is mentally difficult to cope with. You've likely already lived through massive changes during your time on planet Earth. If you were to take someone from 2010 and send them just ten years into the future, they would be completely shocked at the massive penetration of smartphones, AI-assisted voice assistants, cryptocurrencies, RNA vaccines, and the emergence of remote work cultures, ride-sharing vehicles in large cities, and more. It's easy to forget how things we now take for granted didn't exist until quite recently—such as GPS, the internet, and PCs. Equally, it can be hard to imagine a potential future that doesn't yet exist. But to become Future Fit, we must cultivate this ability to understand the trends and capitalize on them.

The key cause of the future's blurriness is innovation. Whenever an innovation is launched, we now quickly expect it to improve and continually get ever better. For example, Wi-Fi on planes was for the majority of aviation history unheard of. However, the moment it was launched (albeit with slow speeds), passengers quickly went from awe to frustration and demanded more speed, better ease of use, and greater reliability. Oh yes, we are spoiled. We demand better, faster, and cheaper all the time. This is the development we are used to, and it is likely to continue.

The other message is that the limits to what is possible are extremely generous. Just think of a butterfly. It starts as an egg, then mysteriously transmutes into a caterpillar larva. Then a pupa. Then a butterfly. Then it flies around. Then it makes perfect copies of itself.

You and I might not understand the science of how that's possible, but it is, and so is precise, satellite-guided navigation. And so is anesthesia, whereby you can cut into a living human without them feeling a thing. And so is sending a message from London to France to China in a split second. The things we can do now already seem like magic, and the things waiting for us out there in the blur will seem even more so. Nature—including our butterfly—is amazing, but so are the things we create.

THE GREAT DIVERGENCE

When it comes to human innovation, we haven't always been so impressive. In fact, for large parts of history we did *not* have crazy, accelerating supertrends. Indeed, compared to today's frantic rate of change, innovation once moved really slowly, if at all.

In those days, lots of people experienced zero innovation throughout their entire lifetime. In fact, for approximately *99.8 percent* of human history, we had no visible innovation and thus no corresponding trend growth in GDP per capita. Instead, people lived in what is now called a **Malthusian economy** (i.e., one in which there was minimal innovation and thus minimal economic growth). And as economies did occasionally grow a little, the result was more people, but not more income per person. In 1798, the pessimistic priest Thomas Malthus, whose name inspired the term Malthusian economy, predicted that the growth of human population would be exponential, whereas growth of food production would be linear. Mass starvation lay ahead, he concluded.

However, just the opposite happened. In his book, *A Farewell to Alms*, economics professor Gregory Clark illustrates it with this graph of what he called "The Malthusian Trap" and the subsequent Great Divergence:[2]

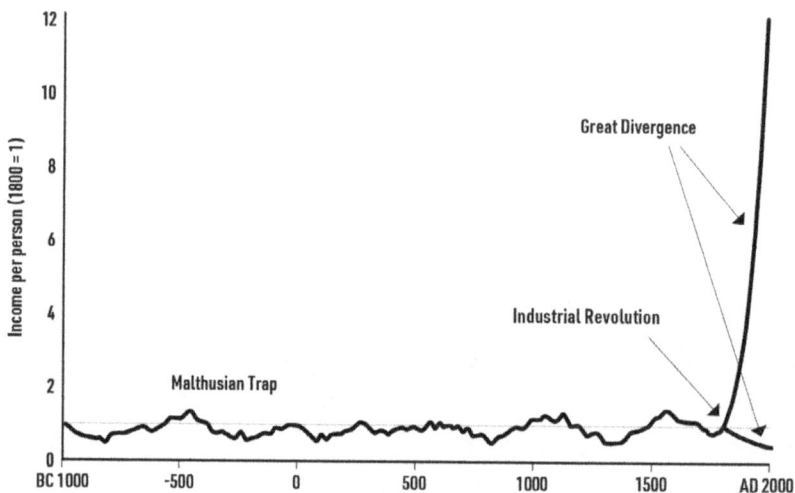

Figure 2.1. How we escaped the Malthusian Trap.

As can be seen, the world's average standard of living remained broadly unchanged for 3,000 years. But then something wild happened: a part of the world's population suddenly experienced exponential growth in living standards, whereas another part (primarily sub-Saharan Africa) experienced declining living standards. That was the Great Divergence.

So why did this happen? The explosively rising standard of living in some parts of the world happened due to innovation. Declining living standards in other parts were due to continued population growth (aided by new access to modern medical care), without corresponding increases in productivity. Fortunately, today only about 15 percent of the world's population seem to be trapped in stagnating or declining communities.

NINE STEPS TOWARD PROSPERITY

We posit that an important corner of the world left the Malthusian Trap around the year 1450—that is, around 570 years before we wrote this book. Since 1450, the world has changed more drastically than during the preceding approximately 300,000-year-long history of *Homo sapiens*. By the way, exactly the same can arguably be said about the world since the year 1800, or perhaps even for the last four decades.

Of course, this raises a question. Our species is some 300,000 years old. So why did all this stuff only begin around 570 years ago? After all, the last 670 years constitute only around 0.2 percent of human history. Why was 99.8 percent of human history spent in the Malthusian Trap? And what got us out of it?

In our opinion, what caused the escape from the Malthusian Trap was primarily events that first took place in a small part of Western Europe and then spread across much of the globe. We can describe this with nine new phenomena:

1. *The Renaissance* (ca. 1200–1600), which promoted artistic expression, humanism, individualism, empirical experimentation, and creativity.

2. *The Age of Discovery* (ca. 1500–1800), involving the European explorations and ultimately the (if partly temporary) European colonization of most of the globe.

3. *The Reformation* (ca. 1520–1650), where the traditionally individualistic Northern Europeans rejected the perceived over-institutionalization of the Catholic Church and replaced it with a more individualistic and decentralized interpretation of religion. This also emphasized literary skills and personal achievement over collective obedience.

4. *The Scientific Revolution* (ca. 1540–), which replaced mysticism with exact, testable knowledge, and which formed the basis for the later Industrial Revolution. It also united people, because whereas people may fight religious wars, they don't fight wars about alternative laws of math, and so on. Testable truth is a peacemaker.

5. *The Enlightenment* (ca. 1600–1800), which placed the ideals of freedom, democracy, science, religious tolerance, the rule of law, division of power, rationality, and common sense as primary values of society.

6. *The Industrial Revolution* (ca. 1750–), in which technical ingenuity brought mass-production and chemical processing, and which led in part to a wealth explosion and in part to mass urbanization and cultural upheavals.

7. *Female Liberation* (ca. 1840–), where women gained access to education and political influence, which greatly increased overall creative output.

8. *The Precision Economy* (ca. 1980–), which was largely driven by IT-led computation capabilities that in many ways far outpace the human mind, as well as the mass digitization of previously non-digital mediums (e.g., audio, images, text). Furthermore, as the internet became available to the public, the quantity of information anyone with a connection could access multiplied by many orders of magnitude. The power of digital products included the fact that they could be replicated at close to zero cost and moved anywhere at the speed of light. Also, following the sequencing of the DNA, the coding of life in its finest details became feasible. DNA is now digitized and increasingly programmable, like a machine.

9. *The Social Networking Revolution* (ca. 2000–), where people, building on the internet, organized into countless social online networks, and anonymous, non-credentialist crowds (i.e., people not formally approved in the form of specific education or union membership) began to collaborate on countless creative tasks.

BUT *WHY*, SHERLOCK?

This explains what happened, but not why. To get toward why, please look at the following graph. It shows the history of human innovation as far back as we can put a person's name to an accomplishment. And it goes forward until the chosen cut-off year of 1950.

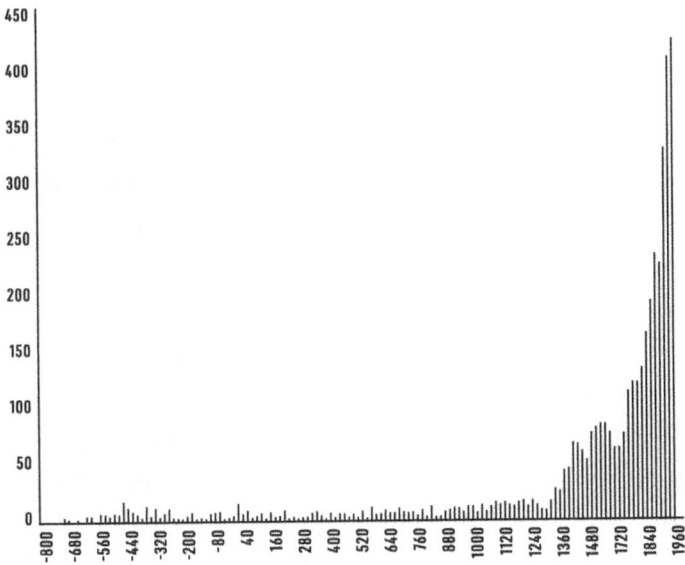

Figure 2.2. Human accomplishment from 800 BC to 1950 AD.

This remarkable graph was created from work done by the American Enterprise Institute (AEI), which used quantitative history tools to study human accomplishment spanning the 2,750 years from 800 BC to 1950 AD.[3] The study's objective was to identify all cases in history where a named person had made a creative innovation in art, science, or technology that was so important that it was quoted in at least half of the leading modern reference books worldwide.

The project took five years to complete and involved fifty people. And it was a huge nerd job that involved poring over 163 modern

sources of human accomplishment (such as encyclopedias) and metic-
ulously recording 1) what each accomplishment was about, 2) the
creative people mentioned, 3) how much print space was allocated to
each of them, 4) when they did what was described, and 5) where they
lived when they did it. So, it was a mapping of the who, what, when,
and where of human accomplishment. This resulted in a list of 4,002
names of prominent philosophers, mathematicians, musicians, poets,
astronomers, physicists, biologists, technological inventors, and so on
who qualified as particularly significant, plus, a corresponding list of
their accomplishments.

As we can see from the graph, the global number of new accomplishments was low and trendless until around the year 1000, where
it started to pick up a bit, but without accelerating any more. Further
examination of the data shows that the accomplishments were not only
trendless, but also scattered around geographically so that bursts of creativity would appear at different spots of the globe, but in each case
only temporarily. Each time, spontaneous innovation would flame up,
then die. And although the accumulated human knowledge and abilities overall increased slightly over the first approximately 300 years on
the graph, there were long, intermittent periods without any accelera-
tion or even with temporary *declines* in global accomplishment. Indeed,
many decades showed *no* recorded innovation at all! Like zero. Which
makes us think of David Deutch's great monotony.

But then—from approximately 1450 onward—global creativity
virtually exploded. If we want to understand why this happened, we
could start by looking at *where* it happened. The AEI study showed that
initially, it happened almost entirely in Western Europe, and as people
from Western Europe later started populating other parts of the world,
such as the US, Canada, Australia, New Zealand, Hong Kong, and so
on, they brought their innovative culture with them. And this time, the
flame didn't die.

Some of the details of the statistics are amazing. For instance, the
study showed that from 800 BC until 1950, no less than 97 percent of

all attributed human accomplishment was created within the territories of the Western civilization. Different indicators that track global innovation or accomplishment after 1950, such as Global Innovation Index, continue to show a very strong Western dominance; although, particularly since the 1980s, the Asian nations China, Japan, and South Korea have been rapidly catching up and, in some areas, taken the lead. Similarly, innovation in India and Israel are on the rise. Indeed, on a per-capita basis, Israel is now among global leaders.

WHY WESTERN EUROPE?

In any case, we must ask the question why the creative explosion originated in Western Europe. Again, we can learn something by looking at where in Western Europe most creativity took place. It largely happened in a corridor that is now sometimes referred to as the *Blue Banana*.

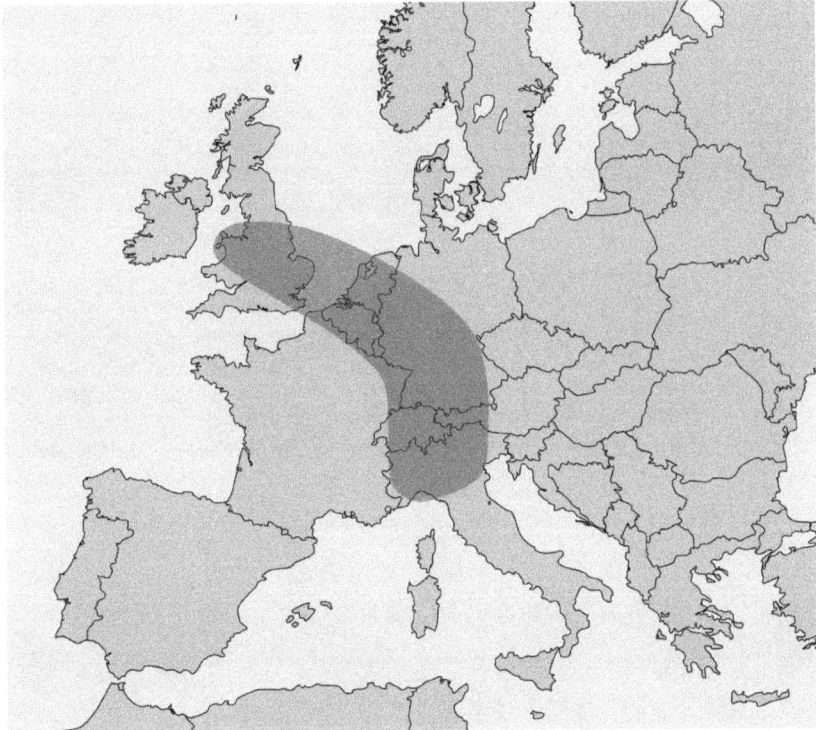

Figure 2.3. The Blue Banana.

The Blue Banana includes modern-day cities such as Milan, Zurich, Munich, Brussels, Amsterdam, and London. Sometimes, when people discuss the Blue Banana, they also include Paris, Florence, and Prague. In either case, this banana has been pointed out as a European area that has particularly high population density. The obvious reason for this is that, on average, this area has offered more prosperity to its citizens than most other parts of the planet, including most other parts of Europe. The Blue Banana is prosperous.

Two of the key reasons the Blue Banana grew in prosperity were the dissemination of knowledge and creativity. Just take a look at Figure 2.4, which shows the location of printing towns in Europe during the fifteenth century, which was when book printing began in Europe:[4]

Figure 2.4. Fifteenth-century printing towns.

Of course, this pattern is not entirely consistent with the Blue Banana, but you definitely see some overlap. And if you check a modern photo of Europe from space, you see a rather similar pattern. The Blue Banana shines at night.

Figure 2.5. Nighttime photo of Europe that illustrates the Blue Banana.

Now here is another map where the overlap with the Blue Banana is more striking. This map shows what AEI's study called Europe's *creative core*: an area where approximately half of all European innovation (or accomplishment) took place, according to its quantitative history mapping.

Figure 2.6. Europe's creative core.

Just to put these results in perspective, this creative core constitutes only 0.01 percent of the global landmass, and it was home to only approximately 1 percent of the global population.

That's actually mind-boggling: over a period of 2,750 years, 1 percent of the global population living on 0.1 percent of the landmass performed approximately half of all attributed accomplishment or innovation! Furthermore, for a long period, almost all the rest of the global innovation was done within the rest of Western Europe, which constituted just 1 percent of the global landmass. This also means that the remaining 99 percent of the global population only did 2.5 percent of its innovation. So to understand the escape from the Malthusian economy and the explosion in spontaneous innovation, we must focus on what happened in this corner of the world leading up to and following the year 1450.

DISINTERMEDIATION THROUGH 10X+ INNOVATION

One event that triggered the innovation boom in Europe's creative core was the introduction of printing. This technology had actually first been developed in China and Korea, but there, the technical advantage derived from it was limited, since their thousands of different characters made it extremely cumbersome to print. So, it didn't really fly there. In contrast, when Gutenberg in 1439 launched movable-type printing in Germany, it quickly took off, mainly because Europeans had far fewer characters, which made their written languages much closer to being digital.

Right from the start, Gutenberg's printing press was what we now call a *10x technology*, which means it solves a problem approximately ten times better than what it replaces. Before Gutenberg, the price for a handwritten Bible was approximately 300 florins. However, in 1454, Gutenberg could sell them for thirty florins each, meaning a 10x improvement. Moreover, just twenty-nine years after that—and forty-four years after the invention of printing technology—Ripoli Press could make books at 1/500 the cost charged by a scribe.[5] This meant that book printing was not only a 10x technology but also had within forty-four years become a 500x technology, equal to a doubling of the cost efficiency roughly every five and half years.

When technologies do 10x leaps (not to mention 500x leaps), it often makes them available for the many instead of the few. In this case, European book production went from 2.8 million copies in the fourteenth century to one billion in the eighteenth century—an increase of approximately 360x.[6]

This empowered people so that they became less dependent on others—the printing press empowered people to obtain information without relying on the church or state for it. In marketing terms, this was perhaps the world's most important case of *disintermediation* (i.e., cutting out the middleman). Ten-times technologies often enable this.

And it was a brilliant example of a third typical consequence of 10x+ technologies, which is that they often change market dynamics from *supplier push* (i.e., proactively pushing products to customers) toward *client pull* (i.e., enabling individual customer activity to automatically determine what is proposed or offered to that specific customer). While before printing, priests and kings pushed information to the people, after the innovation, the people increasingly decided for themselves which books and pamphlets to read. Information thus got weaponized and was used by the people against the centers of power. By the way, a similar phenomenon occurred with the internet where the push models of newspaper, broadcast TV, and radio increasingly got replaced by pull models on the web.

10x+ technologies tend to promote disintermediation, unbundling, and a shift from push to pull dynamics in the markets.

10x+ technologies, such as printing and later the internet, also tend to have widespread cascading consequences—on other technologies, on lifestyles, and on human organizations. In Europe, one of the organizational effects of printing was the emergence of the Protestant faith. This movement began in 1517 in the Blue Banana location of Wittenberg, Kurfürstentum Sachsen (part of present-day Germany). Here, the priest and theologian Martin Luther nailed a document listing ninety-five theses to All Saints' Church.

At that time, the Catholic Church was a major landowner in many nations and had massive income from this and many other sources, including selling indulgences whereby the faithful could allegedly reduce time spent by themselves or their relatives in purgatory. Luther and his Protestants rebelled against this and more. The Protestants' belief was that people should not find their way to God via priests but should instead read the Bible themselves, take responsibility for developing their own moral character, and each find their own journey to salvation. This *decentralized* approach led to a splintering of the Protestant faith into hundreds of branches, whereas Catholicism remained a monolith.

Meanwhile, the printing press also promoted scientific exploration, where sweeping explanations based on faith and imagination were replaced by reductionist thinking. Every question was broken down to multiple sub-questions, on and on in almost perpetual cascades, and each of these—if at all possible—were tested. And we are still at this, now using devices such as the Large Hadron Collider and electronic microscopes to comprehend the smallest of the small.

An intriguing consequence of this development was initially that far more people learned to read. Numerous subsequent studies have shown that far higher literacy developed within Protestant areas than within those that remained Catholic. In addition to this, over time Protestants developed a predominant mentality that was quite unique. In his book *The WEIRDest People in the World*, Harvard anthropologist Joseph Henrich points out various peculiarities among people he calls WEIRD (i.e., Western, Educated, Industrialized, Rich, and Democratic).[7] For instance, WEIRD people who were Westerners, but mainly those who were Protestant or of Protestant origin, tended to focus on personal attributes and intentions, whereas others would focus more on relationships and situations. This has been illustrated by experiments where people from different cultures are asked to complete the following sentence in ten different ways:

I am _____.

WEIRD people would almost always list personal traits such as *creative, curious,* or *impatient,* whereas non-WEIRD people tended to identify themselves through their relationships with other people (i.e., as someone's daughter, someone's mother, etc.). In other words, non-WEIRD people (and thus non-Western people) viewed themselves as more tribal and would be very loyal to their own kin but distrustful of outsiders. WEIRD people, on the other hand, were more trusting of everyone, and because of this were better at forming functioning societies across tribal distinctions. In other words, the WEIRDos were better at creating extended and/or flexible social networks. And when they did join smaller clans, it was on a very flexible basis and would involve *shifting* social groups such as trade groups, expat groups, political parties, and so on. This brings us to a crucial phenomenon called hyper-sociality.

THE EXPLOSION OF HYPER-SOCIALITY

Nature shows that the most efficient way to compete with other species is to develop cooperation, ideally in the form of **hyper-sociality**. In biological ecosystems, hyper-social species tend to do better than less social ones. Apart from earthworms, the now hyper-social humans and their domesticated animals have by far the biggest biomass on Earth today, followed by the hyper-social ants and termites.

> **Hyper-sociality is the ability to cooperate on a vast scale and constitutes one of the most powerful competitive advantages. It is a major stimulant of creativity.**

An effect of hyper-sociality is to create virtual brains. For instance, when a large group of ants are cooperating on a task, they act as if they were a single organism with a single mind. An hour later, each of these ants might be cooperating with a different group of ants tackling different tasks, and they may thus be part of different virtual brains.

What set the Blue Banana apart was largely an explosion in such hyper-sociality. Before this, for example, traditional Catholic religion had been sufficiently powerful to enforce a set of fixed ideas—enforcing Deutsch's hierarchy rule and great monotony. However, from around 1450, we saw more and more advanced sociality—and then hyper-sociality.

However, from the moment of the explosion in the creative core, more and more sociality—and then hyper-sociality—began replacing this hierarchy and monotony. Just think of the nine steps toward prosperity. A major combined effect of the Renaissance, Enlightenment, Age of Discovery, Reformation, Scientific Revolution, and Industrial

Revolution was to set people free to experiment and discover. Now we had more and more individualism, empirical experimentation, scientific endeavor, long-distance travel, and so on, which all involved hyper-sociality. There was also ever more division of labor, which involved trade and combinations of skills, which, again, are hyper-social activities.

Overall, within this exploding hyper-sociality, we had more and more ever-shifting formations of virtual brains—ever-shifting constellations of people cooperating to exchange products, services, and ideas.

Hyper-sociality is a key component of successful, Future Fit individuals and organizations today.

Chapter 3

THE BANANA AND THE FIVE CS OF INNOVATION

In chapter 2, we describe some of the elements that resulted in the Blue Banana. We now go one step deeper and investigate why it happened *in that particular place and time*, what that can teach us about creativity, innovation, and progress, and how it can inspire the way we live our lives and run our organizations.

Let's start with a map of two nations that share almost everything except political and thus economic models: North and South Korea. An often-used example of the contrast between these models is what they look like from space. When you see these two nations from space at night, the communist North, which is a highly centralized society, has hardly any visible light, whereas the South, which has a market economy with millions of competing enterprises, is brimming with light.

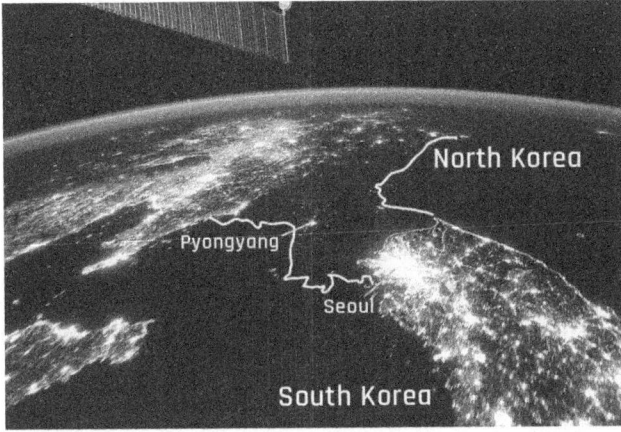

Figure 3.1. Night satellite image of North and South Korea showing the extreme difference in light intensity.

It illustrates what can be seen in many other places on Earth (although never quite as striking): you can have two regions, two companies, two people, or two nations right next to each other, where in each case, one is highly creative while the other is not. The difference is in their mindset and organization. To put it simply, we find that five critical elements need to be in place to enable moves from stagnation to innovation. We call these the Five Cs of Innovation:

- Compact units

- Cooperative networks

- Common codes

- Change agents

- Competition

COMPACT UNITS

Let us start with the units: small, or compact, units are best at dreaming up new ideas, and the smaller the average unit in a network is—and the more of them there are—the more creativity the system generates. Imagine, for instance, that you ask a hundred people in a room to come up with ideas to solve a specific problem. A very efficient way to do this would be to divide them into small teams of two or three to work on the problem independently, then have them take turns presenting their solutions to the assembly so everyone could vote for the best proposals, and then repeat this multiple times. If you have ever had an open logo competition on 99designs, an online graphic design service that supports crowdsourced design, this is pretty much how it works, and it is incredibly efficient. First, you post a brief. Then a lot of designers submit designs. Then you rate each of these, and you can choose to allow the designers to see your responses so they can each go back to the drawing board and submit new and improved designs. This is repeated several times. We can call this the Creative Loop.

DESIGNING HUMANS, ONE LOOP AT A TIME

The efficiency of the Creative Loop is in our opinion universal. In fact, in 2014, paleoanthropologist Ian Tattersall of the American Museum of Natural History proposed a compelling theory that could explain how *humans* could have evolved genetically through a similar process.[1] It goes like this:

- Prehumans lived in Africa, where the climate in many areas alternated between humid jungle and dry savanna.

- These cycles meant that the prehumans oscillated between thriving in the fertile jungle and struggling in the somewhat barren savanna, where they could also easily be spotted by predators.

- Whenever they went through a struggle-on-the-savanna phase, their population declined drastically, which led to *compact units* that necessitated inbreeding and thus accelerated genetic mutation, which of course is a form of genetic creativity. In other words, inbreeding became a *change agent*.

- However, whenever jungles returned, local populations grew and reconnected, resulting in a *competitive battle* of the genes, with the best ones winning. This oscillating pattern of separation versus competition brought rapid genetic change pruned by survival of the fittest—in other words, a pulsating Creative Loop.

This twist adds a dimension to our concepts of sociality and hyper-sociality, which is that they are most efficient when superimposed over an *oscillating* Creative Loop, which we can also call pulsating hyper-sociality.

The Creative Loop is a cyclical process within a social system where creative units are first separated to invent and then confronted to compete and/or cooperate, after which the process is repeated. This can be called pulsating hyper-sociality.

In a compact unit, *insight, decision power*, and *consequence* are closely connected. This means that in such small units, you have the *power* to decide based on your own personal *insight*, and you will quickly feel the *consequences* of your own decisions, whether good or bad. That phenomenon tends to create very fast learning cycles: the compact unit will "fail fast-forward," as entrepreneurs might put it today. Future Fitness for individuals and organizations requires enough insight, decision power, and consequences to be repeated on a continuous basis, with both leaning into the system to shape it and stepping out to maintain creativity.

Fail fast-forward processes work best in small units where insight, decision power, and consequence are closely connected—and where the learning cycle is thus fastest and most precise.

On the other hand, in highly centralized systems, the power to make decisions is often far separated from the insight that should inform those decisions—and it is equally often remote from the consequences of those decisions. For this reason, large and centralized social systems often exhibit far less useful innovation—and are far more likely to head persistently in wrong directions for years if not decades or longer. Think North Korea.

COOPERATIVE NETWORKS

In this era of social media, we hopefully all grasp the enormous power of cooperative networks, but these advantages are also present in other aspects of life—and they were crucial long before the internet. For instance, if we go to Figure 2.4 of printing towns in Europe, we see that these are largely placed along shores of rivers. Why? Because rivers enabled trade.

Trades are what you call win-win transactions, meaning transactions where *both parties gain*. Because they are mutually beneficial, win-win transactions are typically voluntary. And because they are thus both beneficial and voluntary, there is a natural tendency for them to grow in numbers, when at all possible. Often explosively.

Networks can enable movement of people and exchanges of goods, services, and ideas, thereby increasing everyone's ability to see new combinations that can lead to new innovation and new social alliances. This can stimulate hyper-sociality, which is where there is very extensive cooperation between individuals. The biologist Robert Wright has described very well how evolution can be viewed as a gigantic multiplayer game, where the winners overwhelmingly are those who are best at facilitating cooperation (i.e., facilitating win-win transactions). In other words, in this global game, we experience cooperation under competition. The most efficient way to compete is to be good at forming alliances.

To this day, there is still a completely disproportionate concentration of wealth along traditional trade routes throughout the world because that is where you can make the most win-win transactions and thus become hyper-social. Indeed, most of the great, affluent cities around the world are still located along coastlines or rivers because they are nodes of hyper-sociality. And if they're not located along a coastline or river, then they're at least close to a major airport.

Indeed, the power of networks is so strong that it might explain why *Homo sapiens* managed to overcome the Neanderthals in Europe. Neanderthals were physically much better adapted to the cold North, but they didn't trade, whereas *Homo sapiens* did. It seems likely that, since *Homo sapiens* were traders and thus almost certainly better at cooperation under competition, they were much better than Neanderthals at organizing larger armies to attack and eliminate smaller groups of Neanderthals one at a time. The hyper-social won. Again.

This theory aligns with a phenomenon we have seen ever since, which is that *the civilizations that traded most were most successful.* It is even replicated at the individual level: people who excel at sales, marketing, and financial trading are often better off financially than people who excel at production. And companies that facilitate hyper-sociality well have often performed spectacularly. Excelling in voluntary cooperation really pays off.

> In general, those who are best at cooperation do better
> than those who are best at competition. And those who
> perform pulsating hyper-sociality perform best.

COMMON CODES

When people trade and innovate, for many reasons they need standardized and common codes, and this is our third C—Common Codes.

One of the most useful common codes is money: it is far easier to trade if there is a mutually acknowledged medium of exchange. Another useful common code is generally accepted units of weight and volume. For instance, the Roman Empire had its amphora as a uniform size across a vast area. In modern days, we have standardized shipping containers, as well as kilos, liters, gallons, miles, and so on. And as Russia found out when the European Union and NATO in 2022 implemented sanctions that included hindering Russian access to SWIFT (a secure messaging system for international transactions used by more than 200 countries), having a common system for transferring money is essential.

You also need common codes as means of recording results of successful experiments or diligent work. Only if such means exists can you gain from and/or communicate what you have discovered to others so that the success can be replicated, pledged, traded, and rewarded. Property deeds, patents, copyrights, literature, trademarks, accounting systems, measuring units, and more serve these purposes. For example, if you spend money on a logo competition on 99designs, you might want to trademark the result so that your fine logo will not be copied by others.

Another set of common codes are the rules in sports. For instance, football would make no sense unless the players agreed on the rules. It is for a parallel reason that we in modern societies take great effort to make technical trade standards, trade agreements, standard contracts, and so on. Measuring and transportation standards such as the metric system, the shipping container, and internet packages are also hugely helpful. Level the playing field, define the rules, and then let the game begin! In societies where people trade a lot, we often see development of great skills at making such codes for recording, communicating, and protecting the fruits of our labor.

CHANGE AGENTS

Progress requires spontaneous change, even if some of this is negative. We've already seen how *hominins* (i.e., humans' lineal ancestors) probably evolved because of oscillating climate change—so in this case, the climate seems to have been a useful change agent for their periods of inbreeding, which again modified their gene pool. In modern societies, individuals are becoming increasingly powerful.

In isolated communities, or in countries with censorship and severe travel restrictions (think North Korea again), there are fewer change agents, which is why such communities tend to stagnate or collapse. On the other hand, in open societies with free media, free trade, and free social interaction, ideas and change agents tend to flourish, and wealth tends to grow.

So, in summary, the constant flow of people, goods, services, ideas, data, and more provoke and facilitate constant change. However, as Charles Darwin famously pointed out, there is one more thing needed: competition.

COMPETITION

Obviously, competition will usually prevent bad ideas from spreading, whereas the good ones will multiply and be constantly improved upon—like what happens when we rate designs on 99designs for all to see. The same goes for organizations, which, in an era of employee ratings and high occupational mobility, tend to have shorter life spans than ever before.

One important reason competition is essential in a social system is that most ideas are bad. As an example, most genetic change caused by prehuman inbreeding on the savanna must surely have been bad. Nevertheless, in the long run, it was the far rarer *beneficial* mutations that won out. Because of competition.

Experience shows with overwhelming clarity that competition is an essential driver of innovation, and that extreme competition often drives extreme innovation. For instance, major wars are extreme competitions that often trigger extreme bursts of innovation. And the COVID-19 crisis, which was basically a competition between the human species and a virus, led to rapid innovation, both in terms of the RNA vaccines and in viral mutations.

The mirror image of this is that systems with no competition often stagnate or decay completely. This issue is particularly relevant to monopolies such as those that often exist in public sectors. Indeed, studies by McKinsey have shown globally, in the long run and on average, public sectors have approximately zero productivity growth over time.[2] The reason we still achieve around 2 percent overall GDP growth per capita is that productivity grows more than 2 percent annually in the private sector.

BIRTH OF THE BANANA

So those were the Five Cs of Innovation. As we shall see, it was the simultaneous presence of these that made the Blue Banana take off.

The explanation must start with the Roman Empire and what happened when it collapsed. First, the Roman Empire was not particularly creative. Unlike, for instance, the tiny Greek civilization that came before it, the Roman Empire did not invent much, although they ruled up to one-third of the global population for around 1,000 years. Instead, they were able to successfully scale what was already invented by others before them—largely the Greek civilization of antiquity. The Romans were also great at creating infrastructure that facilitated trade. But what they created was in fact the first Renaissance period, since they largely built on ideas previously created in the Greek city-states (which would make what we now call *the Renaissance* the second of its kind).

Yes, the mighty Greeks! So, in terms of creativity, what did these Greeks of antiquity have that the Romans did not? The main answer is multiple compact units. During the period when the classical Greek civilization was most creative, it was not a nation. Instead, it was a loose alliance of between 700 and 1,000 city-states, most of which were tiny. These city-states simultaneously collaborated and competed in rapidly shifting patterns. However, while they competed and sometimes went to war, they also shared a common language, common weight and volume measures, common currency, easy access to sea travel, and much more. In other words, the Five Cs of Innovation were very much present during the Greek city-state period. And they had pulsating hyper-sociality. And thus, spontaneous innovation!

The Greek civilization lost most of its creativity after it became consolidated into an empire by Alexander the Great from 335 BC, but its ideas were revived by the Italian city-state called Rome. Rome then grew into another empire, which was at first quite decentralized but then became ever more centralized. However, the Western Roman Empire fell in 476, weighed down by excessive military expenditures, over-taxation, declining morale, and numerous other problems. Afterward, Western Europe disintegrated into a very large number of states—most of them tiny city-states, similar to what was seen in the previous Greek period of hyper-creativity. In fact, at one point after the fall of Rome, Western Europe contained approximately 5,000 states similar in size to Andorra, Liechtenstein, Luxembourg, Malta, Monaco, San Marino, Vatican City, and the rather autonomous Swiss cantons, which are peculiar remainders from that period.

This triggered a boom in creativity, and interestingly, that boom happened predominantly in the Blue Banana representing just 10 percent of Western Europe. This small but hyper-creative area of Western Europe was distinguished from the rest by having a pattern of numerous small city-states for around 500 years longer than the rest of Europe. To us, it seems extremely likely that this area became so rich because of what happened in its long experience of extreme decentralization.

Make no mistake, whereas many today will think of the medieval age as rather horrible, fewer might know just how much innovation this period exhibited, and the reason was that the Five Cs of Innovation had returned to much of the continent. Not only did Europe now—apart from the role of the Catholic Church—have a highly decentralized political structure, but it also had excellent roads and ports built by the Romans, a common written language (Latin), common weight and measurement units, and a common calendar. Furthermore, due to its city-state period, it had intense competition and cooperation between city-states and companies.

The effects were overwhelming. For instance, by 1900, people of Western European descent controlled approximately 85 percent of all the world's landmass and economy while also ruling the global seas almost unchallenged. All because of innovation. Which was because of a presence of all the Five Cs of Innovation. Which again—in our opinion—was triggered by decentralization.

On this note, it should be mentioned that today, smaller states tend to do better than the bigger ones. In 2014, Credit Suisse demonstrated this by comparing smaller nations (those with fewer than 10 million inhabitants) to the rest, and they found that the small ones on average scored considerably higher on the Human Development Index and Country Strength Indicator.[3] Not only that, but also small nations, such as Croatia, Lithuania, and Kazakhstan, which had emerged from the carving up of larger ones, had on average subsequently improved their relative performance.

THE INITIAL SPARK AND THE ECOSYSTEM

There is a caveat to all of this. Barns made of dry wood and full of dry hay have the potential to burn rapidly, and yet, almost all the time, they're not actually on fire. This is because it takes an initial spark—a strike of lightning, for instance—to get it going, and this doesn't happen often.

The same can be said about any social system where the Five Cs of Innovation are clearly present—someone needs to start the process and thus provide the inspiration for others. This is why we so often see clusters of rather specific creative competence in specific areas. For instance, within the Blue Banana, we have a superyacht builder cluster on the northwestern Italian coast (mainly from La Spezia to Livorno), a supercar cluster in Modena, a fashion cluster in Milano, a watchmaking cluster in Biel, a blockchain/crypto cluster in Zug/Zurich, a pharma cluster in Basel, a car-making cluster in Munich, and so on. These clusters have evolved because there is so-called path dependency in innovation—what has been developed previously in an area has a very strong influence on what is likely to be developed in the future within the same area.

The reverse is also true. When the public turned against nuclear power in many countries, the technology got prevented from mass production that could have driven prices aggressively down and quality progressively up. Later on, the fact that the cost was too high was then used as an argument against nuclear power by the same people.

There is path dependency in innovation. What an area did well in the past will strongly influence what it will do well in the future: excellence is sticky.

The glue that creates these clusters is hyper-sociality. For instance, the superyacht builders in Northern Italy rely on thousands of local sub-suppliers, plus related education systems. There is thus an effect that glues it all together and that is very sticky over time. On another note, when it comes to tech-heavy ecosystems, what is often required to produce hyper-sociality is a combination of the following:

- R&D centers of multinational companies

- Relevant educational institutions

- A thriving local venture finance/private equity environment

- Attractive living conditions for talented people

If you have this combination, a plethora of cool start-ups is likely to follow. Path dependency means that certain industry clusters will likely start to form. However, while it's easy to predict that start-ups will arrive, it's nearly impossible to guess which ones precisely will dominate.

5CS + 3

We now understand more clearly the conditions under which creativity and innovation can thrive, and why the ultra-innovative Blue Banana emerged as it did. A natural question is whether innovation will continue and, if so, where and how. Understanding this is critical to navigating and shaping future trends. In our view, the good news is that innovation will continue at an accelerating pace, and it will be a global phenomenon. This is because of three additional innovation accelerators—namely connectivity, combinatorial explosions, and computerization. More about this will follow.

Chapter 4

INNOVATION ACCELERATORS

The days when a tiny fraction of the global landmass was accountable for the lion's share of innovation are long gone. For example, in recent years, innovation in Asia has exploded. Today, the region produces about 60 percent of the world's smartphones. We are now moving from the Blue Banana to a global innovation bonanza, and the elephant in the room is China. Despite being a relatively marginal player in terms of innovation in the year 2000, this thriving market economy now registers the highest number of new patents globally each year. Furthermore, China boasts around 45 percent of the world's supercomputers, and it also looks set on becoming the leading implementer of 5G connectivity. In addition, it is home to half of the world's electric car manufacturers, it's a leader in high-speed rail, and it is making serious inroads into space exploration, as well as nuclear power, AI, and genomics. Outside its borders, China invests heavily in foreign start-ups, further expanding its reach and influence.

FUTURE POWERHOUSES

Besides China, the remaining top five countries/regions for total patent registrations are the US, Japan, the EU, and South Korea. Russia is in a distant sixth place. These areas, plus a few nations such as Israel and Switzerland, also dominate various rankings of the most innovative cities globally. For example, San Francisco and Silicon Valley remain the leaders in terms of harboring start-ups. Tokyo produces the highest number of patents. Beijing spawns the most unicorns (start-ups that reach a valuation of over $1 billion) and is the third-highest recipient of venture capital financing, while London employs 15 percent of its workforce in high-tech sectors. Paris is the European leader of patent applications, and New York houses the highest number of Fortune 500 headquarters.[1]

However, this does not mean that other cities are sitting idly by—instead of there being "a next Silicon Valley," there will soon be more than thirty such cities/regions. In addition to the usual suspects, they include hubs such as Helsinki, Jakarta, Lagos, Melbourne, Montreal, Moscow, Mumbai, São Paulo, Singapore, Zurich, and Tel Aviv. Many focus on a handful of technologies or industries (e.g., AI in Montreal or fintech in Singapore).[2] Interestingly, with the exit of the UK from the EU, we are seeing an increased focus on forging new alliances, especially with the US and the Commonwealth members. We see similar regional cooperation in other parts of the world. Purchasing power is also shifting, and a new and massive consumer class is emerging across all continents of the globe.

The obvious conclusion is that the Blue Banana's initial dominance in innovation is over. The less obvious implication is how the diversity of innovation hubs will change the relative power of countries and lead to a multipolar world. Innovation leads to future economic growth and money, which over the long run translates into power.

No, the days of being able to threaten others with the biggest army are not over, as Russia unfortunately demonstrated in 2022. But they are waning. We have moved from the missile arms race to a data and innovation arms race. This came to light most evidently during the COVID-19 vaccine race, where the US, EU, Russia, and China all produced a vaccine less than a year after the pandemic was declared. These four power centers were all able to control the production and distribution of the vaccines and guarded them for their own citizens before giving others access to them.

Because intensive innovation has spread from the Blue Banana to all of Western civilization, and now across the globe, we are facing unprecedented and accelerating rates of change. At the same time, humans biologically and mentally have not adapted with nearly the same speed, meaning that we are facing increasing levels of complexity that we are ill-equipped to comprehend and deal with.

VIRAL AND NETWORK EFFECTS (CONNECTIVITY)

On Earth, the most explosive violations of the hierarchy rule and the great monotony often come from viral effects. Just think of COVID-19. Other, less harmful examples include innocent video clips on TikTok or YouTube, which people might share with each other. Virality can thus be harmful, neutral, or beneficial. What is different today, in regard to network effects and digital viral phenomena, is that for the first time in the history of humanity, the world is well and truly connected. Most of the global population is actively online—almost 60 percent of the world, 4.66 billion people, to be precise.[3] In the most developed countries, penetration reaches 95 percent. In terms of social media usage, we now also have over 50 percent of the global population as regular users. Physically, we are also increasingly traveling internationally for living, work, and tourism. Taking tourism as a proxy, there were 25 million international arrivals in 1950, 440 million in 1990, and 1.4 billion in 2018. The number is projected to continue to grow exponentially, with almost 2 billion arrivals in 2030.[4] There is a clear and positive correlation between income and international travel, and in some developed countries, we already see that people on average take more than two trips internationally per year,[5] in addition to greater and greater domestic travel.

All this creates extreme hyper-sociality, which leads to increased potential and potency of network effects and viral phenomena. This again means that ideas, innovations, and new technologies can now travel very quickly. Harking back to the Five Cs of innovation, connectivity puts each of the other Cs on steroids: Compact units now take place at the level of the individual. There are global cooperative networks that can interact in real time. There are global (or at least regional) common codes such as the Apple or Android app stores and 5G networks that increase opportunities for change agents, and competition in more and more industries is almost by nature global. Boom!

COMBINATORIAL EXPLOSIONS AND INTERDEPENDENCE

Knowledge and innovation go hand in hand, and since innovation is chiefly about combining existing things in new ways, the process is inherently explosive: the more we have developed, the more things it will be possible to create. For example, if we only have product types A and B, in the absence of the hierarchy rule, we can combine them in three different two-product ways: AA, AB, and BB. But if we double the number of existing products to four (A, B, C, and D), the number of possible two-product combinations increases from three to fourteen. If we further increase the number of basic building blocks, we get what mathematicians call combinatorial explosions. In other words, explosive innovation instead of dull monotony.

> Innovation begets more innovation, and when the Five Cs of Innovation are present, the process becomes exponential. This is due to coevolution, which means recombining things.

The world is full of examples of how things combine to create greater solutions. For instance, when digital photography was launched, it initially provided far lower quality than analog photography. However, the *combination* of digital imagery with local digital storage, the internet, cloud computing, and social media overcompensated for the initial lack of image resolution. And this, by the way, exemplifies our previously mentioned characteristic of innovation stating that the sequence is somewhat deterministic. Each new core innovation is only possible when certain other innovations have fallen into place. A more recent example of this causality example is the launch of the smartphone. To be compelling, this needed an always-connected feature, a digital camera, accurate touch-screen technology, compass, energy-dense batteries, fast processors, GPS, and more. GPRS had solved the always-connected problem in 2000, and over the following years, all the other needed technologies improved exponentially toward being suitable for a phone. This pointed to a window in 2005–2009 where it was almost inevitable that someone somewhere would launch a smartphone combining it all. However, while incumbent phone providers didn't see this, the team at Apple did, and they launched their first smartphone in 2007.

Historical evidence for this phenomenon is shown in Ian Morris's book *Why the West Rules for Now*. Fifteen out of humanity's first twenty major inventions arose independently in the West and the East—but in the same sequence![6] And, moreover, with approximately 2,000 years of time difference. As Morris writes in his introduction, "East and West have gone through the same stages of social development in the last fifteen thousand years, in the same order . . . they have not done so at the same times or at the same speed."

The difference today is that we are living in a world where there are sufficient numbers of innovations, especially 10x+ innovations, that the overall rate of change is exploding. We are racing into a foggy future, but even if it seems unpredictable, we can actually figure out much of what is likely to happen because in fact, it is largely predetermined.

So is its speed. Many exponential trends are at the cusp of taking off, and as they do so, they will combine in new ways. Because of this interdependence, we must forecast a lot to forecast anything specific with reasonable certainty. We must, in other words, view the world with a radar vision, not just a laser focus. We need to see the detail to then see the big picture.

INNOVATION IS ETERNAL

The phenomenon of innovation through recombination is not only exponential, but actually hyper-exponential as well. In mathematics, there is an operation called a *tetration*, where the exponent in an exponential repetition evolves exponentially. This applies to innovation as a whole, but it is also occasionally observed within more narrow fields, such as the performance improvements in quantum computing.

In his book *The Beginning of Infinity* (2012), David Deutsch argues convincingly that, given such phenomena, innovation is not a bucket of possible ideas that we are emptying rapidly, but rather an endless exponential process.[7] In other words, innovation is, to all practical intents and purposes, endless and limited only by the laws of physics.

The good news is that the laws of physics are extremely generous. For example, the energy potential of our deuterium and tritium is enough to provide Earth with clean, safe energy for between (according to the conservative estimate) 30 million and (by the optimistic estimate) countless billions of years. And in terms of speed, the absolute natural limit given by the speed of light corresponds to flying seven times around Earth in one second.

Whereas the first market response to new core technologies may often seem disappointing, over time people figure out new business models and applications that trigger endless cascades of new business opportunities and technologies.

The strength of this phenomenon leads us to conclude that anything desirable that can be invented within the generous confines of the laws of physics will be invented. And if and when many people feel that anything they can possibly desire technologically is available in abundance, we shall continue to develop new experiences using it—forever.

EXPANDING CREATIVE BOBBLES

The innovation process can largely be described as a flow between three categories, which are well outlined in the book *At Home in the Universe* (1995) by the American professor Stuart Kauffman:

✓ **The actual:** everything that has already been invented

✓ **The adjacent possible:** innovations that in principle could be made by recombining elements of the actual in new ways

✓ **The shadow future:** what is theoretically possible within the laws of physics but not doable now since the necessary subcomponents are not yet part of the actual

Within this creative design field exists an interesting phenomenon: very often, the adjacent possible consists of new applications for actual core technologies. Frequently, when a new core technology has been launched, it struggles commercially for a while, since compelling applications in the adjacent possible have not yet been discovered or launched. As a result, it disappoints initially. One reason for this is that the kinds of people who are good at developing core technologies are often ill-suited for developing the applications for them. For instance, TV broadcast relies on a number of rather nerdy core technologies developed by people with brilliant engineering talents. However, for this to really take off, some trendy people needed to develop compelling media concepts—or applications—such as live sports, talk shows, and soap operas. This all required new ideas, commercial ecosystems, business models, and so on. Having said that, we should mention a glaring example of the opposite: so far, it seems that blockchain was bundled from the start with its ultimate killer app, cryptocurrency, starting with Bitcoin. In this case, the nerds found the killer app from day one.

Amara's law, based on American scientist Roy Amara's observations that "we tend to overestimate the effect of a technology in the short run and underestimate the effect in the long run," predicts these phenomena. This idea was more recently popularized by Bill Gates, who said that "people often overestimate what will happen in the next two years and underestimate what will happen in ten."

Technological breakthroughs often disappoint initially
since there needs to be a shift in emphasis from core
technologies to applications, which often require
completely different people and business models.

MASS COMPUTERIZATION AND 10X+ INNOVATION

Another thing we need to know about the innovation processes is that 10x+ innovations increasingly involve the combination of digitization and automation. It allows computers to take over tasks that have hitherto been performed by humans—and thus constitutes the third central innovation accelerator: computerization. This leads to self-reinforcing intelligence, where we use software to write software, and so on.

THE LIVES OF TECH

Among the earliest models of technical and commercial technological evolution was the *technology adoption lifecycle*, which is based on a model first introduced in 1962 by researcher Everett Rogers and later adapted by American management consultant Geoffrey Moore in his book *Crossing the Chasm* (1991). In this book, Moore describes the importance of ensuring that enough early adopters take sufficient notice of a new innovation that it becomes mainstream and is therefore eventually adopted by a majority of the population.

You also have Gartner's Hype Cycle for emerging technologies, which is a graphic presentation developed by American research and advisory firm Gartner. Gartner's Hype Cycle illustrates the five main phases: Innovation Trigger, Peak of Inflated Expectations, Trough of Disillusionment, Slope of Enlightenment, and Plateau of Productivity. Of course, the trough of disillusionment here often stems from unforeseen technical complications but also from the previously described initial lack of compelling applications.

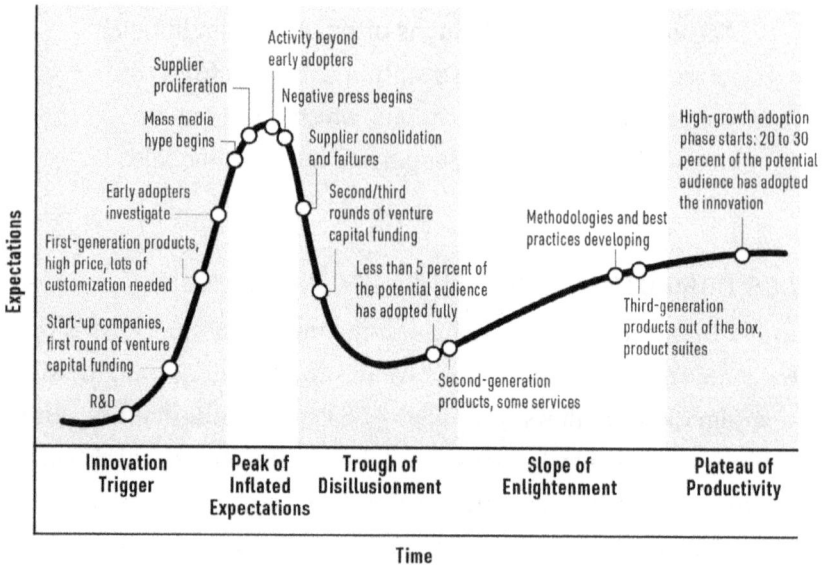

Figure 4.1. Hype Cycle indicators.

Another, more recent model is the 6 Ds of Exponential Growth, formulated by the Greek American physician, doctor, and entrepreneur Peter Diamandis, which states that technology progresses through a predictable path:

- **Digitalization**: When something moves from analogue to digital (or partly digital), it enters exponential growth.

- **Deception**: Initial growth is slow due to a low starting point, but given the nature of exponential growth, things take off rapidly once a threshold is reached.

- **Disruption**: The existing market is disrupted as the new offerings are cheaper, faster, more convenient, or of higher quality. Consumers gradually switch to the new offerings.

- **Demonetization**: The offering becomes cheaper and is eventually offered for free or at minimal cost.

- **Dematerialization:** Physical components are removed and bundled into smaller and smaller packages. Your smartphone is a classic example of this, and so is inbuilt GPS in your car screen.

- **Democratization:** The technology becomes more widely available, and it is eventually available to the majority of the population.

Most often, this path is exponential in nature—for example, digital cameras used to be expensive, stand-alone units but are now expected inclusions in smartphones, of which there are more than three billion globally. Another example is music, which used to be limited to physical formats, but which today is largely free on YouTube or available for a free or low-cost subscription model on platforms such as Spotify, Tidal, and Apple Music.

What these models all have in common is that they describe the somewhat predictable path of technological evolution, moving from the early days where it is unclear whether a technology will survive, to potential mainstream adoption.

Most of these models involve some form of digitization. The transition from physical to digital formats might seem obvious to the world we live in today, but it's worth bearing in mind that MP3s only truly started replacing physical CDs after 2010, and that the last physical edition of *Encyclopedia Britannica* was on sale as late as 2012.

More recently, we are digitizing much more complex things such as DNA, money, decision-making, reality (through VR), and perhaps even consciousness. We posit that anything that can be digitized will be, and when something is digitized, it typically enters exponential growth. This is the future we are entering.

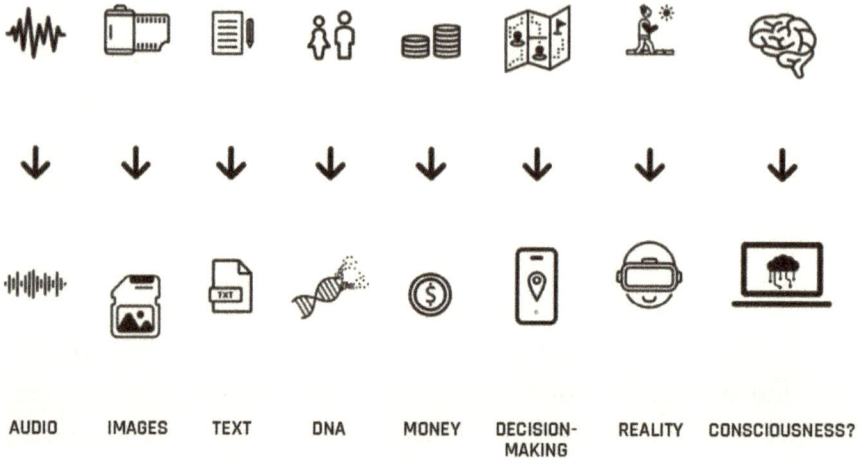

Figure 4.2. Example spheres that are being digitized.

COMBINE TO SHINE

Mass digitization only adds fuel to the fire of combinatorial explosions. Mainstream adoption of technology is very often combined with technological interdependence, and we are now living in an era where a critical mass of digital technologies such as big data analytics, quantum computing, artificial intelligence (AI), blockchain, DNA sequencing, CRISPR, robotics, virtual reality (VR), augmented reality (AR), and the Internet of Things (IoT), plus many others, are high enough up on the technology adoption curves that they can combine with each other in meaningful ways.

The result is convergence, where previously disparate and unrelated technologies and products and services become more closely integrated and even combined. Heart rate monitors, watches, and even sleep monitoring are now combined in smartwatches. Machine learning and robotics are now combining to produce intelligent production machinery, self-driving cars, and robot personal helpers.

These are just a few examples in the endless array of combinatorial possibilities, which all fall under the heading of interdependence. This happens on and on, where one technology or idea combines with another, which then spawns ten more ideas, which each again combine with yet others, which then each spawn ten more, and so forth. This is called coevolution, which is when the development of the technologies become interdependent. People and organizations that are good at developing such interdependency will often find a huge playing field of possibilities to combine and shine. However, they will be best at it if they have a very wide view. In other words, a very effective mental radar.

A high degree of interdependence can foster a high degree of creativity and agility.

On old cave paintings, there are often depictions of Stone Age men hunting massive animals. Among these animals was the aurochs, which weighed between 1,500 and 3,300 pounds. But 8,000 to 10,000 years ago, people began to tame these animals instead of hunting them—and while this original version of the cow became extinct in the seventeenth century, the domesticated version multiplied under human leadership to such an extent that we now have 1.5 billion of them in our custody.

Initially, our motivation for taming cows was certainly for their flesh and skins, and later for their use as draft animals, but at some point, some people started drinking their milk—possibly out of desperation, as it must have seemed strange and probably did not go down well. There were originally no adult humans who could digest lactose, which is part of milk. In fact, no adult mammal could do so at all after childhood. But the potential benefit of human milk consumption was so great that two changes occurred simultaneously. First, it enabled a genetic mutation. Approximately eighty generations after man's first intake of milk, adult lactose tolerance began to spread. And second, the cow's ability to produce milk grew due to selective breeding.

This new ability to digest milk had cascading effects because cow's milk gave approximately five times greater nutritional benefits than meat from the cow. Of course, that was why people wanted to breed selectively for greater milk production, which grew 10x.

This in turn meant that one could feed many more individuals per unit area, which again enabled military concentration, division of labor, and increased trade. In other words, human collaboration with cows stimulated human collaboration with other people and contributed to the development of what we now call civilization.

This is an example of interdependence in the form of coevolution, not only between humans and animals, but also between humans and civilization—mediated by innovation, which involves animals. It is also an example of hyper-sociality.

The story of how cows (or rather, *aurochs*) promoted the evolution of our civilization is also about how innovation develops our lifestyles and consumption patterns.

It is a very widespread phenomenon. For example, the proliferation of cars has created opportunities for living in detached houses in the suburbs. Now, micromobility using electric scooters and so on can reduce the number of cars in the cities, which will free up space for sidewalk cafés, while electric cars will reduce city noise. This makes city life more attractive. However, driverless driving will also make it easier to commute, which will speak for the suburbs again. In other words, both housing alternatives are becoming more attractive due to micromobility. Once quadcopters become widespread, the most desirable lifestyle among the wealthy might be to combine a city apartment and a house somewhere far from the city. One could get to their second home in a snap with their quadcopter. Woo-hoo!

There is not only extensive coevolution between different technologies but also between technologies and lifestyles.

THE EMERGENCE OF CENTAURS, ROBOTS, AND BOTS

Another example of coevolution is the development of centaurs. In Greek mythology, centaurs were half human and half horse. In the world of technology, we refer to humans working very closely with computers or robots this way. While there is much discussion about the competition between man and machines, it is often more relevant to consider the competition between people with machine assistance (e.g., a physician supported by an AI program) and people without such assistance. The combination of humans and machines is typically more efficient than machines alone—at least until the specific technology is sufficiently mature to exhibit human-like (or even human-superior) judgment.

Regarding physical robots, these exist in the form of cooperating co-bots, as they are also called. Imagine, for example, a robot version of a warehouse worker who understands where people are, where all warehouses are at a given time, what the optimal order to pick up item orders is, when things should be packed for shipment, and so forth. A counterpart to this is *internet bots*, which increasingly are used for automating and speeding up customer service and other somewhat repetitive tasks such as answering queries about the use of software, media, or ordering tickets online. Not only can bots—once developed—do this far cheaper than humans, but they can also learn while working and get better automatically. They can also respond within a fraction of a second. More than half of all web traffic is generated by such bots.

While much discussion is about man against machine, what is often more relevant is the competition between people with machines ("centaurs") and people without machines.

When speaking of coevolution, we should mention Yule's law of complementarity: "If two attributes or products are complements, the value/demand of one of the complements will be inversely related to the price of the other complement."[8] For instance, if the price of traveling goes down, then prices of remote holiday properties will go up. The ever-more complex coevolution of advanced technologies makes it ever harder for any individual to get a grip.

Chapter 5

EXPONENTIAL TRENDS FOR THE FUTURE

In 1965, Intel cofounder Gordon Moore famously described how the number of transistors on computer chips had doubled every year between 1958 and 1965. He then predicted that this would continue for at least another decade. In 1975, he revised his prediction going forward to a doubling every two years, which has pretty much held ever since. Today, we know of many parallels to it. For instance, here are some about computer performance:

- Koomey's law: the energy requirement for a given quantity of data processing halves every eighteen months.

- The bits per dollar in random access memory doubles every eighteen months.

- The number of possible qubits in scalable quantum computers doubles each year under Rose's law, but growth can also be double exponential according to Neven's law.

Telecommunication is also evolving exponentially:

- Cooper's law: the number of radio frequency calls that can be made simultaneously in a given area doubles every thirty months.

- Gilder's law: the total bandwidth for communication systems triples every twelve months.

- Nielsen's law: network speeds for advanced private users increase 50 percent per year.

- The throughput cost in fiber networks drops by half every nine months.

- The wavelengths per fiber in fiber optical networks double every nine months.

- Wireless communication speed doubles every ten months.

Production and storage of data follow similar laws:

- Spice law/Kryder's law: performance per unit price for hard drives increases 40 percent yearly.

- The cost of computer memory drops 20–30 percent annually.

- The amount of digital data in the world doubles every two years.

Similar phenomena are also seen within digital sensors:

- The pixels in digital cameras per array double every nineteen months.

- The pixels per dollar of digital cameras double every twelve months.

- The annual growth rate of the number of internet-connected devices (IoT) is 15–20 percent.

Within DNA sequencing and precision fermentation, improvements have been even faster than in most computing, leading to the following laws:

- The Carlson curve: the doubling of performance and the drops in price for DNA-decoding technologies develop at least as fast as Moore's law.

- The dollar cost per base pair sequencing in DNA tests halves every eighteen months.

- The cost of producing one weight unit with precision fermentation drops by a factor of ten every five years, leading to a 10,000x performance increase within twenty years.

Typically, such dramatic doubling rates are seen in technologies that involve information processing on a very small scale. However, they also occur in other markets. Take, for instance, technologies related to the production, storage, and efficiency of use of energy:

- The price per MWh generated from solar cells is halved approximately every thirty-eight months.

- The price per MWh generated from onshore wind energy is halved approximately every seventy months.

- Battery performance doubles every nine to fourteen months.

- Since the 1960s, nuclear fusion experiments have on average doubled the triple product of density, temperature, and inclusion time every 1.8 years.

- Haitz's law: every decade, the price per unit of light generated by LED falls by a factor of ten, while the amount of light produced by an LED unit increases by a factor of twenty.

- The scales at which we can do nanomanufacturing gets smaller by a factor of approximately four every ten years.

And here are three final examples, which relate to human health, the affordability of commodities, and the scientific output:

- Global human life expectancy grows three months per year.

- The amount of labor (measured in time worked) needed to buy the global commodities is halved roughly every twenty years.

- Ziman's law: scientific activity doubles every fifteen years.

Every year, new, similar laws evolve. However, to our knowledge so far, all exponential technologies level off eventually, after which their growth becomes linear or stalls entirely. The general rule is that those relating to the biggest physical objects tend to level off within a few years or decades while often providing rapid, 10x–1000x improvement. However, those relating to the small or microscopic can often go on much longer and double much faster, leading to improvements that can reach tens of thousands to billions times better price-performance. The simplest explanation for this difference is that small things require less energy per performance units as their performance improves.

The fact that exponential laws eventually taper off doesn't mean that innovation will taper off. On the contrary, new technologies will continue to take over and spur new phases of exponential growth so that the overall innovation process is essentially endless.

It should be noted that there are also linear trends. In recent decades, for instance, human life expectancy has grown globally three months per year. This is linear. There are other rules where developments in one variable set up other trends. For instance, when a country's GDP reaches about $5,000 per capita, birth rates typically begin to decline, and when it reaches approximately $10,000, the fertility mostly drops below replacement levels, which signals population decline. Also, according to the Environmental Performance Index (EPI) website, the threshold for environmental improvement is annual incomes around $10,000 per capita. They reached this conclusion by comparing their environmental index scores with national GDP/capita numbers.

CHEAPER AND BETTER

These trends not only make technologies faster and better but also cheaper and more user-friendly. Especially for mass-produced consumer products, we tend to get higher quality at lower and lower prices. For example, most apps on your smartphone are now free or offer a free version, you can now stream virtually all the music in the world for a small monthly fee, and Netflix offers a world of entertainment for the price of one cinema ticket a month. All because of exponential laws.

PREDICTING EXPONENTIAL DEVELOPMENTS

The exponential laws at the beginning of this chapter are just examples among many, and one of the lessons from them is that if you extrapolate such laws, you have a pretty good guess at what is technically and commercially feasible in terms of core technologies and applications two, five, or ten years from now. For instance, the fact that electric cars, vertical farming, and HD streaming would become commercially feasible could have been predicted well in advance since they all depended on stable exponential laws.

Stable exponential laws can enable us to predict when futuristic applications will become possible and economically feasible.

A current example as we write this is the law stating that the global production of OLED screen area is growing by about 30 percent annually, while the cost per screen unit of a given quality tends to fall 25–30 percent annually. This means that increasingly, it makes sense to create whole walls made of digital screens—which again enables a market for artistic applications in our rooms and outside our buildings. The idea is not new. In 2011, designer Zaniz Jakubowski made giant screens on the mega yacht *Luminosity*, which showed a rain forest.[1] And it was interactive: as you walked along the screens, a digital butterfly followed. A building wall as a screen? Your refrigerator door? Dining table surface? Your belt buckles? Why not—it might be only a matter of time before this becomes mass market. And definitely, a very cool home office with lots of screens will be on many shopping lists.

Or, take the Internet of Things (IoT). IoT uses sensors to create huge streams of data, ranging from temperature to speed, location, pressure, light, sound, and much more, which are distributed over the web. As the sensors used for IoT get ever cheaper and telecommunication ever better (such as with 5G), companies can sell more and more products using as-a-service business models, where we remotely monitor local status of things and places and take over the entire resupply and maintenance on a subscription basis. For instance, micromobility with local scooters is a transportation-as-a-service enabled by IoT. Overall, IoT and 5G and future communication protocols will—at exponential rates—promote autonomous driving, augmented and virtual reality, telesurgery, smart cities, and much more.

Another way to put this is that by knowing relevant exponential laws, you can look at the current status of the creative design field and then surf into the likely future and make pretty good predictions about when core technologies and applications will move from the shadow future to the adjacent possible and then further to the actual. Such exercises are part of making ourselves and our organizations Future Fit.

Interestingly, when technological advancements result in price drops, this often leads to an increased consumption of that same resource—this is known as the *Jevons paradox*. For example, as the cost of DNA sequencing has dropped in the past few years, the market for direct-to-consumer DNA testing has grown by around 25 percent.[2] Equally, due to falling costs, music streaming volumes are expected to grow with a CAGR (compound annual growth rate) of 17.5 percent in the next five years, far surpassing the general economic growth.[3] In this way, one exponential law concerning price-performance can create another concerning user penetration—which again feeds back to the former. Similarly, exponential improvements and penetration in one technology can drive exponential growth in many others.

> **One exponential law will often trigger others,**
> **which can feed back on the first in a positive loop.**

RECURSIVE INTELLIGENCE ON STEROIDS

The majority of the exponential laws have been working like a charm for the past many decades, and the level of knowledge on the planet has exponentially grown. Researcher John Ziman has calculated that the planet's scientific activity has long doubled approximately every fifteen years.[4] Some scholars even put the time frame for doubling closer to ten years.[5] When something doubles every fifteen years, it grows—perhaps a little surprising—approximately a hundredfold in 100 years and approximately 10,000 times in 200 years. This is the wild process we are now living in. By the way, if scientific activity doubles every ten years instead of every fifteen, the growth per century is more than 500 times. And in 200 years, it is more than half a million times!

But can it continue? Will we not run out of scientists at some point? Yes, of course, but as an excellent example of recursive intelligence, computers are on the verge of taking over a great deal of our scientific work. When we can run artificial intelligence on quantum computers, the performance in some scientific pursuits will explode.

On that note, according to Supertrends experts, quantum computing will start to impact many markets significantly between 2024 and 2028. A likely example is drug development. It takes up to ten years and costs up to $2 billion to get a drug developed and brought to market. Quantum computers can make this much faster and cheaper, which is why the world's second-largest pharmaceutical company, Swiss Roche, in 2021 initiated the world's first quantum computer-based research into molecular combination options for possible future forms of treatment against Alzheimer's.

This is interesting, and it is also noteworthy that AI can not only answer very complex questions but also deal with very open-ended questions—and generate new hypotheses based on what it observes through "automatic hypothesis generation."

This scenario and its consequences have a great parallel to the situation where Malthus predicted global famine since population growth would be exponential whereas food production would grow linearly. Now, some 200 years later, we are facing a situation where the growth in available digital data is exponential while the addition of scientists to interpret it will simply stall, if not reverse. However, just as food production saved the day by going persistently exponential, so will AI save the day for scientific discovery by assuring that our ability to process data intelligently also goes exponential. If we had a mindset like Malthus, then we would conclude that innovation will flatten out. Abundance happens because we continuously break out of previous restraints.

Here is a fun thought: if the scientific doubling rate remains fifteen years for 2,000 years, it will become about 10^{40} times larger than today, and our *accumulated* knowledge will by that time be even greater. As David Deutsch points out, if our exploratory knowledge at some point will dominate something that is 10^{40} times larger than itself, it is actually equivalent to humans controlling our entire galaxy. Then, he says, the universe will truly "wake up" and the great monotony will truly be broken. Two thousand years from now, that is. Obviously no one has that planning horizon, but perhaps this thought will help shape a part of our mental approaches for the nearer future.

EXPONENTIAL LAWS EXTRAPOLATED

For perspective, we have here extrapolated the previously studied exponential laws from the year 2022, when we're writing this book, to the years 2025, 2030, and 2050. Below are some examples of technologies that have exponentially growing usage or performance:

Technology	2025	2030	2050
Moore's law: the number of transistors on a microchip doubles every two years.	3x	16x	16,384x
The bits per dollar in random access memory doubles every eighteen months.	4x	40x	416,127x
Rose's law: the number of possible qubits in scalable quantum computers doubles each year.	8x	256x	268,435,456x
Cooper's law: the number of radio frequency calls that can be made simultaneously in a given area doubles every thirty months.	2x	9x	2,353x
Gilder's law: the total bandwidth for communication systems triples every twelve months.	27x	6,561x	22,876,792,454,961x
Nielsen's law: network speeds for advanced private users increase 50 percent per year.	3x	26x	85,223x
The wavelengths per fiber in fiber-optic networks double every nine months.	16x	1,625x	173,162,038,545x
Wireless communication speed doubles every ten months.	12x	776x	13,019,952,185
Spice law/Kryder's law: performance per unit price for hard drives increases 40 percent yearly.	3x	15x	12,348x
The amount of digital data in the world doubles every two years.	3x	16x	16,384x
The annual growth rate of the number of internet-connected devices (IoT) is 15-20 percent.	2x	4x	91x
The Carlson curve: doubling performance and dropping price of DNA-decoding technologies develops at least as fast as Moore's law.	3x	16x	16,384x

This simulation shows technology improvements by 2025 (within three years) of two to twenty-seven times (2x–27x).

By 2030, we find 256 times improvement in quantum computing performance, more than 6,000 times bigger telecommunication bandwidth, 16 times improvement in DNA decoding performance, and so on. In essence, these vectors point toward a future with true abundance and to amazing performance at little to no cost to consumers.

Moving further forward in time, many of the numbers seem hard to believe. If we extrapolate global bandwidth to 2030, we reach over 6,500 times, and if, for fun, we run these numbers all the way to the year 2050, the number is 22,876,792,454,961 times.

BUT IS IT TRUE?

Of course, some of these empirical laws may not actually work out that long. For instance, the mother of them all, Moore's law, may indeed run out of steam pretty soon. However, as it does, a number of work-arounds and new core technologies can take its place to continue the forward thrust in computing performance—possibly at the same speed as before, and possibly for many more decades, if not centuries. Among these technologies are 3D chips, optical computing, and quantum computing. So while Moore's law will die, others will take over.

Another thing that may not last much longer is the previous massive price-performance improvements in solar and wind power. However, if some of the emerging nuclear power technologies break through and get rolled out at scale, they may simply take over the mantle and assure that the impressive price-performance improvements in electric energy provision continues for a very long time.

If they do, it ought not surprise us. After all, in 1994, the American economist and Nobel Prize winner William Nordhaus calculated that the time-price of producing light had dropped by a factor 500,000 times since the Stone Age. This, by the way, made him estimate that real economic advance since those days is underestimated by a factor nearly 100,000. Yes, the trend is really our friend, and the future will bring a lot more wealth than many assume.

We must first understand these trends before we can accurately investigate how each of us personally—as well as the organizations we work with and in—must respond to become Future Fit for this environment. In the following chapters, we therefore take a detailed look at a number of different industries and technology areas, and provide markers of the future we are speeding into. For those who would prefer a less technical read, we encourage you to skim the key points and reference the supertrends snapshots in the tables we provide. For readers who want to go deeper, more details can be found in the sources in the endnotes.

Chapter 6

THE ROAD TOWARD ABUNDANCE

One effect of innovation is that the world generally develops for the better, whatever society—including well-educated experts—might believe at a particular moment. Too often, we focus on momentary emergencies, not longstanding trends. Indeed, when we follow the public debate about society and politics, we cannot help but notice that a substantial part of the population seems to believe that we still live in a Malthusian world—even though we broke decisively away from it almost six centuries ago. Essentially, many people view resources as if they're in a bucket that we are gradually emptying. They think that we are "running out," largely because population numbers keep rising. Of course, many people don't notice how many doomsday prophecies fail to come true. For instance, instead of facing the global famine that Malthus predicted in 1798 and many catastrophists predicted as late as the 1960s and '70s, our rapidly growing population has been ever better fed and achieved ever longer average life spans. In fact, for the first time in 300,000 years, today there are more people on Earth who are clinically obese than clinically undernourished.

A substantial part of the population seems to believe that we still live in a Malthusian world—even though we broke decisively away from it almost six centuries ago.

Modern catastrophists' response to such positive news is to simply postpone the predicted date of disaster, or to come up with some other, similar doomsday scenario. If we are not running out of this, then surely we're running out of that!

In our view, these new doomsday scenarios will typically (or consistently) also fail, and the reason is that since the world became truly creative, and since we broke free from the law of monotony, the hierarchy rule, and the Malthusian Trap, resources have not from any practical point of view been a finite limitation. Instead of seeing ever-growing starvation rates on the planet as Malthus predicted, we are now discussing sending people to Mars. How weird is that?

THE ULTIMATE RESOURCE

The deeper reason for this achievement is that—at least for the last six centuries—human ingenuity has been undergoing an exponential process. David Deutsch gave an excellent example in *The Beginning of Infinity*. He points out that at some point in the past, there must have been Stone Age people who died of exposure to cold weather while resting on dead branches. Their problem was that they had not yet invented controlled fire, which could otherwise have changed those dead branches to a warm and pleasant bonfire. We must bear in mind that if you exclude the effects of innovation, cavemen actually had far more resources per person and in total at their disposal per person than we do now. They just couldn't unlock them.

What we must understand is that "the ultimate resource," as the scientist Julian Simon also explained in his book of the same name, is human innovation.

This calls for some context. An economy can grow in two ways, which are sometimes called Smithian and Schumpeterian growth, respectively. Smithian growth is achieved by adding more people, capital, and land to the production process. Schumpeterian growth is based on innovation, which often means doing more with less capital, less people, and less land. Since around 1450, Schumpeterian growth has done most of the work. This shift toward Schumpeterian growth has had propound effect on resource availability partly because it activates potential resources, and partly because it replaces matter with mind.

ENDLESS POWER?

The world is in the early phases of a massive energy transition, which is partly driven by innovation leading to natural market changes but largely by fear of global warming driven at least partly by greenhouse gas emissions. This energy transition will consist of a combination of—

- Energy-efficiency measures

- Technologies to capture and sequester greenhouse gases (mainly CO_2)

- New ways of producing, moving, and storing energy

As for energy efficiency measures, this happens all the time, everywhere. For instance, internal combustion cars have obtained ever greater mileage per liter/gallon of fuel, and old-fashioned light bulbs have been replaced with LED bulbs, which are far more efficient. These technologies continue to improve year after year.

Another interesting field of research is carbon capture and storage (CCS) technologies. Supertrends experts predict a number of breakthroughs for these during the mid-2020s, and if (or when) these become cheap enough, we might not want to skip using coal, oil, and gas after all—instead, we can continue to burn it while capturing the carbon from the process. This can then be sequestered or used for making synthetic fuel, carbon materials, and various chemicals. In any case,

CCS technologies can be mandated in processes such as production of cement, which currently emits lots of CO_2.

However, the most dramatic developments are expected within technologies to produce, move, and store energy. Let's jump straight into one potential development that may eventually change pretty much everything: nuclear power. The sun is powered naturally by nuclear fusion between isotopes of hydrogen, and it is estimated that more than half the heat within Earth (which is approximately 3,500°C/6,332°F at the base of the mantle, and around 5,000°C/9,032°F at the center) is due to natural underground nuclear fission primarily from uranium, thorium, and potassium.[1] The power density of these input materials for nuclear reactions is enormous. If nuclear fusion works commercially, we could supply the total lifetime energy consumption for an average citizen on Earth with the amount of deuterium contained naturally in a single bathtub filled with tap water, plus the lithium contained in two standard notebook batteries.

These amounts of commodities are so small—and the natural occurrence of them so vast—that scientists estimate that commercial nuclear fusion can provide enough energy to supply the world with very safe and clean power for somewhere between 30 million and several billion years.[2] For perspective, the lower of these estimates is approximately 100,000 times as long as our fossil fuel era will last (which we think will be approximately 300 years), and it is even 100 times longer than *Homo sapiens* have so far existed. And that's the *lower* estimate.

Skeptics have long argued that it is not practically possible to get the so-called triple product, which is critical density multiplied by temperature multiplied by time, up to a suitable level. However, the fact is that since the 1960s, triple product in experimental reactors has followed a positive trajectory, with average triple product doubling every 1.8 years. This is a Moore's law for nuclear fusion, and we all know how much Moore's laws led to within computing: a lot!

In terms of timing, if the experiments continue to follow this exponential trend, sustained fusion should be achieved in an experimental

reactor within a few years. If indeed this happens, then it will probably take another ten to twenty years to develop commercial reactors
that are easy to build and maintain—and then we shall begin a major
transformation into what will provide essentially endless, very cheap
and compact energy for humanity. Most experimental fusion reactors
now fall into the categories of tokamak and stellarator (the former looking like a doughnut and the latter like a twisted doughnut), where fuel
plasma is retained in an extreme magnetic field and heated to temperatures higher than those in the center of the sun. (It must be hotter than
in the sun because the pressure is lower than in the sun.)

Other reactors are based on periodically hitting very small flying fuel
particles with very strong laser beams. This triggers nuclear fusion—
think of it as the world's most advanced clay pigeon shooting. In 2021,
this was particularly successful in an experiment at the NIF experimental reactor in California, where the explosion from a hydrogen ball of
less than 1 millimeter (0.04 inches) in a split second produced 10 percent of all the heat energy the sun supplies to the entire globe.[3]

In 2022, the English company First Light Fusion demonstrated a very
creative approach: Minimal strips of fuel were encapsulated in a cube
of approximately 1 cm^2 (0.4 square inches), which contained a series of
bubbles around the fuel.[4] This cube was dropped from the rifle muzzle
of a so-called ray gun, after which it was hit from behind by a projectile
from the same. This projectile flew at 3.7 miles per second (6 km/sec),
and when it hit the cube, its bubbles collapsed in a cavitation process that
accelerated the fuel particles around them to psychedelic 43 miles per
second (69 km/sec). This triggered nuclear fusion.

According to the company, such a single shot provides enough
energy to power the average UK home for over two years. If the machine
constantly fires two shots per minute, you can continuously supply all
the energy to approximately four million people. The reactor will be
housed in a fairly small and utterly harmless building. Plus, the otherwise minimal amount of waste will be helium, which is used to inflate
balloons for children's birthdays.

When nuclear fusion works, we can embark on a greater transformation into that which will supply humanity with virtually endless, secure, very cheap, and compact energy. And we really do mean compact: The power source for nuclear fusion is more than ten million times as compact as coal.[5] Two kitchen spoons could hold all the nuclear fusion fuel you would need for all your energy consumption your entire life.

Partly for this reason, a general rule about nuclear power is that the cost of constructing the plant is far higher than the cost of supplying the commodity for the plant during its lifetime. A nuclear fusion power plant will be able to substitute for windmills and solar panels hundreds or thousands of times its size. As with gas turbines, you will also be able to throttle a fusion reactor up and down like the speedometer of a car, which makes it suitable for baseload power to fill in the gaps created by solar and wind power, which are unstable due to fluctuating weather. As of 2021, there were twenty-three experimental nuclear fusion reactors globally, up from eight in 2010. Their private funding totaled $1.8 billion and included investments from Amazon founder Jeff Bezos, Vulcan Capital (from the late Microsoft cofounder Paul Allen), LinkedIn founder Reid Hoffman, and a range of large corporations and leading venture funds.

There has been a plethora of other exciting developments in nuclear research and development, including thorium reactors. With thorium power, a modern person's lifetime supply of energy for all purposes could be accommodated in a mass the size of a golf ball and with a weight of approximately 100 grams (3.5 oz). If they entered mass production, they would cost no more than a few dollars. Thorium is very safe, and the waste deteriorates orders of magnitude faster than the waste from uranium-based fission reactors. For such reasons, one of the US presidential candidates in 2020, Andrew Yang, would spend $50 billion to intensify thorium research and have a reactor ready by 2027. However, he wasn't elected, but China just launched an experimental thorium reactor in 2021.[6] And if the whole world were powered entirely with thorium, we could probably do it for around 100,000 years, which is thirty times as long as our 300-year fossil fuel age will last.

What's more, Terra Power, which is financially supported by Microsoft founder Bill Gates and former Microsoft CTO Nathan Myhrvold, has designed a potential "traveling wave" technology, which, through transmutation, might be able to utilize much of the remaining energy in nuclear waste (currently, approximately 98 percent of the energy potential from uranium-based nuclear power is wasted).[7] Transmutation is the process of transforming one element into another, like medieval alchemists dreamed of doing. If traveling wave reactors work, they could deliver the US energy supply for some 600 years with the current global energy consumption—all with the world's current supply of nuclear waste. Incidentally, a Nobel laureate in 2019 proposed a technology that could transmute nuclear waste into something harmless in half an hour.[8]

The power source for nuclear fusion is more than 10 million times as compact as coal.

Snapshot Sample of Future Nuclear Power Breakthroughs Predicted by Supertrends Experts	
2025	Sustained nuclear fusion is achieved in an experimental reactor.
2025	A nano nuclear reactor that runs on spent nuclear fuel is built.
2030	A transportable nuclear microreactor is developed in the US.
2030	A full-scale demonstrator Traveling Wave Reactor (TWR®) is built.
2030	A sodium fast reactor with a molten salt storage system is commercialized.
2032	An advanced modular nuclear reactor is used for the first time in industry.
2033	The world's first economically viable commercial fusion power plant is built.
2050	Power of two gigawatts is generated by a nuclear fusion power plant.

There is also great progress being made with energy storage and transmission. This includes vast improvements in battery-based technologies and a number of breakthroughs in the use of hydrogen and synthetic fuel created by windmills, solar panels, bacteria, microalgae, and nuclear power plants.

Power-to-X is an umbrella term for a number of conversion, storage, and reconversion pathways that use surplus electric power from renewable energy, typically solar and wind. "X" stands for the type of energy into which the electricity surplus is being converted. These are generally gases, liquids, or heat. Hydrogen fits into power-to-X concepts where temporary production surplus from, for instance, windmill parks, could be stored by manufacturing hydrogen.

Hydrogen can be made in five ways: "Black" hydrogen is made from coal and "gray" hydrogen is made from natural gas. If these two methods were combined with carbon capture, we would have "blue" hydrogen. And if it is made via hydrolysis powered by electricity from nuclear power plants, it is "pink." Finally, if the energy comes instead from wind or solar energy, it is called "green" hydrogen.

In 2022, gray hydrogen cost about two dollars per pound (a dollar per kilogram), whereas the price of all the "colored" varieties was higher. For green hydrogen, for example, the price was ten dollars per pound. However, experts expect that those prices will fall to around two dollars per pound by 2030. For perspective, one kilo of hydrogen has an energy potential similar to three kilos of oil, which means that all else being equal, a price of one dollar per kilo hydrogen would be similar to around fifty-five dollars per barrel of oil, which sounds competitive. Having said that, handling hydrogen is typically far more complex than handling oil, which distorts that comparison somewhat. In any case, an exponential improvement in the efficiency of hydrogen production is expected, corresponding to an annual efficiency improvement of just over 25 percent. (Morgan Stanley, however, has predicted much faster progress.)

It also has the advantage that it can to some extent be transported via existing technologies and networks for the transportation of natural gas. In fact, you can in some cases mix up to 30 percent hydrogen directly in natural gas and thus—if the hydrogen is green—make the gas greener. One could store huge amounts of hydrogen to even out variations in primary energy supplies. Hydrogen can also be used in a number of industrial processes, as is already common today, as well as in combined heat and power plants (CPH). When used for transport, it may be converted into ammonia or, for instance, dimethyl ether for easier transport, and then back to hydrogen in the transport unit. It can also be used for aircraft; for example, it has three times higher energy density per kilo as the aviation fuel kerosene. However, hydrogen is an extremely volatile gas, and before it is compressed, its energy density in gaseous form is only 1/3,000 of that of aviation fuel. Here it is predicted that you will instead use ammonia based partly on hydrogen.

As for use in cars, a KPMG survey of 1,154 automotive executives revealed that they expected the global car fleet by 2030 to be split almost evenly between internal combustion engine, battery electric, hybrid, and fuel cell electric (which is powered by hydrogen).[9] The prediction for 2040 was almost the same, with fuel cells remaining at 24 percent. Here is the rollout timeline predicted by consulting company Arthur D. Little:[10]

Estimate of how different applications of hydrogen become technologically and commercially possible.

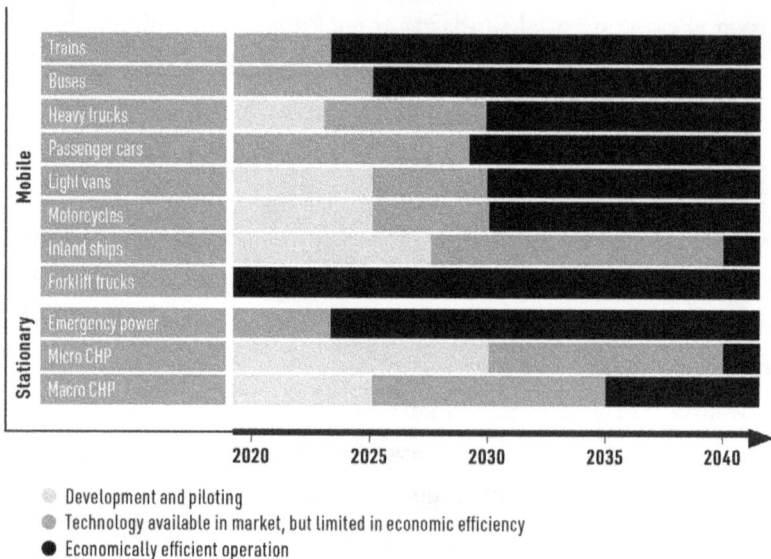

Development and piloting
Technology available in market, but limited in economic efficiency
Economically efficient operation

Figure 6.1. Estimate of how different applications of hydrogen become technically and commercially possible.

What follows from this timeline is that in most cases hydrogen is expected to become commercially sustainable by 2030, including in passenger cars. A probable development is therefore that after 2030 an exponentially growing number of trains and vehicles will be switched to green hydrogen, and that pink hydrogen from new forms of nuclear power will be encountered later.

We constantly see breakthroughs and exciting forecasts for other technologies as well. For the purpose of nuclear fusion, a technology called millimeter-wave beam has been developed. This technology, some researchers now believe, can be used to drill a hole nearly thirteen miles deep in just a hundred days.[11] This brings you down to temperatures of around 500°C (932°F) and thus directly taps the results of the planet's natural fission energy.

Another example is the harvesting of energy via membranes with boron nitride nanotubes (BNNTs), which exploit differences in the osmotic pressure between salt and fresh water. The forecasts for what it may bring are not modest. For example, a source recently stated that such a so-called blue membrane of just one square meter could generate about thirty megawatt hours per year, which is enough to power three homes.[12] And another stated a global energy potential from the technology of two terawatts—equivalent to about 2,000 nuclear reactors.[13]

What follows are some examples of various energy storage and charging technologies predicted by supertrends experts.

Snapshot Sample of Future Energy Storage Breakthroughs Predicted by Supertrends Experts	
2023	Nuclear waste diamond batteries are commercially employed.
2023	The average lithium-ion battery pack price falls to $137/kWh.
2024	Solar photocatalysis is used to treat wastewater and generate hydrogen fuel.
2024	Electric vehicles can be charged via lamp posts.
2024	Electric vehicles can be charged while moving.
2025	California installs its 200th hydrogen fueling station.
2025	Hydrogen plant driven by 4 GW of wind and solar is completed in Saudi Arabia.
2025	A lithium battery with an energy density above 500 Wh/kg is on the market.

continued

Snapshot Sample of Future Energy Storage Breakthroughs Predicted by Supertrends Experts	
2025	First washable battery is commercially available.
2027	Potassium-ion batteries become feasible alternative to lithium-ion batteries.
2027	Electric vehicles are fitted with graphene batteries.
2027	Biomorphic batteries for robots are commercially available.
2030	An over 100-seat, zero-emission fuel cell aviation powertrain takes flight.
2030	Shadow-effect energy generator panels are developed.
2030	First ammonia-fueled aircraft propulsion system is available.
2030	Mobile robots are wirelessly charged while in operation.
2030	Total distribution costs of hydrogen fall to $0.80/pound ($0.40/kg).
2030	Cost of renewable hydrogen in China, India, and Western Europe falls to $4.00/pound ($2.00/kg).
2030	Global production of green hydrogen reaches three exajoules.
2030	A commercial saltwater battery launches.
2030	First "lifetime" battery is installed in commercial IoT sensors.
2031	Batteries that can be charged within seconds are developed.
2031	The first phone battery that doesn't lose capacity over time is on the market.
2032	First zero-emission hydrogen aircraft is in service.
2032	First nanotech-based hydrogen storage device is commercially released.
2032	Green hydrogen becomes economically competitive.
2032	A battery-less and chip-less sensor node is commercially released.
2033	Aerial drones are wirelessly charged while flying.
2034	First smartphone is powered by self-charging batteries.
2036	Microwaves are utilized to convert electricity into green hydrogen.
2036	A hydrogen factory powered by bacteria is developed.
2036	A smartphone with a battery runtime of one month is commercially available.
2038	Hydrogen produced from microalgae is sold commercially.
2045	A nuclear power plant powers the production of hydrogen.

The conclusion is clear—we will not run out of energy, and we will be able to shift to alternative and sustainable energies through new innovations and technologies.

However, having said that, we should not become too optimistic about how long the entire energy transition toward zero greenhouse gas and particle emission will take. For perspective, in his book *Energy Transitions* (2018), Vaclav Smil showed how each of three former global energy transitions took approximately fifty years to reach 40 percent,

30 percent, and 20 percent of global supply, respectively. And that was after they first gained a 5 percent market share.

Global growth in market share for various energy sources after they had previously achieved a five percent market share

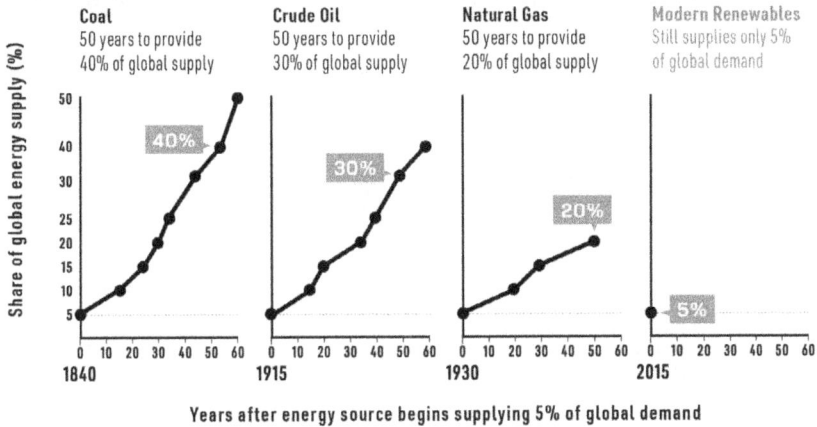

Figure 6.2. Global growth in market share for various energy sources after they had previously achieved a 5 percent market share.

As we write this, the global energy industry constitutes approximately $5 trillion, which amounts to around 5 percent of the roughly $100 trillion global economy. To be clear, this is not like silicon chips, where performance can be improved at the speed of Moore's law. The reality is that it mostly takes years, if not decades, to develop and build new power plants. They are also very expensive to build, but once you have them, they often produce enormous amounts of power at competitive costs. If we develop one that is 20 percent better than the previous version, it rarely pays to just pull down what already exists.

No matter how many climate summits and national commitments we see, it seems most realistic to us that this combined undertaking will take at least fifty years. And it has to be *combined*. For starters, we cannot fix everything by simply using wind, for instance. Not even the combination of wind and solar power would be sufficient. First, in many areas, solar panels and windmills would take up too much space, as seen in the following table.

Energy Source	Watts per Square Meter
Fossil fuel	500–1,000
Nuclear	500–1,000
Solar	5–20
Hydropower (dams)	5–50
Wind	1–2
Wood and other biomass	Less than 1

Solar and wind power are also highly unstable, which means they have massive requirements for associated storage and transmission of energy—which again require a lot of industrial metals. Currently, storing excess power from wind or solar for just one day costs approximately twice as much as generating it in the first place.[14] In his book *How to Avoid a Climate Disaster*, Bill Gates runs the numbers for how much it would take to store backup power for Tokyo for just three days. The answer is $400 billion for purchasing the batteries, equal to an annual expense of $27 billion plus the costs of installation and maintenance. Furthermore, wind, solar, and the associated backup and storage infrastructure would require far more industrial metals than the mining industry can deliver within a reasonable time frame, even if that time frame is a whole century! For instance, just generating power with offshore wind requires approximately fifteen times as much industrial metals as it takes to generate the same power with gas turbines. Gas turbines can also be throttled up and down to meet demand at any given time, whereas windmills can't.

If we should alternatively address the entire greenhouse gas issue with CCP technologies, and if we assume that the cost of this goes below a hundred dollars per ton, it would still cost around 5 percent of global GDP every year (current emissions are ca. 50 billion tons, so the cost would be $5 trillion). That would double global energy costs.

The essential point here is that we need to combine a broad range of technologies—partly to avoid excessive short-term demand for single resources such as copper or lithium, and partly because different situations call for different solutions in order to be reliable, cheap, and practical. For example, per weight unit, gasoline today delivers approximately thirty-five times as much energy as lithium-ion batteries. That is why batteries in airplanes are impractical, whereas they make sense in cars. Solar panels require sunlight, wind power requires wind, and both

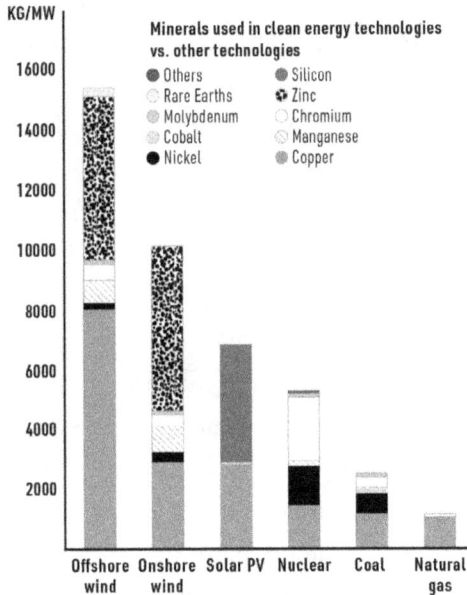

Figure 6.3. Minerals used in clean energy technologies vs. other technologies.

tend to take up a lot of space. Furthermore, any unstable solution requires at least some power storage solutions plus significant backup power in the form of peaker plants, which are additional plants that only operate when there is high demand. If peakers are not to be based on coal, gas, or hydropower, new forms of nuclear power are a strong option. Nuclear power could also be used in container ships. Some industrial processes such as cement production can be made to emit less CO_2, and any remaining emissions can then be sequestered via CPP solutions.

In any case, the amount of innovation within the energy sector will be enormous and exciting. But also very, very complex. And it will take its sweet time.

CREATING HOW NATURE DOES IT

The story of the gigantic energy transition is an example of the technological revolutions toward greater efficiency. One of the general technologies supporting efficiency is 3D printing. The standard approach in industrial production (and most craftsmanship) is subtraction. You take a piece of metal, wood, or marble and then you cut away what you don't need.

However, living organisms are built in *additive* ways, meaning from the ground up, layer upon layer, and with incredible precision. As anyone can see, this approach enables far more delicate and complex objects—like butterflies or humans. Interestingly, there is now an evolving revolution in manufacturing where we can do more and more products in an additive way. This means that we can create more and more complex and tailored products. For instance, this is already used extensively in customized dental implants and crowns, and it can have exotic uses, from printing tools on spaceships to kitchenware, 3D logos, organs, beefsteaks, reefs, nanobatteries, and human skin. Recently, scientists even managed to produce flexible OLED screens with a tabletop 3D printer.[15]

Snapshot Sample of Future 3D Printing Breakthroughs Predicted by Supertrends Experts	
2023	3D-printed anatomical models become standard for complex medical surgeries.
2023	A commercial 3D printer for latex is released.
2024	3D printers capable of printing at microscopic level are sold commercially.
2024	3D-printed aerogel is used in transplants.
2024	The first 3D-printed car is commercially available.
2024	Volumetric 3D-printed polymers are commercially available.
2025	3D-printed hybrid meat products hit supermarket shelves across the EU.
2025	A 3D-printed rocket is launched.
2025	The first artificial 3D-printed coral reef is constructed.
2025	Solar-powered prosthetics are 3D printed.
2026	3D-printed medical devices and simulations are regularly used in complex surgeries.
2026	3D-printed skin is approved for use in skin transplant.
2027	Construction of the first 3D-printed high rise is completed.
2029	A 3D-printed liver is transplanted into a human patient.
2030	A 3D-printed heart is successfully transplanted.
2031	Spaceship parts are 3D printed in orbit.
2035	Housing Infrastructure is 3D printed in space.
2045	3D printing reduces shipping volumes of finished goods by 7 percent relative to 2018.
2056	3D-printed artificial leaves are used to create oxygen and energy on Mars.

COMPACT FOOD PRODUCTION

Other examples of compact technologies are now being rolled out in the food industry. Today, approximately 11 percent of the globe's landmass surface is farmland. For perspective, 11 percent is equal to the mighty size of Russia. Or to the combined size of the United States, India, Argentina, Greenland, and South Africa. As we know, farmland offers far less biodiversity than the free nature that we see in natural parks and so on. It has therefore been a common concern that as we cut down forests and such to make more farmland, biodiversity drops and species go extinct.

In some places, catastrophic destruction of habitat is still happening, but in other places, farmland is now returning to nature. The total amount of farmland on Earth has actually been roughly unchanged since the 1980s. This, we should add, despite a doubling of the population plus a substantial increase in calorie intake per capita over the last four decades. One reason is the rollout of various degrees of "precision farming," which may use, for instance, a wide range of real-time data such as weather flows, water and nitrogen levels, air quality, and disease spread to generate precise instructions to the farmer about what needs to be done on the land. It's called precision because the system uses GPS and precise instruments to create specific instructions for each inch of farmland, rather than each acre. Eventually, tractors will become autonomous, and the various robots and sensors will speak to each other to the extent that the job of the farmer will be to control the various pieces of equipment and machinery remotely—perhaps from an iPad in the comfort of their office. Similar trends can be seen in industries like construction, architecture, and transport.

We now have substantial indicators that we are in the midst of a turning point in global farmland. There are seven major reasons for that:

- A continued development and rollout of highly effective precision farming, including use of genetically modified species, which require a lot fewer resources

- Rising concentrations of CO_2 in the atmosphere, leading to faster plant growth through aerial fermentation

- Global population growth, which is constantly slowing and likely to stop and reverse around the middle of this century

- Introduction of vertical farming, which uses far less water, no pesticides, and typically around fifty times less land per produced unit than traditionally farmed crops

- Use of precision fermentation to make milk proteins and similar products

- Growing use of faux meat, which is actually made of plants or other protein sources that take up less land than animal farming

- Introduction of cultured meat (meat cells growing in steel tanks), which, like vertical farming, also require only around fifty times less land per produced unit when compared to traditional farming

Cultured meat and vertical farming technologies typically reduce land use necessary to produce one pound of food by 98 percent.

The last four require some explanation. Vertical farming is the practice of growing crops on top of each other in a controlled, indoor environment. Vertical farming utilizes artificial light and hydroponic feeding, which means the roots are suspended in water-based nutrient solutions. Some of these controlled environments are shipping container-sized or—for home use—even smaller, but others are big. Additional plans may produce seafood in vertical stacks, and there are interesting combinations where waste from vertical seafood farming feeds plants in neighboring vertical plant farms.

In San Francisco, a company called Plenty runs an 8,100-square-meter (5-square-mile) vertical farm, which they claim produces over 300 times as many crops per square meter as traditional farming. This is possible because of constantly optimized growth conditions, lack of inhibiting seasons, and the stacking of multiple layers of plants.

So, in terms of land use, this is a 300x+ technology. There are even so-called deep farm projects located in abandoned mine shafts, refurbished underground tunnels, or the like, where the footprint on land is completely eliminated. Vertical farming also recycles most of their water and minimizes unwanted microbes. Furthermore, it can entirely avoid insects, weeds, and other pests—partly because the environment is sealed, and partly because many pests require soil for their life cycles.

As we write this, there are plans to build very large-scale vertical farms in at least Switzerland and the UAE. The Swiss project will be a "semi-deep" (partly under the natural land surface), one-million-square-mile (ca. 100,000-square-meter) farm located in 300-foot-deep holes within abandoned limestone mines. This should produce some 3,525 tons of food annually. Since an average person eats roughly 0.5 tons of food annually, this should be equivalent to feeding some 7,000 people. Switzerland has approximately 8.65 million inhabitants, which means fewer than 1,250 of these farms could feed the entire population, provided they were all vegans. Those 1,250 farms would take up around 48 mile² (125 km²), equal to 0.3 percent of the land area of this densely populated nation. The limited water needed will be captured on the roof. Heat will come from geothermal heat pumps, and biowaste will be reused to generate electricity. At this point we don't know if the reactor will be built or if it would be economically feasible, but the perspectives for the world's resource use are promising indeed.

Precision fermentation is higher tech. We know fermentation from the production of beer, wine, and other alcohols, for instance, and precision fermentation is similar, but uses genetically engineered microorganisms to produce complex organic molecules like proteins. This has been used commercially since the 1980s and has since become ever cheaper. Initially, it was only used for production of very expensive compounds such as human insulin, vitamins, flavoring agents, supplements, growth hormones, and rennet. However, typical production costs have dropped from $2 million per pound in 2000 to around $200 per pound in 2020—a compound annual cost reduction of some 60 percent. This has opened markets for precision-fermented, premium cosmetic products such as collagen and then for precision-fermented materials for the construction, clothing, and furnishings industries, including synthetic leather and spiders' silk.

PF disrupting more industries as costs fall

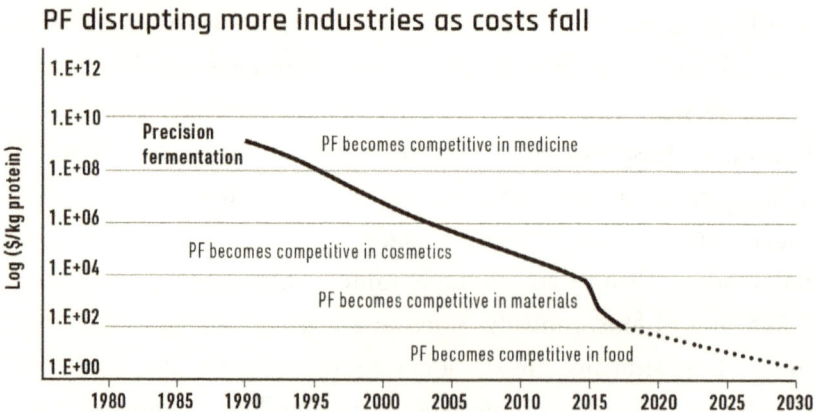

Figure 6.4. How falling prices of precision fermentation open up new markets.[16]

The next step is for this process to becomes price competitive for production of food ingredients and then bulk food. This will lead to mass production of precision-designed food and ingredients that can take place anywhere, at any time. For instance, you could use genetically modified microorganisms to produce casein and whey for animal-free dairy products.

Many precision-fermented products are used as ingredients in other products, including plant-based meat substitutes. This market is growing rapidly and includes fake minced meat, bacon, and more. To obtain a meaty taste and structure, Impossible Foods uses precision-fermented leghemoglobin. We are shifting from the ancient extraction model to the future model of creation. As with 3D printing, we use information to design what we want, and then we build it—in this case using biological replicators. Here is a snapshot of relevant predictions made by the supertrends experts:

Snapshot Sample of Future Cultured Meat Breakthroughs Predicted by Supertrends Experts	
2023	Lab-grown caviar is commercialized.
2024	Cell-based crabmeat is commercialized.
2024	Lab-grown bluefin tuna is commercially available.
2024	Bioengineered fish meal is used in commercial aquaculture.
2024	Precision fermentation reaches cost parity with animal protein molecules.
2025	Lab-grown kangaroo meat is commercially available.
2025	Vertical fish farms are cost competitive with traditional fish farms.
2025	The first cell-based cow milk is available on B2B market.
2026	Cultured elk meat is commercially available.
2026	Continuous bioreactors for production of cultured meat are available for cell culture.
2030	50 percent of protein production comes from precision fermentation.
2034	50 percent of global collagen and gelatin use is cell-based.
2035	Proteins produced by precision fermentation are 10x cheaper than animal proteins.
2038	Small-scale cultured meat system for family or personal use is available.
2060	Cultured and plant-based meats make up more than 60 percent of global meat supply.

Whereas the exact timing is very difficult to assess, it seems clear that food and farming is on the cusp of a massive revolution. In their report "Rethinking Food and Agriculture 2020–2030," the Rethink X organization writes, "The current industrialized, animal-agriculture system will be replaced with a Food-as-Software model, where foods are engineered by scientists at a molecular level and uploaded to databases that can be accessed by food designers anywhere in the world. This will result in a far more distributed, localized food production system that is more stable and resilient than the one it replaces. The new production system will be shielded from volume and price volatility due to the vagaries of seasonality, weather, drought, disease, and other natural, economic, and political factors. Geography will no longer offer any competitive advantage. We will move from a centralized system dependent on scarce resources to a distributed system based on abundant resources."

A likely outcome of the growth of precision farming, aerial fermentation, declining population growth, vertical farming, precision fermentation, faux meat, and cultured meat is a massive reduction in global farmland in the coming decades, particularly in the second half of this century. Because of this, the future is likely to offer far more national parks and biodiversity.

We can expect a massive reduction in the global farmland in the coming decades, particularly in the second half of this century.

Snapshot Sample of Future Food and Farming Sector Technology Breakthroughs Predicted by Supertrends Experts	
2023	Pollination machines are used in commercial agriculture.
2023	Biodegradable alginate capsules (alternative fertilizers) are on the market.
2023	Subscription service for biweekly satellite data of crop fields is launched.
2023	Plant-based egg is on B2B market.

Snapshot Sample of Future Food and Farming Sector Technology Breakthroughs Predicted by Supertrends Experts	
2023	Proteins made from thin air are commercialized.
2025	RNAi-based biocontrol is used as an alternative to pesticides in commercial agriculture.
2025	Genetically modified banana variety resistant to Panama disease is commercially grown.
2025	Biowaste-fed insects are used as livestock feed.
2025	Tinted greenhouses that generate electricity reach the market.
2025	Cotton-based textiles are chemically recycled into glucose.
2026	A hatchery produces a batch of 100 percent female chickens.
2027	Genetically modified decaf coffee with improved taste is on the market.
2027	Fiber made from agricultural waste is used in 1 percent of textile products.
2028	Greenhouses powered by transparent solar panels are built.
2028	Less-allergenic varieties of wheat and peanuts are produced.
2029	Lab-grown hair enters the market.
2030	Heat-tolerant wheat is achieved by gene editing.
2030	A bioengineered cow breed combines the genetic traits of African and European cattle.
2030	A protein made out of CO_2 and water is produced off-Earth.
2031	Transgenic food crops that require less water are approved for wholesale production.
2032	Radically altered GMO foods appear on grocery shelves.
2032	Seeds for suberin-charged carbon-capturing crops are approved by regulators.
2035	Market share of high-tech vertical farming companies surpasses that of traditional vegetable producers in the EU.
2038	Gene-edited super horses compete in a race.
2050	A major desert is transformed into agricultural land.

We are even likely to reintroduce extinct species into these growing natural parks. As described in the book and movie *Jurassic Park*, this possibility has over the last few years moved from the shadow future to currently the adjacent possible. Yes, today we are technically capable of reengineering extinct species in cases where we know their DNA sequence: a lot of what was lost the last 10,000–15,000 years can be brought back. In this connection, here are a few predictions from the Supertrends company's experts:

Snapshot Sample of Future De-Extinction Breakthroughs Predicted by Supertrends Experts	
2025	The first viable embryo of a formerly extinct species is cloned.
2025	The first functional species proxies are introduced into the wild.
2025	The first extinct species is brought back to life by back breeding.
2027	A formerly extinct species is reintroduced into the wild.
2030	Two-million-year-old DNA is sequenced.
2034	The first extinct bird species is revived.
2042	A non-avian dinosaur is brought to life.

10x+ innovations of similar magnitude will be seen across almost all other industries. Here are just a few predicted breakthroughs that illustrate the art of the possible, before we move on:

Snapshot Sample of Future Breakthroughs for Various Industries Predicted by Supertrends Experts	
2029	Light-transmitting concrete is used as structural material.
2032	A personalized cancer vaccine is approved by the FDA.
2035	Methane rocket fuel is made on Mars.
2039	The majority of automobiles in one country are autonomous vehicles.
2043	Malaria is eradicated.
2061	The first space hotel opens.
2083	Humans live permanently on Mars.

WELCOME TO THE PRECISION ECONOMY

As these examples show, our ability to get more with less—as in more food with less land—has accelerated substantially, especially since the 1980s.

Throughout the vast majority of human life, our means of production have been overwhelmingly based on extraction—we killed or collected stuff from nature, then reformatted it to meet our needs. By cutting wood and stones, for instance, or by cutting and cooking meat. However, we are now increasingly designing products on digital networks, then creating them in labs from the ground up using DNA, electrons, photons, and atoms. And soon, perhaps, we'll be using qubits, which are the basic units of quantum information used in quantum computing.

This is a great violation of David Deutsch's hierarchy rule, and we are thereby increasingly living in what we could call a precision economy, where things become ever smarter and more compact—and increasingly created rather than extracted. A good example of the trend toward smart and compact solutions is in mobile phones, which were initially dumb and could weigh around fifty pounds, but today they weigh around 300–700 ounces, even though they now have computer power that far surpasses a 1980s mainframe computer that would fill out a big room and weigh several tons. In fact, a study published on Nature.com in June 2018 by Arnulf Grubler et al found that smartphones had reduced materials consumption by a factor 300, power by a factor 100, and standby power by a factor 30.

Smartphones exemplify what the invention of the printing press also demonstrated: they led to cascading changes across a number of industries, as well as in lifestyles and organizational forms. For instance, they enabled billions of people to work from wherever they were. They also enabled people to order stuff from anywhere, which helped the takeout business explode and enabled Transport-as-a-Service (TaaS) in the form of Uber and other rideshare platforms. Smartphones revolutionized music, media, travel, education and more.

Ultimately, a smartphone becomes like a magic wand. It can control what you hear and see and instruct stuff to come to you. In many cases, such as TaaS and streaming music services, the solutions deliver 10x+ disruption. However, the huge popularity of smartphones also improved the cost/performance ratios of technology they require, including lithium-ion batteries, sensors, digital cameras, and more, to the benefit of countless other products and sectors.

Since the 1980s, an ever-increasing part of the world has entered the precision economy.

Incidentally, the Russian attack on Ukraine in 2022 provided an example of a confrontation between heavy (Russian) industrial technologies and compact (Ukrainian) precision technologies. Russia's top-commanded army invaded with a huge arsenal of heavy tanks and artillery, as well as with aircraft that quickly ran short of laser-guided weapons. Here, they largely fell short of Ukrainian forces, which responded with a decentralized approach focused much more on compact precision weapons such as shoulder-bearing Javelin rockets with fire-and-forget features, which could hit Russian tanks and other targets up to 2.5 miles away with great certainty and without the Russians being able to see where they were coming from. Javelins leave no revealing traces of smoke, and the soldier who fires them may be in hiding before they hit their target.[17] The Ukrainians also used Stingers, which are shoulder-bearing rockets that can shoot down planes and helicopters,[18] and Switchblades, which are remote-controlled, propeller-driven grenades that weigh just five kilos[19] and can fly for a quarter of an hour before the sender detonates them from a screen right on the head of the enemy. They also used Turkish TB-2 drones, which can fly for twenty-four hours while searching for targets for their laser-guided missiles.[20] In the face of this, the heavy industrial equipment of the Russians often fell completely short.

Similar processes are everywhere, and generally in modern economies, the precision economy has enabled us to produce more wealth without using more resources. In fact, we often even use fewer resources as our wealth grows. For instance, in the US, the consumption of many commodities peaked in the 1980s, even though American GDP per capita has risen massively since then. This leads us to a distinction—resource availability can be divided into three degrees:

- Scarcity: resources are limited, and if there are too many people spending too much, we will run short or out.

- Abundance: through combinations of Smithian and Schumpeterian growth, we manage to increase resource output to meet our growing demands.

- Superabundance: growth in population and average wealth leads to even faster Schumpeterian growth in total innovation, which means that available resources per capita also grow.

When people talk about humans exceeding the "carrying capacity" of the globe, or, for instance, that "we are currently using the resources of 1.7 Earths," their underlying assumption is that we are still in a scarcity economy. This may be understandable, since all other species on Earth are subject to rules of natural scarcity, whether it is bacteria growing in a petri dish or bears living in a forest. However, humans are very different from bacteria and bears because we innovate and trade. No other species than humans would ever trade an item for a completely different one with a perfect stranger, and no other species exhibit innovation that is even remotely equal to what humans perform.

Because of this unique behavior of humans, we have long since entered an era of not only abundance, but superabundance as well. The best way to measure this is by how many hours the average citizen of the world needs to work to acquire a fixed basket of commodities. This is called the "time-price," and it gives the best measure of scarcity because money is essentially tokenized time. One measure of this phenomenon is the Simon Abundance Index (SAI)—an index of the fifty most used commodities in the world. This index is named after Julian Simon, who, in the 1970s, went against the grain and predicted ever-increasing abundance. This index shows us that the average time-price fell by 74.2 percent from 1980 to 2019. In fact, not even a single one of these fifty commodities required more work to afford in 2019 than they had thirty-nine years earlier—every single one had become *more* affordable. Overall, the compound annual growth rate in affordability of these commodities was 3.63 percent, which implies a doubling of abundance every twenty years. This is yet another exponential law. There are some excellent studies of this phenomenon in the book *Superabundance* by Marian Tupy and Gale Pooley. Here, they noted that between 1850 and 2018, where global population grew approximately 630 percent, the time-price of twenty-six commonly used commodities throughout the period dropped 98 percent for American blue-collar workers and 96 percent for unskilled workers. Furthermore, every single one of these twenty-six commodities was superabundant.

A related observation is that electricity became approximately 200 times more affordable from 1900 to 2000.[21] That means compounding affordability improvements by 5.5 percent annually. (Of course, there are certain goods and services that have become relatively less affordable for large parts of the population, such as housing and higher education, but this is not because of resource scarcity.)

Experience so far shows us that abundance of commodities doubles roughly every twenty years.

The precision economy also seems to promote peace. In the extraction-based economy there was competition for scarce resources, which bred a strong win-lose mentality where a common route to success was to capture land through warfare. As these economies matured, the route to success was innovation and hyper-sociality, which changed mindsets from win-lose to win-win.

Of course, there are nations with leaders who still look for land grabs through violence or threats thereof, but that is because their mentality has not yet caught up with the precision economy. Instead of abundance mindsets, they still have extractive mindsets. There are also nations that destroy natural habitats on a massive scale to extract rather than create. If they had a creator's mindset, they would realize that such habitats contain species with DNA that will in the future enable endless digital replication in compact lab environments. These environments could become a huge resource for the emerging experience economy as well. However, more and more leaders are shifting to the mindset of the emerging economic models.

> **In the Malthusian and industrial extraction economies, control of resources is important for economic success. This promotes aggressive win-lose behaviors such as conquest wars. However, in the precision economy, the primary road to riches is innovation through skilled hyper-sociality, which promotes win-win activity and thus peace.**

INNOVATING TOWARD WEALTH

We have now studied a range of emerging 10x+ technologies, which tells us that the most likely future will bring a wide range of far cleaner, cheaper, and more productive technologies.

The overall conclusion is this: innovation is humanity's most important resource. Only through innovation can we address poverty and environmental challenges and obtain new resources. And since our innovation process is exponential, our access to affordable resources will also be. That is why innovative societies do not run out of resources. We know we will solve climate challenges largely with technologies not in existence today. We know we will never run out of food. The future might seem like a blur, but we can rest assured that more super-abundance is a part of what is waiting.

Chapter 7

HEY, WE CAN CODE LIFE NOW!

We now know that life has always been code-based, since it builds on the digital language of DNA and RNA. Now we can read and rewrite that code with ever greater ease and precision. For instance, we can—

- Eliminate existing species (specicide)
- Change, heal, and "tune" species
- Create hybrid species using genes from several different species (interspecies chimera)
- Make extinct species reappear (de-extinction)
- Create new species

Of course, the first three of these processes are not new to us. Humans have indeed eliminated species, and most of what we eat is very tuned versions of what nature originally developed—often to the degree that it is difficult with the naked eye to spot any relationship to the original source at all. We have also created hybrid species such as wheat.

So much more is possible now. We can design viruses that are optimized for "gene surgery," as they can insert genetic corrections for people with genetic diseases. We can also reprogram soil microbes to enhance growth conditions for our plants or use gene drives to eradicate natural pests or mosquitoes that carry malaria.[1] We can make RNA-based pesticides to avoid resistance development. We can even re-create species that went extinct thousands—if not millions—of years ago.[2]

As a radical example of recurring intelligence, we can also recode our own species, and we have no doubt that we eventually will. We will also code cells as if they are robots at our service so that they can perform magic for us, for instance, by programming microorganisms for precision fermentation of countless compounds. In short, we are the new programmers, and nature is our new computer.

> **With genetic engineering, we can create, re-create, eradicate, tune, and heal species.**

ANTIAGING TECHNOLOGIES

The emerging antiaging technologies illustrate our evolving capabilities well. Most people wish to extend their life span and their "health span," which is the number of years where they feel great and healthy. Ideally, sixty should become the new forty, and eighty should become the new sixty. (We actually believe 120, even 150, could eventually become the new eighty.) And we seem to be getting there; according to a study by the Pew Research Center, only 35 percent of all people aged seventy-five or over considered themselves "old."

Since the year 1800, the global average life expectancy has increased from twenty-nine years to seventy-three years now. This is due to combinations of medical progress, better lifestyles, less violence, and safer environments. Global life expectancy is rising approximately three months per year. However, even as we now manage to dodge plague, cholera, and hunger, we do still age.

Simply stated, there are two elements of aging. The first is mechanical wear and tear, which we can increasingly fix with procedures such as hip replacements and dental surgery. However, the far more complicated challenge—and one of the reasons for much mechanical breakdown—is the genetic breakdown, which is essentially loss of genetic information.

Snapshot Sample of Future Antiaging Breakthroughs Predicted by Supertrends Experts	
2025	The first Telomerase gene therapy enters clinical trial.
2026	An effective assessment tool kit is developed for standard aging evaluation.
2026	Retina image is used as a biomarker for aging.
2029	An antiaging drug that improves at least one aging parameter is approved by the FDA.
2033	A country's average human life span reaches 100 years.
2035	Smart toilets for automated gut microbiome analysis are commercially available.
2035	A human clinical trial that targets brain aging as its primary outcome is conducted.
2036	A CRISPR-based therapy is developed to alter gut microbiome.
2090	The human life span record reaches 150 years.

ERASING THE RECIPE

For the foreseeable future, primary genetic decay seems unavoidable. The average adult human has more than thirty-five trillion cells, and during an average human life span, there are ten quadrillion cell divisions. Some of these divisions create unfortunate mutations, where useful genetic data is lost. Furthermore, our DNA is also exposed to radiation, harmful chemicals, virus infections, and more, which also contribute to genetic degradation. For instance, there are more than 10,000 cases of oxidative damage per cell per day. Most will be fixed through automatic error correction, but some daily damage remains unfixed, and over time, the errors accumulate and lead to the overall loss of information.

It is a genetic breakdown that creates cancer, but even if we could cure all cancer, it would only extend the average human life span by approximately three years, because if aging doesn't kill us through cancer, it makes even simple diseases like the flu significantly more lethal.

However, there are now many R&D projects aiming to slow down or even temporarily reverse the natural aging processes, and this field is about to get rather more interesting, since it often works well when tested on animals. One of the approaches scientists are now working on is making cells closer to immortal. In 1961, US anatomist Leonard Hayflick discovered that human cells in culture would only divide between forty and seventy times—and then stop. This phenomenon is now known as the Hayflick limit. It happens because all chromosomes have telomeres on their ends, which are sections of DNA with no useful genetic code that are there to protect them from other chromosomes. Every time the cell divides, some of the edges break off. For as long as these chromosome edges are protected by the codeless telomeres, you are fine, but after enough divisions, you start to lose useful coding DNA, and then the cell stops dividing and may enter *senescence*, a state of gradual degradation in which it essentially becomes a zombie.

Some cells avoid this with an enzyme called telomerase, which restores telomeres. This can make cells virtually immortal. Scientists have now created mice with extended telomeres, and these had longer health and life spans. A related study of 65,000 people found that those who naturally had longer telomeres also had longer and healthier lives. In other words, protecting or expanding telomeres might slow aging.

We all know that as we age, we naturally lose muscle, and eventually, this alone can kill us. Furthermore, we also lose cells necessary for immunity defense, for processing sugar, and more. This is largely because of loss of stem cells. Stem cells are special cells that can self-renew indefinitely due to telomerase and that can later turn into anything that is needed in your body. Unfortunately, as you age, you have fewer and fewer of them, and this means you lose the ability to replace old or damaged cells. However, in 2006, Shinya Yamanaka discovered how we can turn any cell into a stem cell by adding just four genes. (Yamanaka won a Nobel Prize for this discovery in 2012.) Interestingly, scientists have treated mice with stem cells, and they became healthier and lived longer. This antiaging approach is also promising.

This is the precision economy on steroids, and there are many more emerging antiaging approaches, including treatment with rapamycin, which has extended life spans significantly in yeast, flies, worms, and mice. Numerous other approaches have demonstrated clear antiaging effects in other living organisms than humans.

We are the first species in the history of Earth who consciously and with considerable precision can modify its own genes. This is striking, and if the techniques available to us today can be deployed to enhance not only human health and life span, but also human intelligence (thus creating recursive intelligence in yet another way), we will have reached escape velocity in terms of biological intelligence. This phenomenon will be comparable to the creative processes that took us out of the Malthusian Trap—just at another level. Perhaps this will even replace war as a means of gaining power.

Genetic engineering of humans for higher intelligence might become a future instrument in the battles for geopolitical power.

Much of the genetic revolution is already in process, but far more will materialize over the coming decades. Here are some examples of likely results:

- Precision fermentation or genetically engineered plants or algae will be used to produce raw materials, fabrics, medicines, and food.

- Cancer will commonly be treated via immunotherapy.

- Body parts will often be replaced with new ones created by 3D printing and stem cells.

- We will be able to vaccinate against allergies, addiction, diabetes, cancer, and countless other health threats.

We are approaching the ability to do a genetic analysis on any person (or pet, for that matter) to identify which forms of cancer they might be at risk for. We can then vaccinate them against those specific cancers by injecting them with small strings of RNA, which create antibodies against specific molecular markers that would appear on the surface of the relevant cancer cells, should they ever appear.

So here we are, in a world where living cells are now our computers that can print 3D copies of themselves according to digital instructions that we can control. And we are improving those skills at exponential rates. So much so, in fact, that scientists have even speculated that in the future, humans might have an extra Z chromosome that will act as a genetic app store for added features.

Snapshot Sample of Future for Health-Care and Biotech Breakthroughs Predicted by Supertrends Experts	
2023	The first epigenetic reprogramming therapy targeting tissue regeneration enters clinical trial.
2023	The first gene therapy for treating visual impairments gets FDA approval.
2023	The first cancer treatment is undertaken using nanomagnets.
2023	3D-printed anatomical models become standard for complex medical surgeries.
2024	The first mRNA influenza vaccine is available.
2024	An mRNA vaccine is available for malaria.
2024	An mRNA treatment targeting missing or defective proteins is approved.
2024	3D-printed aerogel is used in transplants.
2025	The one-dollar hearing aid is certified as a medical device.
2025	First functional species proxies are introduced into the wild.
2025	Stem-cell "bandages" are used to treat broken bones.
2025	A vaccine is available for preventing/slowing Alzheimer's disease.
2025	Solar-powered prosthetics are 3D printed.
2025	A highly effective malaria vaccine is approved.
2025	Ultrasound-guided precision delivery of drugs in the brain is approved for clinical practice.
2025	The first telomerase gene therapy enters clinical trial.
2025	3D-bioprinted mesh is used to repair hernias.
2026	A robot is approved clinically to draw blood from patients.

continued

Snapshot Sample of Future for Health-Care and Biotech Breakthroughs Predicted by Supertrends Experts	
2026	3D-printed skin is approved for use in skin transplants.
2027	A patient has nerve damage repaired by a biodegradable electric device.
2028	Medical smart contact lenses are approved for sale.
2028	A virus that makes cancer tumors destroy themselves comes on the market.
2029	CAR-Treg cell therapy research leads to the first living cell vaccines.
2030	Gene and cell therapy for type 1 diabetes based on CAR Tregs is available.
2030	Pancreatic islet transplantations can treat late-stage type 2 diabetes.
2030	A patient undergoes surgery performed by micro-bots.
2032	The first monogenic disease is cured by genetic engineering therapy.
2032	Whole genome sequencing is included in newborn screen tests.
2034	A treatment to cure HIV is approved by the FDA.
2036	Life is synthetically created from nonliving material.
2038	The first quantum computer laptop is commercially available.
2038	There is a cure for Parkinson's disease.
2042	Human germline editing is approved to fight infectious diseases.
2045	Gene editing is routinely utilized to cure hereditary disorders.
2049	There is a cure for Alzheimer's disease.
2073	Humans can theoretically become immortal.
2143	The first human who will live to the age of 1,000 is born.

Chapter 8

AWAKENING THE WORLD WITH I.T.

A recurring theme, when you study the progress of technology, is how much in particular information technology begins to resemble what we see in natural species and biological ecosystems. Technology entrepreneurs have long referred to their collaborative systems as "ecosystems." Just like we find in nature, computers have "viruses," "worms," and "crawlers." One of the most striking elements of this is how computing technologies now add sensors and brains to man-made objects that were previously dumb, blind, and numb. The other similarity is how the innovation of the digital stimulates more of the same in a virtuous loop, whereby we get recursive intelligence. These feedback loops can accelerate, allowing for exponential self-improvement, theoretically with no upper limit. They can essentially take on a life of their own.

If the Five Cs of Innovation are all in place, anything digital that replicates itself is likely to gain recursive intelligence.

**A key component of recursive intelligence is the
presence of digital replicators.**

That being said, much of AI and machine learning today focuses on narrow sets of tasks. Impressive systems such as the AlphaGo, AlphaZero, and MuZero consistently beat world champions in the most complex games on Earth, oftentimes by learning the rules by themselves.[1] Nevertheless, they would struggle to adapt their intelligence to different problems the way humans can. The ability to build an AI system that can adapt to all situations, known as Artificial *General* Intelligence (AGI), is only expected to surpass human intelligence in 2036 at the earliest, according to the Supertrends company's experts.

Some of the most striking recent examples of self-reinforcing intelligence are found in artificial intelligence. For example, the program DALL·E 2, which was launched in April 2022, can enter a simple text description of almost anything, after which the program creates a photorealistic image that represents what you typed. You can also upload a picture, put a frame around part of the picture, and then write how it should be changed, after which—voila!—the desired change magically happens. Or you can upload an image and then ask to get a number of variations of it. In 2018, the Christie's auction house in New York sold, as the first in the world, a work of art produced by an artificial intelligence. A French art group called Obvious had trained the algorithm on a dataset of 15,000 portraits painted by human visual artists between the fourteenth and twentieth centuries, until the algorithm itself concocted an original portrait. The work was printed on canvas, valued at $10,000, and sold for $432,000.

After DALL-E 2 came the even more radical ChatGBT, which at lightening speed can answer almost any question, plus—and this is radical—write software codes reflecting simple oral descriptions of what they are supposed to achieve.

AUTOMATIC HYPOTHESIS GENERATION

More interesting and relevant for the next decade is the application of current forms of AI to ever more specific tasks currently done by humans. An example is automatic hypothesis generation. This works because AI-powered computers are phenomenally fast at reading through massive amounts of scientific papers and drawing overall conclusions from them. They can also sift through extremely complex and overwhelmingly massive amounts of biochemical data and draw conclusions from it in a way no human could, even if given years and years to investigate. Basically, there are three ways to explore potential solutions to developing new medicines:

- *In vivo*, where they are tested on plants, animals, or humans

- *In vitro*, where they are tested on microorganisms, cells, or biological molecules in a lab

- *In silico*, where they are tested through computer simulations

It typically costs more than $40,000 to conduct an *in vivo* test on a single human.[2] *In vitro* is typically quite a lot cheaper. However, the cost of *in silico* can over time drift toward zero and thus constitute a 10x+ technology. This also means that it can be personalized to a single individual.

The point of automatic hypothesis generation is that computers and their software have reached the point where they are not only good at providing answers but can also ask intelligent and meaningful *questions* and form plausible hypotheses. They develop exploratory knowledge. This is recursive intelligence, ladies and gentlemen!

They can also devise solutions that humans would not be able to. In 2012, genetic engineer Craig Venter expressed his expectations for biocomputation in an interview in *Wired*: "I think we can make a robot that learns 10,000 times faster than a scientist can. And then all bets are off on the rate of new discovery."[3]

As we write this, what Venter dreamed of in 2012 has moved from the shadow future into the adjacent possible, and even to the actual. And this is yet another example of recursive intelligence, which at some point indeed should enable AI software to learn "10,000 times faster than a scientist can"—at least in some domains.

Already, AI seems ever more human-like. We are seeing AI that can compose music, draw, create poems, and write ad copy in ways that are impossible to distinguish from human work. And this is just the beginning.

How do these AI-powered computers get their information? Of course, they can read scientific literature or be fed data manually by a human. However, often and increasingly, their data input comes from sensors on internet-connected devices. When things get equipped with sensors that communicate via the web, we talk about IoT, or Internet of Things. That combination creates man-made objects with lifelike behavior, and central computers with human-like situational awareness.

DASHBOARDS, DIGITAL TWINS, AND NOWCASTING

One of the consequences of improvements in IoT is the growth of the "digital twin" phenomenon, where real structures are duplicated virtually for monitoring and simulation purposes. For instance, a modern nuclear reactor obviously has a digital twin, but a more common example is a large retail group with tens of thousands of suppliers and outlets, which tracks everything in real time and uses AI to predict where bottlenecks could occur. For instance, if the weather forecast in an area says warm and sunny, do the stores need to stock up on more cold drinks? You could also make a model of a school to enable experiments with alternative teaching approaches.

BIO-TRACKING AND TELEHEALTH

A big growth area is wearable health trackers—also called bio-trackers—which enable consumers to monitor their health status on various dashboards. This can be used for tracking personal sleep rhythms, glucose levels, blood pressure, steps walked, body temperature, and more. If you add frequent blood tests, such personal health dashboards could be expanded to include smart surveillance of hundreds of health indicators, where data such as sleep and movement tracking is IoT-based and real-time updated, and where health adjustment recommendations could be at your fingertips.

This is called telehealth, and a similar approach can be used for remote patient monitoring (RPM). RPM can enable release of patients from clinics much faster, which both saves money and brings social and health benefits.

In more extreme cases, AI can be used to offer digital biomarkers that track not only physical indicators but also things like how people interact with different apps. Subtle changes in this may indicate the beginning of depression, anxiety, and more. The solutions to these and other health issues could come in the form of digital therapeutics, which are evidence-based treatments delivered through software and devices. In other words, IT providers can create digital twins in order to support your health.

Here are a few examples of anticipated future breakthroughs in these technologies:

Snapshot Sample of Future Bio-Tracking and Telehealth Breakthroughs Predicted by Supertrends Experts	
2023	The global fitness tracker market exceeds $50 billion.
2025	Smartphone-based diagnostic method is developed for a common medical condition.
2026	Electronic skin is used for health monitor.
2026	The first commercially available textile antenna for millimeter wave bands is launched.
2034	Underwear that monitors health is developed.

FROM FORECASTING TO NOWCASTING

Taking it to an even higher level, we can use IoT to vastly improve macroeconomic management. Indeed, economics has already entered what *The Economist* has called its "third wave," which is where real-time processing of vast amounts of data dominates. This is a major shift, because until quite recently, the vast majority of statistical data available to economists was dated by months, quarters, or years since it took time to collect. This led to the kind of problems described by *The Economist*: "If you look at the data right now . . . we are not in what would normally be characterized as a recession," argued Edward Lazear, then chairman of the White House Council of Economic Advisers, in May 2008. Five months later, after Lehman Brothers had collapsed, the IMF noted that America was "not necessarily" heading for a deep recession. In fact, America had entered a recession in December 2007.

That was then, but in the precision economy, real-time economics is getting ever more accurate. We can now capture real-time dataflows such as purchases from Amazon or Alibaba, use of Uber and other rideshare and micromobility services, credit card spending, electricity consumption, physical movements of people into shopping and tourist areas, jet engines in operation plus aircraft flying right now, new car registrations today, oil sales right now, containers leaving from—or arriving in—ports, OpenTable bookings this evening, and our personal portfolios of financial investments all in real time or close to real time. Economically, our fingers are increasingly on the pulse.

PRECISION MONEY

Leading investment banks such as the management consulting company McKinsey & Company are already using such input a lot, as is the Atlanta Federal Reserve, which runs the GDPNow model to nowcast (i.e., estimate in real time) the state of GDP. Such data can vastly improve corporate inventory management, financial investment decisions, and fiscal and monetary policy adjustments. As an example, if the central bank knows pretty much in real time when the economy is overheating or in danger of going into recession, they can react much faster and thus lessen the blow. This can be combined with issuing digital money that expires after a limited time so that people will indeed spend it—an approach that Hong Kong has already experimented with. Call it precision money if you will. Such money for the precision economy can even be dedicated for use in specific sectors.

DECENTRALIZATION THROUGH TECH

An interesting tension in our organizations is the conflict or dichotomy between those with inherent tendencies toward centralization and those that tend toward decentralization. First, we believe that in any company and nation, there is an inherent tendency toward greater centralization of power and toward over-institutionalization. This phenomenon is well described, for instance, by scientists such as Caroll Quigley (spontaneous over-institutionalization in civilizations) and Mancur Olson (centralization and bureaucracy in public sectors and companies).

During the Industrial Revolution, such centralization was reinforced by the technology-driven desire to reach economies of scale in mass production, so it often made sense: almost all the innovations driving productivity forward in the *industrial economy* were about centralized mass production on a huge scale. The massive productivity increases of the Industrial Revolution were created by cascades of 10x+ innovations. For instance, the Bessemer process brought the cost of steel production for railways down from $170 per ton in 1867 to $15 per ton in 1898—a 10x+ improvement within thirty-one years.[4] With the invention of the container, plus other shipping innovations, the cost of shipping across the Atlantic dropped from $420 in the 1950s to 50 dollars today, which when corrected for inflation, equals an improvement of 80x within seventy years.

However, in the precision economy, far more of the 10x+ technologies depend on or promote *decentralization*. For instance, with homeworking, teleconferencing, and crowdsourcing, products are increasingly developed by teams scattered all over. With vertical farming, precision fermentation, and cultured meat, it becomes far easier to produce food anywhere. And with solar, wind, and new nuclear power technologies, you can produce energy virtually anywhere. Indeed, you will be able to use wind, photons, thorium, nuclear waste, or deuterium and tritium to produce electric power, which again can be used to produce fluid fuel such as hydrogen, syngas, and ammonia at or very close to the locations where it's desired. The small, the local, and the decentralized will thus shape the big, adding organically from below instead of designing from the top—all of which puts Deutsch's hierarchy rule on its head. Ultimately, we will take such small-to-big assembly technologies to the stage where self-sufficient habitats can be produced in spaceships, on the moon, and even on Mars.

Back on Earth, blockchain is another technology promoting decentralization and transparency. With this, you can to some extent replace states, banks, lawyers, and more. And with 3D printing, you can manufacture anywhere. Cloud computing, app stores, blockchain, crowdsourcing, sharing economy, online education, social media, micromobility, and the rating economy are also technologies that facilitate decentralization.

In this economy, creativity and design is done in global digital networks where it's much easier for anyone anywhere to contribute to innovation, as well as to production. These trends will affect how people live and how we run efficient organizations.

THE MAGIC QUARTET OF IOT, BIG DATA, AI, AND ROBOTICS

To process data captured through IoT and other means, we frequently use big data approaches. These approaches differ from traditional statistical sampling in the following ways:

- They use continuous, rather than periodical analysis.

- They follow all relevant data instead of selected representative sample data.

- They are often based on so-called data exhaust: data that was not primarily created with the intention of analyzing it—but which is now analyzed anyway.

- They are capable of pattern recognition, which means that if some data is missing, they can extrapolate from other data to fill in the gaps. This is called "synthetic data."

- They can simulate future projections of even very complex processes—often via AI.

This means that AI, IoT, and big data are highly complementary technologies. And together, they are making ever more of the physical world "wake up." As this happens, more and more of the things in our environment become active and adaptive. And as already mentioned, sometimes almost living, like in the biological ecosystems.

You are probably a user of cloud computing, which is on-demand availability of computer data storage (cloud storage) and/or computing power without direct active management by the user. Gmail is a cloud-based service, and phones and computers routinely store data in the cloud. But now there is another cloud: the cloud of things, which is what IoT is about. Indeed, the trio of IoT, big data, and AI increasingly enables massive intelligent communication with the edge of IT systems, which in this case is sensors.

Interestingly, AI is tied in with open-source solutions so that AI components can be freely accessed online and used as modules for processing real data—in the same vein that websites are typically created from ready-to-use templates.

> **The IoT, big data, AI, and robotics quartet is making ever more of the physical world "wake up" and become smart.**

However, in many cases, this AI/IoT/big data technology trio is further connected with robotics. This technology quartet is currently being rolled out in the American military. Today, the US military forces depend to a large degree on relatively few important nodes, like aircraft carriers, communication satellites, and JSTARS (converted

Boeing jumbo jets). However, as Will Roper, the US Air Force's head of acquisitions has stated, a JSTARS has become "a sluggish flying bull's eye." It can be shot down with weapons that increasingly can be afforded by much smaller armies. Satellites can also be destroyed, although that costs more. Even a mighty aircraft carrier is increasingly vulnerable.

KILLED BY THE SWARM

For these reasons, the US Department of Defense has launched a concept called "Joint All-Domain Command and Control," or JADC2, which aims to completely decentralize and partly automate military processes while still maintaining the military hierarchy/chain of command. Instead of relying on a few central nodes, the idea is to create a peer-to-peer network that uses countless sensors and nodes, and where data will automatically reroute if some of the nodes become incapacitated—just like how the internet works. In this way, they aim to link "every sensor to every shooter." Sensors might lie on the ground and look like natural stones, or they may be tiny drones that could even emulate birds or insects. Shooters might be robots, and cars might be self-driven. AI massively reduces the time it takes to process data and detect or select targets. It might also propose unusual approaches like triggering fire alarms in buildings before they are destroyed by a military attack so people have time to get out.

Of course, similar approaches could be used in civilian life to protect parking lots and other residential areas. This can be done by continuously checking whether something looks right, which can be facilitated with AI. These technologies might also be used by companies to run parts of civilian businesses.

In financial services, robo-advisers are increasingly prevalent. We could also imagine governments using many of these techniques: feed the macroeconomic models and all the laws and regulations to AI, and it might suggest how to simplify rules, optimize tax structures, improve monetary policies, and much more.

On a personal level, we might imagine robotics, IoT, big data, and AI combining in the form of a personal assistant, who not only caters to your wishes but also often predicts your needs better than you do yourself. Warm bath already prepared after biking home in the rain? Automatic ordering of household goods, based on typical consumption? Preventive maintenance on your self-driving car, carried out while you're at work? Yes please. And with regular feedback from you, the robot will only collect more data and get to know you even better. This feedback loop might even create recursive intelligence where you and your robot learn from each other.

THE DIGITAL WHIRLWIND

Data is sometimes referred to as the oil of our time. From the 1940s to the 1970s, there were seven huge oil companies, known as "the Seven Sisters," which dominated the global oil business and made tons of money. Now we have seven new sisters, and their names are Facebook (Meta), Apple, Amazon, Google (Alphabet), Baidu, Alibaba, and Tencent. But these seven sisters are all *data* companies.

In other words, really big money is now made in areas such as computing power, AI, connectivity, sensors and IoT, and blockchain. One sector after another is going digital, and one digital technology after another is going exponential. This is compounded by technology convergence, network effects, AI, and recursive intelligence.

Digitalization also brings about lower unit costs. An increasing number of sectors are evolving. At one time, they emphasized manual work, then they moved to mechanical operation, and now their work is finally digital. This means that productivity changes from being static to growing linearly, and then to growing exponentially. Organizations often need to move from hierarchical systems optimized for the industrial extraction economies to the decentralized optimized for precision and experience economies.

VIRTUAL AND AUGMENTED REALITY

Virtual reality (VR) is a simulated environment, often accessed via goggles that give a 3D effect. Augmented reality (AR) is an extension of this where the virtual reality is overlaid on the real world and visible, for instance, via smartphones, GPS monitors, or smart glasses. Jointly, these are called immersive technologies. Among the weird effects that these technologies can enable are artificial limbs, artificial senses, and virtual powers. For instance, a paralyzed person can learn to control artificial limbs entirely by thinking about it. If we extend this to a VR game, imagine that your avatar is Superman and that you can make this avatar, which feels like you, fly only by thinking about it!

Some of this relates to devices that interact directly with the brain—a radical form of IoT. This comes in the form of noninvasive devices, which use focused ultrasound (FUS), and invasive devices using deep brain stimulation or optogenetics. In the future, we might even engage such technologies to erase negative memories such as of violence, or even introduce new false memories to combat self-destructive behavior. Closed-loop mechanical devices can also amplify brain activities that assist in things like getting a good night's sleep.

THE METAVERSE

In video games, you often become the player that you see on the screen. Now imagine that instead of controlling the character with a limited set of moves through a joystick, you feel like you actually become the main character. Or the character becomes you in the form of an avatar. How fun would it be to dictate your avatar's identity and actions, interact with the avatars of other real people, and perhaps even get married and have children in cyberspace? You could escape from your current physical reality and forge a completely new online reality. This game might well become a bestseller if it were produced.

Except it's not a game. It's already happening through the metaverse, and there is big money behind it. The company previously called Facebook has defined building this as one of its major future missions and even renamed itself Meta. In 2020, 27.7 million players attended *Fortnite*'s Travis Scott's virtual concert in the metaverse, and in 2021, Microsoft secured a $21.9 billion contract to produce AR headsets for the US Army. That same year, almost $2 billion worth of virtual land in the metaverse was purchased. Through a combination of a single common platform that connects people, virtual reality headsets, and wearable body sensors, a metaverse means that you will be able to enter a new digital universe and live out your dreams. The boundaries between what is real and what is not are blurring, and an increasing number of people are choosing to substitute this virtual world for their everyday reality. When you enter the metaverse, not only is your physical location irrelevant, but to a larger and larger extent so is your physical reality. You can now shape and mold your identity and actions and, as one early adopter of the metaverse has said, "dream with your eyes open."

What is clear is that information technology is not standing still, and there is a whole host of "new tech" that is still very much at the emerging stages, such as quantum computing, blockchain, and the metaverse. And many of these technologies are converging in totally new ways.

Following is a snapshot of the IT predictions made by the Supertrends experts:

Snapshot Sample of Future Information Technology Breakthroughs Predicted by Supertrends Experts	
2023	A government replaces its census with big data.
2024	Small modular quantum computers are networked together in a data center.
2024	AI-based, no-touch technology is used in public spaces instead of touch screens for the first time.
2024	A hotel offers an immersive virtual reality experience.
2024	Voice assistants can anticipate users' needs.
2024	An AI fashion designer outperforms a human designer.
2025	Passengers can pay with their face on city public transport.
2025	Quantum computing and quantum finance theory are used in market forecasting.
2025	Guided bullets are employed in military operations.
2025	A magnetic shield successfully prevents a drone attack.

continued

Snapshot Sample of Future Information Technology Breakthroughs Predicted by Supertrends Experts	
2025	The first robot is fitted with carbon nanotube muscles.
2025	A smartphone app that judges whether meat is safe to eat is launched.
2026	An artificial intelligence is part of a corporate board of directors.
2026	An algorithm identifies a viral outbreak from anonymous cell phone data.
2026	Self-charging electronics are embedded in everyday objects.
2026	Quantum computing is used to improve weather forecasting.
2026	A chatbot that allows people to speak to the dead is launched.
2026	A major retailer rolls out augmented reality mirrors in all stores.
2027	A quantum simulator is used to develop a video game.
2027	Half of worldwide IT infrastructure spend is generated through cloud products.
2027	75 percent of all blockchain traffic relies on technologies with low energy consumption.
2028	Smartphones can project holograms.
2029	A major social media platform integrates blockchain into its login system.
2029	The first school that teaches only in VR opens.
2030	The computational capacity of personal computers surpasses that of humans.
2032	Whole genome sequencing is included in newborn screen tests.
2032	Ambient light and radio signals are utilized to power electronic devices.
2032	The first computer passes an official Turing test.
2033	The first anticipatory AI home assistant is launched commercially.
2033	Virtual reality headsets are replaced by smart contact lenses.
2034	6G networks accommodate 10 million IoT devices per square kilometer.
2034	Objects can be made invisible to the human eye.
2035	First commercial optical computer goes on sale.
2035	Electronic devices can be charged using Wi-Fi signals.
2037	An AI claims to be self-aware.
2038	Half of all cars on US highways are self-driving.
2038	The first quantum computer laptop is commercially available.
2038	Full-immersion virtual reality becomes possible.
2042	Over 10 percent of the worldwide computer power is based on quantum computing.
2042	Universal household robots are commercially available.

Chapter 9

FROM BOOMERS TO ZOOMERS

Myriad forces affect how consumers choose to spend their time and money. This phenomenon is complicated by the difference in habits and values between generations. That difference is growing because of accelerating technological changes and the fact that younger people change lifestyles faster than older people. The current workforce and consuming class comprises five generations (if we include traditionalists/the silent generation born between 1928 and 1945), and it is probably the most culturally diverse population the world has ever had. While marketing and sociology professionals often talk of the "zeitgeist" that comes with any generation, the issue here is that we have multiple different zeitgeists simultaneously. The rate of technological change is tearing generations apart.

> The current population comprises five generations.
> Each of these has its own predominant values
> and habits, and these are often conflicting.

What follows are profiles of different generations. Please note that these are generalizations and must therefore be taken with some caveats. For more insight into the issue, we recommend *The Generation Myth* by Bobby Duffy, where Duffy points out that the attitudes of the generations change as they age, and we aren't necessarily going to see more generation wars than we've seen in the past.

BABY BOOMERS (BORN 1946-1964)

Baby boomers have grown up with memories or real stories from their parents of World War II. They've seen the advent of the audio cassette, personal computer, dial-up internet, space travel, and popularization of inventions such as the television, radio, and telephone. They are used to stable work environments with hierarchical leadership structures, and they have typically been loyal to their organizations in return for stability and job security. They witnessed the great resource and environment panics of the 1960s and '70s, and they experienced the transition from traditional printed marketing toward mass broadcast marketing on radio and TV.

GENERATION X (BORN 1965-1980)

Gen X has experienced the shift from analogue to digital, fondly remembering the days of Walkmans and the bulky Discmans that followed, before the move to smartphones and MP3 audio. They might also have sported pagers and PDAs (personal digital assistants) for a short period, and generally managed the transition to digital well. They remember a world separated during the Cold War and the fall of the Berlin Wall, and the bold proclamations of liberal democracy as the "end of history." They are typically used to a more participative organizational culture and are prepared to work hard to further their goals but also focus on "work-life balance" (a term coined in 1986). About one in four Xers in OECD had earned a college degree by age thirty-three.

GENERATION Y/MILLENNIALS (BORN 1981-1996)

Millennials have grown up with access to the internet from an early age and remember receiving their first mobile phones during their childhood or teenage years. For many, these were brick-like devices that bear little resemblance to the smartphones of today. This generation grew up with globalization, global scares, shocks, and threats such as the Y2K bug, the 9/11 attacks, the 2008 financial crisis, and the COVID-19 pandemic. They demand empowerment and continuous development on the job and are less focused on job security than previous generations. The majority of them are expected to change jobs every three years or so, with an increasing share considering freelancing as a viable career option. Although about one in three millennials have a college degree, there is evidence that in some wealthy nations, they will be the first generation to earn less than the one before them.[1]

GENERATION Z/ZOOMERS (BORN 1997-2010)

Zoomers have grown up with smartphones, smart TVs, digital assistants in the home, and the advent of social media. They are true digital natives and are often part of multiple social networks. They prioritize access rather than ownership and take a greater interest in the ethical considerations around their purchases and around company behavior. They harbor real expectations of living to at least a hundred years old through biological engineering, and perhaps one day visiting space as a tourist. They're already the biggest global generation ever, with almost 2 billion of them alive today. It is forecasted that up to one in two will go on to earn college degrees, although there is also an opposite trend toward shorter, skill-based diplomas and micro-accreditations instead of degrees. Over their lifetime, they are forecasted to hold eighteen jobs across six careers and to live in fifteen homes.[2] At the same time, this generation has been shown to be the most stressed and anxious, and many are pessimistic about issues such as climate change, the rise of authoritarianism, and growing inequality.

Over their lifetime, Generation Z/zoomers are forecasted to hold eighteen jobs across six careers and to live in fifteen homes.

For the moment, we will leave out Generation Alpha (born between 2010 and 2024), as the oldest of them will be twenty years old by 2030. However, there is evidence that they again have important differences in how they view the world compared to previous generations, and they are a rapidly growing generation (2.7 million new alphas born each week!), so they will be important to study at a later point.

Each new generation brings clear shifts in perceptions, expectations, and behaviors, many of which are unidirectional. By *unidirectional*, we mean that they are moving in a specific direction that is expected to continue in the future, even if there are occasional bumps along the way. For example, the world generally cares more about the environment, not less. The world is generally becoming more tolerant of LGBTQ+ rights, not less. Demographically, Generation Z is more open-minded and tolerant of differences than millennials, for example, in terms of supporting same-sex adoption, same-sex marriage, and racial equality. Millennials, in turn, are more open-minded and tolerant than Generation X and baby boomers.

Millennials and Generation Z are also increasingly atheist or have no stated or formal religion, are more likely to mobilize around causes they care about, more likely to believe climate change is dangerous and predominantly human-caused, more comfortable as self-learners (having grown up with Google at their fingertips), more likely to freelance, more likely to value job flexibility in terms of hours and location, and are more likely to spend time online and be part of multiple online communities. Furthermore, the newer generations are more likely to pay a premium for personalized offerings, more willing to pay more for brands that embrace causes they identify with, and more likely to value brands that don't classify as male or female. Also, they are more comfortable with using ratings as guidelines for purchase decisions and thus more willing to shop for unfamiliar brands, as long as ratings are good.

Younger people are more comfortable with buying unfamiliar brands, as long as their ratings are good.

A few things break with the trends. Having a job is still important and relatively consistent among generations. This is likely due to the innate human desire to do something valuable, and also the more disruptive macroeconomic upbringings millennials and Gen Z have faced in terms of multiple economic crises, soaring costs of real estate relative to real wages, and epidemics and pandemics. In fact, while up to 71 percent of millennials would prefer work-life balance over a well-paying job, this number falls to 58 percent for Gen Z. Furthermore, despite their desire for more flexible and self-guided careers with a new employer every few years and potentially a freelancing side gig, millennials and Gen Z are still career-focused and typically make deliberate decisions to enhance their skills, job responsibilities, and pay. Finally, there is a consistent discomfort across generations when it comes to sharing personal data with companies, with only 10–15 percent of consumers declaring that they have no issues with doing so.[3]

In 2030, we will see some significant demographic shifts. By this time, up to 700 million baby boomers will reach retirement age, as the youngest of this generation will be sixty-five years old. Interestingly, a majority plan to work past the age of sixty-five, or already do so. Generation Xers will be between fifty and sixty-five. The oldest millennials will likewise be fifty years old. During the same time period, 1.3 billion Generation Z workers will enter the workforce and become the largest share of the workforce (as well as the global population), overtaking millennials as the dominant group. Combined, millennials and Gen Z will make up more than two-thirds of the global workforce.[4]

While boomers still hold large swaths of purchasing power in many parts of the world (and their retirement wave will benefit industries such as travel and leisure, health care, vitamins and functional food, traditional retail, and DIY stores), these shifts will bring important changes in terms of consumption, work expectations, social interactions, and voting behavior.

> A majority of people now plan to work past
> the age of sixty-five, or already do so.

THE RISK AVERSION-BRUTALIZATION DICHOTOMY

We have previously discussed the dichotomy between forces promoting centralization versus decentralization in our societies and organizations. This is a very high-level phenomenon, but there is a parallel one worth noticing: over time, our societies continuously promote more safety in products, work, free time, and so on. Similar forces create greater adversity against hardship and risk. However, human genes don't change nearly as fast, and the result is that many people (especially men, it seems) feel a residual desire for risk and hardship. This is then played out in often rather violent and sometimes extreme sports, and in movies and games that are often extremely and increasingly brutal. We don't see any immediate reason why both of these opposing trends won't continue.

PEAK CHILD VS. CONTINUED ABUNDANCE

Measured as a percentage, the global population growth peaked in 1964 and has declined every year since. When measured in actual numbers, it peaked with 93 million people added in 1988, but again, this number has also declined since (it was 81 million in 2020). Furthermore, on a global basis, we have now reached "peak child," which means that the number of children in the world is no longer rising but has reached a plateau.[5] Indeed, according to the UN median estimates, the global number of children aged five and fifteen will stay pretty much unchanged during the rest of this century.

This means that while our technologies continue to evolve exponentially, population growth is constantly decreasing and will sooner or later be reversed into population decline. A consequence of this is that more and more people will feel the effects of abundance and make lifestyle choices where they choose not to increase their material wealth anymore. They will prioritize better quality over quantity.

It should be added that the *nouveau riche* are often greater material spenders than people who grew up in affluence. A typical pattern will often be that those who were born feeling shortage of material wealth will overcompensate later in life, if they can, but that their children who are born with "enough" will not make that choice. This sense of having enough is often called *enoughism*.

As more and more grow up in affluence, more will prioritize quality over quantity. This is so-called enoughism.

MOVING UP MASLOW

The Maslow pyramid is a visual representation of Maslow's hierarchy of needs, which is a description of human needs ranging from basic ones such as food and shelter toward higher ones such as love, esteem, and self-actualization. It has been shown that the needs Maslow identified are not always sought in a strictly chronological way, from bottom to top. Those with more time and money do typically seek higher needs to a greater extent than those with less, however.

There is more of a widespread focus today on finding your purpose and self-actualization. This is reflected, for instance, in considerable differences between the typical values of baby boomers and Generation Y/millennials. For the latter, spare time and freedom of choice are becoming a new currency of the wealthy, and they are using that time to meet new needs, develop themselves to pursue higher levels of purpose, and focus on social causes.

There is more of a widespread focus today on finding your purpose and self-actualization.

LOW-TECH AT THE PEAK

One mistake often seen in older science fiction movies is a depiction of a future where everything is very high-tech and artificial. By now, we have passed the years that many of these movies were about, and what we see is often rather different. Yes, many places employ high-tech solutions, but as people get wealthier, they often prefer much more expensive low-tech—or retro—lifestyles. For instance, in many places, hunting is now a sport mainly for the most affluent, even though there exists no more expensive way to get fed. Even though we all can check what time it is on our smartphones, the market for less-precise hand-made mechanical watches is booming—among the wealthy. In the European Alps, the most affluent remove new wood from walls and surfaces of the mountain lodges and replace it with old and worn wood that cost four times as much. And so on. What happens here is that the prosperity brought from high-tech and the many 10x+ technologies around us enable more and more of us to choose low-tech options when we find them more charming, pleasant, cozy, or whatever. Handmade production is often very inefficient, but it becomes more desirable as it becomes rarer. This applies to the maker movement as well, which is about doing the manufacturing yourself at home and is another revolt against industrial mass production. Really, it is about increases in wealth created by the industrial and precision economies allowing us to afford more of the lovely but inefficient experience economy.

PERCEPTION GAPS

Just as well as gaps in perception can arise between people and cultures because some have a mistrust-based win-lose/dominance/conquest men-tality and others have a trust-based win-win cooperation mentality, other mental gaps can also arise. There can, for instance, be gaps between the experience economy and the precision economy's often conflicting approaches to reality. For example, the experience economy serves up an initially very appealing story about healthy and nature-friendly organic food. But here the supporters of the precision economy can then point out that if the entire world's food production was actually organic, we would either have to convert huge natural areas into agriculture—or let billions of people starve. Organic food requires far more land per produced unit than modern industrial or precision-based agriculture.

Correspondingly, conflicts of perception and thus prescription can arise when young people who—perhaps unlike their parents or grandparents—were born in safe and wealthy societies are fascinated by experience economy stories but forget how it is all based on the at times less charming efficiency of industrial and precision economies.

Chapter 10

THE VISIBLE HAND
OF THE MICRO-MARKET

As technologies and consumer preferences evolve, so do markets. Driven by mass digitalization, technological convergence, and changing consumer preferences, there are a number of significant shifts that all industries are going through.

INCREASED PRODUCT DIVERSITY

Let's recall again David Deutsch's great monotony and hierarchy rule. In nature, this was brought to an end because of the re-combinatory potential of DNA. The same happens regarding products and marketing in our commercial markets: digitalization and replicators lead to vastly increased diversity in the offerings. Digital data meets online and combines in countless ways, and with the digitalization of our manufacturing processes, we can create greater diversity and prosperity.

Since the widespread adoption of the internet, the number of media anyone can access has virtually exploded, and many of us now subscribe to hundreds of groups and streams of all sorts—most of them free and interactive.

Prosperity gives us ever more choice. Have you noticed what has happened to coffee during the last decades? We got more brands and variants. Like, *a lot* more. Of course, this happens partly because with prosperity we can afford more choices and higher quality. Thus today, we get a lot more choice when it comes to coffee, but also to beer due to the proliferation of microbreweries. In many cases, digital technologies make this possible.

Something similar has happened to bread, watches, fashion, gin, and so on. Within all these markets, we are combining the advantages of the industrial economy with precision economy and experience economy. Not only do we get more products and brands, but we also get seasonal and event-related specials, collector- and limited-edition versions, and more. In many cases, products and services foster tribes, which give a more exclusive sense of identity and belonging—not just in products like craft beer at your local microbrewery, but also in niche fitness concepts, clothing, and coworking spaces.

> **More prosperity also brings more product diversity. This in turn makes consumers self-organize into tribes rallying around different product clusters. Companies can tap into this.**

THE SEGMENT OF ONE

At the extreme end, we get the entirely tailor-made versions, targeting a market segment of one—you! Online shopping, AI, and self-measurement plus self-tracking technologies can serve the purpose. So can 3D printing: walk into a shop, get your feet scanned, and then the 3D printer will print a pair of shoes that fit you—*exactly*. A sector that may be impacted massively by this is the fashion industry, where so-called soft robotics is improving toward being able to sew and knit individualized clothes at a competitive cost.

Snapshot Samples of Future On-Demand Fashion Breakthroughs Predicted by Supertrends Experts	
2026	A major retailer rolls out augmented reality mirrors in all stores.
2028	A brand employs an AI-powered virtual influencer.
2031	Prescription glasses that update themselves are commercially launched.
2033	End customers can design their own clothes with the help of AI.
2035	Chatbot fashion stylists are used more than human stylists.
2041	A skilled robotic makeup artist is developed.
2042	People commonly purchase augmented reality clothing.
2045	Clothes can be 3D printed at home.

Equally, telecommunication and the telecommunication-facilitated developments in computing have contributed toward a diversity of offerings. While the first computers were highly centralized (think mainframe computing), the evolution toward networks, internet-connected computing, cloud computing, and then edge computing via IoT, big data, and AI has meant ever more decentralized computing. This has facilitated an explosion in the diversity of our digital offerings, as well as increased personalization.

Increased wealth combined with digitalization leads to ever finer segment targeting, with a rapid growth in segment-of-one marketing.

FROM PUSH TO PULL

One consequence of these developments is a shift from push marketing toward pull marketing. The clients are increasingly equipped to make very precise demands, which can trigger an order—and they are less willing to be bombarded with offers that are often not tailored exactly for them.

We also see this push-to-pull shift evolving in knowledge seeking and education. Rather than going through a very long academic education where much of what we learn is pushed to us and may never be used, while some of the rest is forgotten by the time we need it, we get more and more inclined to find relevant and up-to-date information just in time via Google searches, YouTube, Wikipedia, and so on. Even within formal education programs, the future is likely to deploy AI to customize the training of every single student, who then truly becomes a segment of one. For instance, AI can offer tailored learning journeys. This means a move away from the industrial economy–style mass education of students to the precision economy–inspired mass customization. A part of that can be the so-called flipped classroom, where homework comes before the lessons. Another is multi-disciplinary super-labs and totally immersive teaching experiences.

> **Mass-personalization technologies support**
> **a shift from vendor push to client pull.**

THE GROWTH OF THE EXPERIENCE ECONOMY

Similarly, we are moving toward the experience economy. We have long since seen a shift toward selling experiences rather than selling just products, which, for example, is part of the reason why consumers might pay ten dollars for a cup of coffee at a waterfront café, even though it only costs a fraction of that to actually produce it. As more and more things are packaged and sold as experiences, brands are competing to further differentiate themselves. From an economic perspective, the Industrial Revolution—which is still ongoing—and the precision economy—which began around 1980—are creating the wealth that moves us toward the experience economy. These three will all coexist, but ultimately, the attributes of the experience economy will dominate. Whereas a few decades ago, the world's most valuable companies were related to the industrial economy and they now are actors in the precision economy, it wouldn't surprise us if a few decades from now, they are mainly leaders from the experience economy.

As a part of this, we will also gain access to more excitement. Some of this will come from new computer games and associated e-sports, new types of media, and the likes of virtual and ambient computing: in other words, from electronics. There will also be a growth in fascinating new hybrid experiences that will enrich all our senses and play on all our feelings, not to mention new combinations of physical and electronic experiences as in augmented reality. Even established industries will be transformed. Just think about how construction, education, or health care could be transformed to provide a more precise and meaningful experience to consumers, rather than just covering a basic need. Disney, for example, has ventured into developing residential communities in order to bring storytelling to "storyliving." The company aims to "bring the magic of Disney to people wherever they are."[1] This is an example of product diversity, push-to-pull dynamics, and a focus on experiences, all in one, and we're excited!

WHEN *YOU* ARE THE PRODUCT

Interestingly, many new services and products are emerging where you as a consumer essentially are the product. This includes coaching, wellness workshops, healing, body shaping, debate clubs, personalized clothing and interior design, personalized foods, and anything where what you buy enhances you in some way, where you are essentially buying a better you.

> **In the growing experience economy,**
> **the client is often the product.**

Linked to all this is the growth of the participation society, where we are not only consumers of stuff that others produced, but also producers of it—"prosumers." This happens, for instance, on social media, where we all consume and produce content. And it happens on Spotify where we produce and consume playlists. Even things like homemade gin, homegrown vegetables, and homemade artisan products are booming, while partial participation is growing too, for example in terms of DJing and editing songs, which can now be done much more easily with the latest software and equipment. Sometimes you choose to sell what you produce, sometimes it is your way of promoting yourself or building your network, while often you do it purely for the joy of the activity and personal consumption.

Just as we merge with machines to become centaurs, we merge consumption with production and become prosumers.

THE GROWTH IN AS-A-SERVICE SOLUTIONS

One of the most significant shifts is the move to an on-tap economy. In countries that are wealthy now, life was very different a few hundred years ago. Back then, most people lived in the countryside, and absolutely everything they needed in their home—apart from air—would be manually carried in. They got their water from wells and carried it in with buckets. Heat came from wood, but this was also carried in. The same with coal and coke. Information came in the form of letters and perhaps newspapers, but again, this was carried physically into the house, although it was less heavy than buckets of coal!

But then they got tap water. Water would now simply flow into the building on command, and you would pay for whatever you happened to use. How nice! After this came power on tap in the form of electricity. And perhaps also natural gas, which, unlike firewood, coal, or coke, also flowed seamlessly into the house. Then came news and data on tap via the internet. Then access to data storage and computing power on tap via cloud computing. And now via IoT, we are increasingly getting data from devices on tap.

Such on-tap models are often extremely convenient for sellers, as well as buyers, and that is why they keep growing. Countless industries have already been converting to on-tap business models—or as-a-service, as it is often called. Numerous more will follow. This also means there is a shift in many industries toward renting rather than owning (or subscribing rather than buying).

As we digitize the economies, we increasingly shift from owning
to renting and from buying to subscribing.

SIMPLIFICATION AND AUTOMATION

As more and more shopping is done online, shopping becomes increasingly algorithm driven and simplified for the consumer (e.g., one-click checkout). Amazon's recommendation engine generates upward of 30 percent of its revenue, while music streaming services such as Spotify also increase the number of streams from targeted artist and song suggestions. Sometimes we don't even know what we want, or we wish to be pleasantly surprised, and the machine algorithm can help us. The fact that the back end may be extremely complex in order to make the consumer experience great and simple is invisible to us.

However, the trend is moving toward something even more extreme—fully automated actions and even purchases based on needs that you don't even know you have. Can you imagine if you check your phone one day and see that your electric, self-driving car has gone ahead and changed its tires, using your credit card on file? We would hope that it would at least ask for permission first, but maybe that's even one click too many for some consumers.

SHARING AND RATING

We are also seeing an increase in the sharing economy. There are three forms here:

- As-a-service models (e.g., car lease, bicycle rental, short-term jobs)

- Crowdsourcing from people rather than companies, (e.g., Airbnb, dog-walking services, or cloud kitchens with freelance chefs that provide takeaway meals)

- Peer-to-peer, which is similar to crowdsourcing but without an intermediary (e.g., BitTorrent filesharing)

Blockchain technology can further enhance trust in such systems, as it maintains a decentralized register of transactions, removing the need for an intermediary as a safeguarding mechanism. Interestingly, these trends also make markets significantly more global as you can now share with virtually anyone around the world.

We have also entered the **rating economy**, where customers provide transparent feedback on products and services, which empowers the end user and continuously enhances quality levels. In many cases prices are even transparent and fluctuate in real time based on supply and demand—leading to the invisible hand of the market becoming increasingly visible. This is particularly useful for the sharing economy since offerings here are not necessarily offered in homogeneous quality. Of course, it can cut both ways. Drivers on vehicle hiring platforms also rate the passengers.

DISINTERMEDIATION AND PLATFORMS

Another important trend is **disintermediation**, which is where products and services are sold directly to the consumer. This is typically done through an open platform where consumers can see available offerings (and prices, and ratings, and availability in the case of physical products). These platforms have strong network effects where more users make the platform better, which in turn entices more users. Digitalization and globalization can often create winner-takes-all market dynamics, which helps explain why some tech companies have been able to grow huge.

Chapter 11

THE FAST, FLUID, AND FLEXIBLE FUTURE OF WORK

The world of work is evolving more rapidly than ever, and the COVID-19 pandemic created new ways of working—a transformation that happened within weeks instead of years. We believe that the notion of work as we know it has changed for good, and that there will be four overarching trends going forward:

1. Workers will continue to migrate from the industrial economy to the precision and experience economies.

2. Increased demand for emotional fulfillment and increased enoughism will be reflected in work preferences.

3. Work-life patterns will become faster, more fluid, and more flexible.

4. Jobs will increasingly chase talent online, instead of talent chasing jobs.

PRECISION AND EXPERIENCES

Since our machines, robots, and computers are increasingly conducting more routine and basic types of work in the industrial economy, human capacity is freed up to focus on more creative and higher-level cognitive tasks. Of course, a huge area is the precision economy with its IT and bioengineering, as well as the precision manufacturing with 3D printing and more. Indeed, new industry-related jobs such as SEO expert, blogger, app designer, app developer, cloud services specialist, AI specialist, big data analyst, robotics engineer, full stack engineer, customer success specialist, cybersecurity expert, and behavioral health expert have emerged or become mainstream. Coming up next might be organ creation, AR customer journey building, digital currency adviser, drone traffic controller, self-driving mechanic, and active contact lens creator.

More will also work in intersections between the precision economy and the experience economy. As computers increasingly handle routine call center jobs (e.g., changing an address in the system, ordering a new debit card, or booking a flight), call center representatives can focus on providing superb customer service and a personalized touch on topics such as charge disputes and personalized recommendations and bookings. Other industries such as education, health care, and retail are also seeing a shift toward humans interacting with machinery to focus on facilitating more complex discussions and topics with clients and consumers.

Other industries such as education, health care, and retail are also shifting toward human interaction with machines so that the focus can be on facilitating more complex discussions and topics with customers and consumers. Such centaur constellations will in other words increasingly involve machines for most of the work but remain under human supervision. However, the opposite also happens. Machines are used for monitoring people while they perform their work, for instance in order to prevent them from making catastrophic errors. Distance control system in cars is an early example of this.

Ultimately, we should expect the experience economy to become the greatest job provider. We already see the beginning of this in the most affluent segments of the world with its significant growth in lifestyle-oriented jobs like life coaches, fitness coaches, wellness practitioners, healers, and designers. This will continue. For instance, we may see lots of new jobs within transcendental experiences, assisted self-help, dream linking, active skin scientists who use tiny capsules embedded in the skin to enhance sensory experiences (e.g., reliving old feelings or enhancing movie or video game experiences), live medicine biologists, screen wall designers, and video tattoo artists.

While this happens, we will experience again, as we consistently have throughout human history, that net-net: Technology doesn't kill jobs; it just changes them. In fact, this phenomenon has been with us for centuries and is described in Say's law, which states that supply creates its own demand—in the sense that if we automate something, the increased wealth this creates just goes into something else. This is also sometimes called recycled demand.

PURPOSE AND FULFILLMENT

As we have already seen, younger generations are increasingly looking for purpose in their lives, and this will also reflect on their work preferences. They will increasingly expect that what they work for serves meaningful purposes, and also that it enriches their own lives with more than money.

Also, as prosperity increases and the opportunities for leisure become more attractive, more people will choose to work less and thus earn less, because they are already earning enough to cover their basic needs and finance their higher-level ones. This is one of several kinds of enoughism, where in this case more work for more money will not be what people want.

THE HUMAN CLOUD

Faster innovation cycles, more complexity, and the digitization of work processes has led to products, services, and labor being broken down into smaller and smaller units, which we call micro-objects. Not only is there more specialization (e.g., product manager, UI expert, design specialist, and coder to build an app), but also work tasks are often short term and project- or task-based.

This has led to a situation where instead of asking, "Where do you work now?" a more meaningful question is often, "What are you working on now?" And the answer to this question is increasingly likely to be that you work in parallel on several different projects for a number of people or clients. In other words, there is a trend toward micro-work and gigs.

> **Instead of asking, "Where do you work now?"**
> **a more meaningful question is often "What**
> **are you working on now?" Increasingly,**
> **people do micro-work in ad hoc gigs.**

One technology that enables increased choice and flexibility is digital clouds, including the ability to access computer power online. We are seeing the same shift in the labor market. As consumption increasingly moves toward more choice and on-tap models, demographic shifts bring new work-life desires, and work processes become increasingly granular, labor markets must do likewise. In other words, we now have three types of clouds: computer clouds, the cloud of things (IoT), and human clouds.

Human clouds enable us to break human services down into smaller, tradeable microunits so that they become available on tap. According to a Supertrends panel estimate, over half of the US workforce will be freelance by 2060. Such microunits of products, services, and data may be subject to ratings, digital analysis, real-time pricing, and transparent competition. This will both constitute a significant refinement of our market economies and counteract inflation, since it will increase competition.

We are moving toward microunits of products, services, and data, which become available as-a-service at prices that often fluctuate in real time, and which are often subject to ratings, digital analysis, real-time pricing, and transparent competition.

Concurrent with these changes, we see an increased blurring and integration between private life and work life, and between leisure time and work time. This was accelerated by the COVID-19 pandemic, and the accelerated shift forced many organizations into a radical rethink about where and when work gets done, but these trends were already underway. It is safe to say that ways of working will not return to how they were pre-pandemic—there has simply been too much change already to imagine that employee expectations and corporate cultures would revert back to how they were in the past.

We will likely see hybrid models emerging, to various degrees. A study from 2021 showed that 83 percent of employees wanted a hybrid work environment that combines in-person interaction with flexibility for remote work.[1] Another study found that 20 percent of workers want to return to the office five days a week post-pandemic, 30 percent want to work from home five days a week, and the remaining 50 percent fall somewhere in between.[2]

Overall, with the shifts toward more cloud-based and distributed micro-work, people increasingly have

- No fixed working hours

- No permanent designation as an employee, consultant, or freelancer

- No fixed workplace

- No clear holidays

- No title

- No fixed pension age

Instead, everything becomes faster, more fluid, and more flexible.

For sure, everything also can become more uncertain. However, for many, it becomes *less* uncertain in the sense that you are no longer at risk of losing "your job," only losing a given project or two.

Increasingly, work hours, job functions, workplaces, holidays, titles, and pension ages become more unsettled. The fast, fluid, and flexible world is getting blurrier.

THE REVERSED TALENT FUNNEL

In a reversal of the talent funnel, organizations are no longer the sole custodians of jobs or expertise. Many people have grown up in a world where if you had a work capacity, a service, a product, or perhaps a special talent, you almost invariably had to send an application to a powerful gatekeeper to activate it. You had to send your music to a record label, your job application to an employer, your start-up pitch to a venture fund, or your newspaper article to an editor. After you had sent it, you would wait hat-in-hand and pray. And then, mostly, you would get no for an answer, if you got an answer at all.

Of course, these approaches and gatekeepers still exist, but it is remarkable how often the process is now reversing or reversed. Today, journalists are increasingly monitoring what influential people are posting on the web, because not only might that content be interesting by its own merits, but also the fact that the influencer chose to post it in the first place might be a story in itself. Then, the journalist will write a story about the story and possibly request an interview about it. Elon Musk tweets are examples.

With social media, the talent funnel is often inversed so that more and more brand owners and employers are scanning the internet for talent rather than talent scanning brand owners and employers for opportunities.

Increasingly, employers are checking how active and liked job applicants are on social media. Indicators include numbers of friends, followers, views, engagements, upvotes, and shares. For instance, if a software developer is liked or upvoted on Hacker News or Stack Overflow, this could be indicative of special initiative and talent.

Traditional gatekeepers in the arts are also scanning the web for talent instead of waiting for demos to come in. One example is the record label Twin Music. While you can always submit demos to Twin, their main road to talent is to systematically scan the web for the most liked and shared indie music, then approach those who made it and offer them help.

As the number of freelancers grows, they create their online profiles, including portfolios of work. Many platforms include the ability to get, for instance, 1–5-star ratings from their clients. Companies discover this and are increasingly reaching out to talented individuals to pitch a project. This is a complete reversal of how employment contracts are usually structured. A quick look at platforms such as Upwork and Fiverr shows prominent categories such as digital marketing, graphic design, writing/translation services, and strategy analysis.

The posting of views, talent, and samples on social media is now far ahead of the systematic search for it, but we think that will change. Indeed, we expect massive growth in the use of highly organized scraping, text mining, machine learning, and other tools to find untapped human resources of all kinds. One advantage of this is that the web acts as a massive real-time test bed: markets talk, and if someone is popular on the web, it's probably for a reason.

The value of that insight is considerable when we consider how often the alternative model fails. Every year, gatekeepers recruit employees, performers, or artists who don't deliver. Perhaps even worse, they fail to engage with many talents who could succeed massively. For instance, J.K. Rowling's pitch for *Harry Potter* was rejected by a dozen publishers before being accepted by Bloomsbury. Stephen King's first book was rejected some thirty times, and even Madonna and The Beatles initially had a hard time getting through the bottleneck. Only after they were published did markets really talk.

While the reversal of the talent funnel is often very convenient for both buyers and sellers of human labor and talent, it is also great for the world. After all, when markets work like that, it matters less where you are born or how well connected you are. The web can shine the spotlight directly at you.

Chapter 12

TWENTY-FIVE VECTORS FOR THE FUTURE

The future we are describing includes some rather radical stuff: quantum computers that will conduct certain types of computing *millions* of times faster than the fastest existing supercomputers; innovations in food production that may ultimately reduce global farmland by more than 90 percent; power generation with thorium, deuterium, and tritium, which will provide millions of times more energy per weight unit than coal; a prediction that scientific discovery might grow a hundredfold over the next hundred years; 3D-printed human organs; and smartphones producing holograms, to name but a few extreme predictions.

What follows are twenty-five key vectors that point into the blur ahead of us:

1. *Many supertrends are only now at the cusp of truly taking off.* A number of supertrends as we know them today have only begun to gain momentum in the past decades or less, and only recently became truly global phenomena.

2. *There is no end to innovation since innovation is essentially about recombining what already exists.* The more things we have developed, the more new things it will be possible to create in the future.

3. *Our scientific activity doubles at least every fifteen years and grows approximately a hundredfold for every hundred years.* According to Ziman's law, this can continue indefinitely.

4. *The key driver of these processes is our Five Cs of Innovation:* (1) compact units, (2) cooperative networks, (3) common codes, (4) change agents, and (5) competition.

5. *The most hyper-social tend to win.* In general, those who are best at cooperation do better than those who are best at competition: win-win beats win-lose. Those who master pulsating hyper-sociality perform the best of all.

6. *Exponential laws provide predictability.* Stable exponential laws can enable us to predict when futuristic applications will become possible and economically feasible.

7. *Average real income per capita rises approximately 20 percent per decade.* This is surprisingly stable. Recessions typically lead to rapid reversals in order to catch up to this exponential trend line.

8. *There is ever more abundance.* The average time-price of commodities reduced by half approximately every twenty years, which means superabundance. For this reason, more wealth is created through innovation than through ownership of the commodities and resources that enable their production. We also know that as people meet their basic and foundational needs, such as food and safety, they focus on higher-level needs such as well-being and self-actualization.

9. *The precision economy means more for less.* Precision technologies enable us to create ever more value with ever smaller physical footprints.

10. *The adjacent possible that follows breakthroughs in new core technologies is often applications.* Whereas often, the first market response to new core technologies may seem disappointing, over time, people figure out new business models and applications, which trigger endless cascades of new business opportunities and technologies. This means that when a new core technology moves into the actual, derived applications always appear in the adjacent possible.

11. *AI and quantum computers are leading us toward recursive super-intelligence.* In an increasing number of disciplines, computers beat the human mind, and this is now also happening in areas that we think of as intuitive. Furthermore, quantum computers are boosting some areas of computation with factors of millions or billions. One of the effects of this will be computers that are able to program other computers better than we can and formulate theses and ask questions in ways that defy human capability. Intelligence will thereby spontaneously create more intelligence.

12. *More and more of us will become centaurs.* It will become ever more common that humans and machines help, guide, and supervise each other.

13. *Technology will become part of every fabric of our lives.* Everything that can be digitized has been or will be, and we are seeing new types of hardware and software across all spheres of life. Furthermore, as one technology after another goes exponential, unit costs drop rapidly while the technological capabilities increase. This is compounded by technology convergence, network effects, AI, and recursive intelligence.

14. *Biology has become a computing platform.* We can increasingly create, destroy, tune, and modify life at will. One of the effects of this is a new industrial revolution where we recode cells as if they are robots at our service so that they can function as factories

that manufacture what we need with remarkable precision. The products we get from this will include food, pharmaceuticals, and building materials.

15. *Demographic changes will be the most disruptive ever.* We are entering a period with the most diverse working and consuming class ever. Newer generations tend to vote more liberally, to be more focused on pursuing a personal purpose, to take a stand on social and ethical causes, and to value flexibility and work-life balance.

16. *Cultural differences between generations will rise.* New technologies trigger new attitudes, lifestyles, and consumer preferences, but since adoption of these are different among generations, generational differences grow as innovation accelerates.

17. *Prosperity leads to product diversity.* Once we reach market saturation in terms of quantity, the innovation effort moves to increased choice and thus diversity in offerings.

18. *As we move from analog to digital, we also move from the batch delivery–based economy toward the on-tap model.* The triple cloud of computer capacity, human gig services, and data from things are just a few examples of this broad trend. There is also a shift from vendor push to client pull. Overall, this will make our economies much more efficient and our lives much more convenient.

19. *Marketing is becoming personalized and intelligent.* Advanced algorithms are increasingly able to target a segment of one, and can provide personalized recommendations where and when we need them—often before we even know that we need them ourselves.

20. *Markets are becoming visible in real time.* As we move toward microunits of products, services, and data that are available as-a-service and hosted on global platforms, prices are often visible to all and fluctuate in real time, while users are enabled to give instant feedback and ratings.

21. *Industries will be transformed.* Every industry is being touched by technology, and many will be unrecognizable in ten years. Particularly big shifts can be expected in transportation, health care, education, media, urban development and real estate, energy, farming, finance, professional service sectors, retail, and manufacturing.

22. *Workers will continue to migrate from the industrial economy to the precision and experience economies.* Increasingly, machines, robots, and computers handle tasks in the industrial economy so that human labor increasingly flows to the precision economy and the experience economy, where humans have greater competitive advantage over machines.

23. *Work-life patterns will become faster, more fluid, and more flexible.* COVID-19 has accelerated trends toward the granularization, digitization, and increased distribution of work across internal and external gig workers. Our work and personal lives are becoming further integrated. People increasingly have no fixed workplace, working hours, holidays, or even pension age. Instead, they are more prone to live their adult lives in fluid combinations of work, leisure, and learning—but they may never retire.

24. *Increased demand for fulfillment and increased enoughism is reflected in human preferences.* This goes for consumption patterns, as well as work preferences.

25. *Jobs will increasingly chase talent, instead of talent chasing jobs.* This means that talented people get discovered online instead of chasing opportunities to sell their labor.

Along the way, all sorts of startling things will occur. Some of these we can predict with a fair degree of certainty, while for others we can only offer conjecture. Still others will materialize like a bolt from the blue. How then should individuals adapt to these changes?

PART 2

MINDSETS FOR FUTURE FITNESS

THIS BOOK IS FULL OF AMAZING STUFF that's about to happen. What we know of today is really only just a fraction of the many developments that will happen in the future. How lucky are we?

It's not all flowers and sunshine, though. With increased possibilities like the metaverse also comes increased demands for you as an individual. In the past decades we have seen increasing levels of stress, depression, and other mental health issues, physical illnesses and obesity, and more self-consciousness and insecurity due to constant comparison on social media.[1] Furthermore, according to a study by the OECD, almost half of young people between eighteen and twenty-four do not believe there will be demand for their skills and knowledge in the future, and that they will struggle to access full-time jobs due to digitization.[2] In short, a great number of people are feeling ill-equipped to deal with the many changes that are coming.

Such pressures mean that you as an individual must look after yourself in completely new ways if you wish to stay physically, mentally, emotionally, and spiritually fit.[3] This is the focus of part 2—namely how to become more Future Fit as an individual. This includes the extent to which you shape the world around you from the inside out, your ability to navigate supertrends, how you make sense of new information, how you learn, how you deal with the effects of an increasingly interconnected and wealthy world, how you create your own luck, how you take action, and how you stay on course.

We focus on not only the types of behaviors and tools that may help, but also the mindsets required. This is because it is only by changing our underlying beliefs and mindsets that we can sustainably shift our way of learning, living, and leading for the better. You will encounter eight mindsets that are pivotal to strengthen your Future Fitness. Some of the mindsets you may have heard of before, and we include them because, while important today, they are becoming even more important in the future. Other mindsets are likely to be new. Each one is valuable in its own right, yet they are all interrelated and mutually reinforcing, so maintaining an overview of how they complement one another is key.

There is no doubt that the future is exciting, yet the ride will become bumpier. Achieving your most desired future requires you to continuously develop yourself and your capacity to deal with the coming changes. Framed in the right way, however, the journey will be an exciting one, and the rewards will be worth it!

Chapter 13

DEALING WITH DURKHEIM

David Émile Durkheim (born 1858) is frequently called the founder of sociology. One of his many interesting observations concerned what he called "anomie," which is a situation without social norms. Babies start their life with maximum anomie since they have close to zero social norms from the outset. However, as they grow up, they learn. For instance, when they are one year old, their eating habits may be pretty close to those of adults 2,000 years ago. By the age of ten, their eating habits may have reached what was common 1,000 years ago. And hopefully, by the time they turn twenty, they will have caught up with modern eating manners.

Well except perhaps—and here comes the point—if they are in college or similar new surroundings. This is because when young adults leave home, their table manners and propensity to tidy up their rooms, and so on, often retreat for a while to lower levels of civilization—such as the norms of the medieval ages—since they have now departed from the constraining social order previously imposed by their parents. Their first years in college might be a new experience of Durkheim's anomie.

We mention this because as we move into the world described in part 1, a lot of supertrends will continuously disrupt our comfy worlds. And that means that just like young adults when they leave home, the social orders we are used to might disappear. And that can create a state of anomie.

EIGHTEEN JOBS, SIX CAREERS, AND FIFTEEN HOMES

Again and again, our jobs, habits, cultures, technologies, and homes disappear from our lives in exchange for new ones. For instance, the concept of a lifelong job in a single organization where you perhaps work yourself up the hierarchy over the decades is becoming less and less common. As previously mentioned, one estimate shows that zoomers (born 1997–2010) over their lifetime will hold on average eighteen jobs across six careers and live in fifteen homes. This means that they must deal with Durkheim. Of course, much of this change is good, if not truly great. Opportunities, my friend! Lots of them!!

Yet too many choices can lead to problems of their own. You may have seen some of these YouTube videos of a lion preparing to attack one of hundreds of buffaloes stampeding past it—only to fail to make any attack at all—due to the overwhelming speed, chaos, and choice. Something similar can happen to us. In this ever-changing world with so many possibilities, some of us feel a constant anomie and never get a grip. If the lion had only faced just *one* buffalo, its dinner would be assured. Equally, if it was a given in your life that you would work on your parents' farm and marry the neighbor's son or daughter, things would be simple, and you would probably get that done. However, in the modern world, many get lost.

So, let's look at some of the mindsets and behaviors that can help us get a grip.

FROM DEPENDENCE TO INTERDEPENDENCE

In 1989, Stephen Covey published a global bestseller called *The 7 Habits of Highly Effective People*. In this book, which was based on a lifetime of psychological studies, he described three possible phases of a human life: (1) dependence, (2) independence, and (3) interdependence.

Babies and young children are not only challenged by anomie, but they are surely also *dependent* on people. They depend on those who raise them.

Some people never get beyond that—as they leave home, their parents might keep stopping by to pick up their laundry because it won't otherwise get washed. Or they might, for instance, immediately become dependent on a welfare state, which simply replaces their parents. Or they might become dependent on a know-all ideology that does the same and tells them everything they must do, just like their parents previously did.

Fortunately, many children start taking ownership of their lives somewhere between their early teenage years and their early twenties. Of course, one may well have a sense of self-ownership and therefore be committed to responsibility for their own actions, but nevertheless choose to devote their life to an external course.

But the feeling of self-ownership makes people *independent*. Independence can have many facets. One is the ability to think for oneself, even when they're up against the wind—very independent people tend to do what they think is right, even if others may disagree. Another typical feature of independence is not being a slave to constant recognition from others. Independent people can pat themselves on the back if others do not. And truly effective independent people also think very proactively, take full responsibility for their own lives, and think and plan toward goals. This is extremely useful in a chaotic world—much more so than in a world where fate is a given.

However, if your personal development stops there, you might become somewhat of a navel-gazer with little interest in things other than yourself: me, me, me. Covey's highly effective people take the additional third step toward *interdependence*, whereby they become very good at making voluntary win-win transactions with others. In other words, interdependent people have mastered the independent stage, and on top of that are good at cooperating within teams and at sharing ideas, friends, products, services, and so forth. They are constructive networkers and thus efficient contributors to human hyper-sociality.

This is really important because as we move into a more complex and dynamic world, we actually do need to excel at interacting with others. The clearest way to excellence in complex systems typically requires hyper-sociality.

Thriving in complex and rapidly evolving systems requires hyper-sociality, and as a person, you can excel in that if you become an interdependent person with a strong win-win mentality.

DROPPING THE DRAMA

One sign that you may not really have left the initial dependence stage is if you live in the so-called Karpman drama triangle, which was first described by Stephen Karpman in 1961.[1] It has three roles:

- **Rescuers** look for apparent victims so that they can play a savior role. This makes them feel good and fulfilled in life. In extreme cases, their actual role is to call for others to do the rescuing while they personally signal their virtues as rescuers on social media, for instance. "Save the world!" they may frequently yell, while perhaps doing nothing of the sort themselves. This is called virtue signaling.

- **Persecutors** point at someone and blame them for everything. "It's all your fault" is their mantra. Frequently, this is because they have low self-esteem and thus need someone else to blame for their own lack of progress in life. Alternatively, victims and rescuers may invent imaginary persecutors to make their stories add up.

- **Victims** seek to victimize themselves, even though they are not really victims. "Poor me!" is then their constant stance, and to remain in that preferred role, they actively look for people who can play the roles of the persecutors and rescuers in their lives.

Of course, the world does have real victims, real rescuers, and real persecutors, and the Karpman drama triangle isn't about them. Instead, it is about people who *actively seek or make up* one of these roles in their lives, and who thus also actively try to orchestrate the drama and drag others into it. These are Karpman's victims, rescuers, and persecutors. And they are dependent people.

The consequence of this behavior is that each drama triangle participant deflects responsibility for their own life. For instance, the rescuer prevents the victim from taking responsibility for their own life, but they often use their personal rescuer activities as guises to shield their personal lack of responsibility. And the persecutor also deflects responsibility for their own life. They believe everything bad in their life is someone else's fault. This means that neither of the three players in the drama really becomes independent—their drama game keeps them stuck in the dependent stage. They never really grow up.

This was about what might prevent you from moving from a dependent to an independent stage, but are there also signs that you have not moved on from independent to interdependent? One could be that all you post on social media is photos of yourself. Another possible indicator is that your life has no meaning or purpose apart from serving your own short-term pleasure. "Look, here I am with a gin & tonic." Of course, enjoying life now is great, but what else do we live for? Luckily, there are some practical life hacks that can help you become an independent or (better) interdependent person and successfully navigate the complex world of the future.

KNOWING YOURSELF AND OTHERS

The first is to truly know yourself. If you haven't already achieved that, an easy start is to take a bunch of personality tests such as the Big Five, Hogan, DiSC, Barrett Values, and Strengths Finder (to name just a few). And then think about how they might explain (1) how you behave, (2) what underlying beliefs cause you to behave the way you do, (3) what works for you and what doesn't, (4) in which situations you feel flow and purpose, (5) in which you feel boredom or emptiness, and (6) why you spend your time as you do.

Secondly, before you tell people what you're working on, make it a habit to tell them *why* you're working on that—tell them why you think it is useful and meaningful. If you know yourself well, this should be possible.

Think also about how you learn most efficiently—is it by reading, writing, speaking, listening, or doing? Tell people about this so they can adapt to you, at least in a work environment, and ask them about how *they* best learn so that *you* as an efficient interdependent person can adapt to that.

UNDERSTAND YOUR ETHICS AND DEFINE YOUR VALUES

In a complex world with a confusing array of choices, it becomes more important to be guided by a deeply felt sense of what is right. Ethics are the moral principles that guide your conduct. Values are derived from ethics and are principles and ideals that help us judge and prioritize in life. If people in the future on average will go through anywhere near eighteen jobs across six careers while living in fifteen homes, their lives will be complex, but perhaps the backbone to their decisions can be clear sets of ethics and values.

A mental hack is to ask yourself which values you would like others to see in you. Which ones will give true meaning to your life? A strong focus on values can provide a backbone in your behavior so that you don't act on temporary feelings but instead on which behaviors are consistent with your values. Having a strong focus on clear values will also make it easier to create your own destiny instead of living someone else's life—or no life at all.

When you navigate a blurry world, you need a strong backbone. Let that be strong ethics and values.

INTERNAL LOCUS OF CONTROL

Another useful mental foundation is shifting from an **external** to an **internal locus of control**, which means thinking "I am happening to the world," rather than "The world is happening to me." This concept was introduced by Julian B. Rotter in 1954, and his main point was that people with a strong internal locus of control assumed that most of what happened in their lives was directly or indirectly due to their own decisions. On the other hand, people with a strong *external* locus of control tend to blame the outside world for whatever goes wrong in their lives, and they will thus also often play around in the Karpman drama. What comes naturally from that is to focus your actions mostly on what you can influence or control. Moaning about others or about the weather may feel good, but it doesn't bring you anywhere—your own action does.

"There's no such thing as bad weather, only bad clothes" is a (somewhat exaggerated) Scandinavian saying that encapsulates this mindset well. However, the overall takeaway is that with an internal locus of control, you shape yourself and choose your actions to shape your life and the world around you. You are a creator of your destiny, not a helpless pawn in the game of life. This doesn't mean that you can become anything, as some motivational speakers sometimes say. You can't, but you can become a lot more if you have an internal locus of control than if you don't.

Mold yourself and the world around you through deliberate and intentional actions.

A helpful way to strengthen an internal locus of control is to observe yourself as if from the outside and then assume that you are responsible for the person you see. This is like looking in the mirror and considering whether what you see seems okay and giving yourself some advice from time to time. The same applies to how you judge if your actions meet your ethical standards and values.

MINDSET 1: OWNERSHIP MINDSET

These various approaches can be summed up in what we call an ownership mindset. This mindset has to do with the degree to which you take accountability for what happens in your life. It can be contrasted with a victim mindset, where you wait to be told what to do, believe you don't really have control over the outcomes of your actions, and blame others when things don't go your way.

An ownership mindset is becoming increasingly important because of the growing number of the opportunities we have in front of us. As social structures and norms around us dissolve (Durkheim's anomie), it is up to us to define what we want with our lives and, more importantly, to take responsibility for getting there.

Core beliefs of an ownership mindset include the following:

- I can influence what happens around me and can improve my situation regardless of where I am today.
- Achieving the results I want depends primarily on my ability and effort.
- I am responsible for what happens in my life.
- I take action before I am told what to do.
- It is up to me to shape my life and make decisions based on my priorities and values.

As mentioned, taking ownership of your life and becoming independent is important but not sufficient. Interdependence is the next stage, and we expand on this concept and the importance of an abundance and win-win mindset in subsequent chapters.

THE GOOD KARPMAN

An alternative version of Karpman's drama triangle, which is actually productive for all and which can provide a way out of the bad dramas, is called TED for "The Empowerment Dynamic." TED aims at constructive goals and positive outcomes. Yes, in TED there is a social triangle, but instead of being played by dependent people, it is played with constructive interdependence. The concept was introduced in 2005 by medical doctor and coach David Emerald and based on his extensive experience with coaching efficient self-leadership. Here, the roles change as follows:

- The victim becomes a creator.

- The rescuer becomes a coach.

- The persecutor becomes a challenger.

Let's say, for instance, that you realize you are wasting your time and that of others by always playing the victim. One way out, according to Emerald, is to do much of what we have described above while defining your values and long-term goals. Focus on what you can control and your desired outcomes as opposed to your problems while you embark on your journey from dependent to independent and finally interdependent.

Or let's say, alternatively, that your preferred role in life has been to "save" people who should rather learn to take responsibility for themselves. You have been a Karpman rescuer, in other words. Changing from this to coach can be done by starting to help them help themselves through their own informed choices. Don't give the victim a fish, so to speak, but teach them to fish. Help them escape from their role of victim.

Finally, could it be that your preferred role in life has been Karpman persecutor? Might it be that this was because you have inherently low self-esteem? The first step here, according to Emerald, is to give yourself a break. Cultivate compassion toward yourself and embark on a personal growth process. Then, if you want to become a challenger toward others, always do so with a positive, learning intent. If you are a truth teller for others, do it not to alleviate your own minority complexes but to nudge them gently toward a better future. As inspiration, think of those times in your life when teachers, bosses, grandparents, or friends compassionately and efficiently nudged you in better directions or toward better goals. Now, be them, and do that for others.

What follows is a list of tips to help you develop an ownership mindset to help shape the world around you, inside out.

1. **Know thyself:** Take the time to get to know yourself at a deeper level through personal reflection, discussions with friends, family, and potentially a coach.

2. **Define your values or life principles:** There are countless articles and books on how to define your values. Most of them include looking at a long list of values and choosing the handful that are most important to you, taking a values test, reflecting on times when you were most fulfilled (or unfulfilled) to understand the common denominators, and identifying the traits and values of the people you most admire. Although you will likely not feel like you are completely "done" the first time you write down your values, persevere with the exercise and be open to tweaking them on a regular basis.

3. **Take an oath:** Many countries have an "oath of allegiance" for incoming presidents, members of the government, and citizens. This ritual symbolizes the start of something new and outlines what the person commits to uphold. Similarly, undertaking a personal oath where you commit to taking full responsibility for your life can be a powerful enabler as you begin to craft your most desired future. A part of this can be a commitment to always try to grow, and to improve how you interact constructively with others to mutual benefit.

4. **Listen to your inner voice:** Catch yourself when your inner voice is limiting you or holding you back. Shift from "I can't" or "It will always be like this" to "I have the power to change my situation."

5. **Reflect:** Get into the habit of reflecting regularly on what is going well in your life, what you can further develop, and how you can move forward. The very act of setting an intention about your future self will help steer you toward that vision.

Chapter 14

NAVIGATE THE WORLD—NIMBLY

Every day, we make decisions that are guided by our understanding, hopes, and beliefs about the future. This includes how we spend our time each day, but also what job we take, which country we live in, and where we prioritize our investments. Even though we might not necessarily think of ourselves as futurists, that is what we are. And being a futurist can be demanding, since in a rapidly changing world driven largely by exponential advancement in technologies, it is becoming increasingly difficult to understand what's going on, let alone deal with it.

How then can we all ensure that we are not completely blindsided and that we become reasonably good at spotting opportunities early on? There are a number of tools and approaches that professional futurists, companies, and other future-facing organizations employ—and that we can each to some degree apply in our own lives. Indeed, these tools are not only applicable, but they can also be critical as we speed into the blur. Here is the first tool:

BUILD YOUR INTERACTIVE INFORMATION NETWORK

One way highly efficient people have changed over recent years is by using social media efficiently. A good framework here is the Personal Knowledge Management (PKM) approach described by Canadian management consultant Harold Jarche. PKM describes a distinction between seeking information, thinking about information, and sharing information and thoughts about it.

That last part is the most intriguing to us. If you are good at sharing interesting information, you will become engaged in a network of people interested in the same subject areas. These are your online friends and followers, and they will share other information about your interest areas and may frequently send you private messages with relevant tips and information.

In other words, they become your eyes and ears. Your personal advisory board, so to speak. And while this happens, you are actually creating your personal network effect: the more friends and followers you have, the more attractive it becomes to join your network. You begin to excel in hyper-sociality. Just be sure to remain critical of the data sources you follow and whose voices you choose to listen to.

> Your friends and followers on social media can
> become your personal advisory board.

The sharing of information on social media can have another powerful effect: because of your increased visibility, you become far more likely to be approached with ideas and solutions you can use, as well as by people who would like to use your services. In this way, you can take advantage of the inversed talent funnel that we describe earlier, which may furthermore increase your chances of finding serendipitous opportunities.

If you build a professional ecosystem around you on social media, you will gain more ideas and insights, and the network will also increase your chances of finding serendipitous opportunities.

Becoming hyper-social via social media (even if in private you might be an introvert) will empower you with a hyper-social meta-brain. And just think about it—more than 50 percent of LinkedIn users have more than 500 connections, and it's not uncommon for regular users to have thousands.[1] The same goes for people and organizations on networks such as Facebook, Twitter, Sina Weibo, Instagram, and TikTok. Yes, many participate mostly for fun, and others don't like it. But it can be a useful tool in a world where hyper-sociality can provide critical advantages. Of course, a social following can also be a bad tool if it is used entirely to collect likes. However, that would be the approach of a fixed mindset rather than growth mindset.

APPLYING A MENTAL OSCILLATION

Most Western education systems and business schools focus on root-cause problem-solving as the key analytical tool to crack tough problems. This is called **convergent thinking**. You analyze different sources to solve a problem. This approach is essential for scientists when they test hypotheses, and it is extremely efficient for those purposes.

However, the future is neither inherently knowable nor a well-defined problem to be solved. It is rather a huge, almost endless, foggy landscape to be navigated in ways that are optimal for each of us. As such, a supplementary approach is needed: divergent thinking. **Divergent thinking** is about continuously generating alternative responses, ideas, and scenarios. This includes wildcard ideas and unexpected or totally unusual scenarios. Very efficient scientists do this often, combining convergent and divergent thinking.

The point is that in our journey into the future blur, we need to oscillate between laser vision and radar scanning. Both convergent and divergent thinking are needed. We need to foster both convergent and divergent thinking and problem-solving as we navigate the future in our daily lives. If you think this sounds a lot like our Creative Loop, you're right. It is indeed an oscillating process performed by one person—about that person's life. However, if you are skilled at social networking and information seeking in general, you will also involve hyper-sociality in how you do this. Divergent thinking can often be inspired by others. In the same way we can't tickle ourselves, it's hard to truly surprise ourselves. Other people are needed for that.

**In observing and thinking,
oscillate between laser and radar.**

STRATEGIC FORESIGHT

Now that we have looked at the processes for gathering information and inspiration, let's move on to a couple of mental techniques to put this to use in your Future Fitness approach. A widely conceived approach to futurism is called strategic foresight. It consists of six steps:

- *Frame the domain*: What focus area and outcome are you interested in?

- *Scan for forces and trends*: Look for relevant data, weak signals, and trend timing.

- *Forecast scenarios*: Create a list of plausible futures.

- *Envision the future*: What does success look like for you in these scenarios?

- *Backcast*: What milestones must you reach to achieve this future success?

- *Implement*: What must you do now to begin the journey?

In a personal foresight process, you oscillate between laser and radar in your information search and between convergent and divergent thinking. Converge around your focus areas and the outcomes you are interested in. Then diverge as you explore trends and make observations from a wide variety of sources. After that, converge as you analyze trends. Then diverge as you think about different potential futures. Then converge on your decisions, action plan, and next steps.

EXPONENTIAL MINDSET

All this makes you grow, but you can become even better at it by including exponential thinking. It's true that some things in life barely change, and others evolve linearly, but the rate of change for most things is increasingly exponential, and exponential trends create future developments that are anti-intuitive. If you had told Thomas Malthus in 1798 that 200 years later, the world's population would be around 7.5 times bigger *and* much better fed, he would not have believed you at all. "How would that be even remotely possible?" he would surely think. Exponential thinking was close to nonexistent back then.

Nor would a person watching the Wright brothers' first fragile flying machine in 1903 easily imagine that on any normal day 100 years later, more than a million people would be speeding forward in airborne machines!

And today, if someone states that in the year 2100, the world's population is likely to be a good deal smaller than today, that real GDP per capita probably will be 6–8 times larger, that farmland perhaps will have declined 90 percent, that almost all energy will be generated by nuclear fusion and building-integrated solar panels, and that we will have avid space tourism and perhaps even a colony on Mars, people without an exponential mindset will be puzzled. Seen over longer time spans, the world seems to make frequent radical jumps, but if you investigate each of them, they are typically not the result of an instant change, but instead of something that changed exponentially. And this is why futurism has to incorporate exponential developments.

MINDSET 2: EXPONENTIAL MINDSET

As the world around us changes, so must we. And we know that many of the changes are exponential in nature, typically driven by digitization. As such, we too must learn how to think exponentially.

This means being able to understand the power of digitalization and how trends will develop in the future, using facts and data. It means being able to envision a future that doesn't yet exist, including imagining many different possible futures. And it means *reinventing* yourself and your business, not just improving it.

Core beliefs underpinning an exponential mindset include the following:

- The future will be *different* from today, not just incrementally better or worse.
- The pace of change a year from now will be far greater than the pace of change today (for a given trend, technology, or context).
- Changes in the future will be 10x, not 10 percent.
- We will solve the problems of today with innovations and methods that aren't yet fully applicable today.

The opposite of an exponential mindset is a linear mindset, where you believe that a change in one quantity will continue to produce a proportionate change in another—similar to how things are today.

Here are seven ways to combat linear thinking as you craft your most desired future:

1. Read up on exponential technologies and the power of compounding. Ask yourself what you can do today that you couldn't do even in the recent past, and how you can use these advances in your life.

2. Plot the linear and exponential trends that are important to your decisions to get a better sense of where they might be heading. Compare these trends with trends that had similar trajectories three to five years ago.

3. Think about which trends and technologies are in the actual, which opportunities lie in the adjacent possible (if you were to recombine existing technologies), and what is theoretically possible if new technologies are developed (the shadow future).

4. Ask yourself what would need to be true for the current number to be 10x or 100x bigger in the next decade, and then assess whether those assumptions could be plausible.

5. Look at trends that are converging and think about how they can complement one another to create something entirely new. Technological convergence means that the whole is not just the sum of the parts, but it can also be infinitely more powerful.

6. Focus on attractive outcomes rather than the underlying indicators—sometimes it is helpful to set a bold vision without considering how it might get done, and then work backwards from there.

7. Crowdsource ideas and questions to your network, using seek-sense-share loops.

We return to exponentiality in a couple of chapters when we discuss abundance mindsets and how to think bigger.

NAVIGATING THE COMPLEXITY

In addition to thinking realistically about how the world evolves, to thrive, you must know yourself. The obvious starting point is to converge about who you really are. What are your talents, moral instincts, interests, ethics, and values? Spend time in deep reflection in order to converge on this.

Then think deeply about the kinds of education, employment sectors, jobs, lifestyles, and places that would make *you feel personally* successful. For instance, if you really like stability, you'll want to stay clear of jobs or sectors where exponential laws will constantly change everything. Or if you want to work with something that doesn't really exist yet, try to figure out when it will.

In such exercises, it is normally recommended to think quite far ahead, as in imagining your dream life twenty years in the future given what you think is possible for you now and what will be possible for you then. Ideally, try to close your eyes and imagine a really great day in your life twenty years from now. Who are you with on that day? Where do you live? What is your work? What are you known for?

As you try to envisage your life on that future day, try perhaps also to envision even sounds, colors, and smells. Then imagine another great day in that desired future life of yours. And then reflect upon what these visions tell you about where you want to go. Now you have a mission!

Try to envision a day in your dream life twenty years from now. And then another day. And then perhaps a third day. Now, how can you get there?

The next step is to identify important trends that will impact your domain. These trends must have meaningful rates of change. They can, for instance, be social, political, economic, or—by far the most important—technological trends. When companies do this exercise, they often make "trend cards" where information about each important trend is noted. If these trends include exponential developments, such as those discussed in part 1, try to plot the exponential progress into a spreadsheet and check where the relevant technology (or whatever it is) will be three, ten, and twenty years from now. Will your dreams converge with some supertrends?

Also think about the first- (direct), second- (indirect), and third- (even more indirect) order effects. For example, a positive first-order effect of more autonomous vehicles on the road is fewer traffic accidents. However, a second-order effect of this will be fewer organ donations available for hospitals, as one of their biggest sources is from car accidents.

Now, as you think about trends in *your* life, ask yourself what will happen if that trend reaches this level, and write down four to eight implications that you might find relevant. Then for the key implications, ask yourself the question again. This can keep going, but typically stops at second- or third-order effects.

Based on this, move on to describe some alternative scenarios that are each plausible, relevant, and different from today in meaningful ways. Imagine them, like they were shown in a movie to you. If you can, envision specific events that they would entail. And again, make it real in your imagination. It is important to think about alternative futures because in reality, baseline forecasts are almost always wrong.

Then think about whether there are factors or issues that show up in several of your desired scenarios. For instance, do these involve that you need to be particularly fit, or live in a specific place, or become good at AI, cooking, visual design, or psychology? Are they *converging* on this?

These competencies or actions are called **transformational factors**, and the next step is to imagine outrageous success for you in a world where such transformations are happening or have already taken place to your benefit. What would such outrageous success require from you?

Now, move back from the desired future scenarios, both the ones you first imagined and then the ones involving trend cards. Choose what dreams you now have and then consider what you need to do between that time in the dream future and now in order to get there successfully. What do you need to start on very soon or right now?

And then create milestones for these action points. For instance, completing a bachelor's degree three years from now, moving to British Columbia five years from now, becoming a well-known blogger about haute couture within four years, or whatever.

A personal foresight process can help you find your personal direction in a chaotic world with ever more choices.

CREATE AN EARLY WARNING SIGNAL

We might sometimes feel that the future is predictable, and perhaps in the short term it is becoming more so as we get ever more precise flight, train, and bus timings, preelection polls, sports probability statistics, and ever earlier weather forecasts. However, this is where a lot of people go wrong. Strategic forecasting is much more about developing a radar for continuously observing and interpreting what's going on around you, rather than defining a precise road map.

One way to sharpen your radar is to look out for weak signals in trends that matter to you (i.e., the first indicator of change that may become significant in the future). You can formalize this for critical indicators by setting breakout points that you believe will require you to act in a different way.

What follows are some tips to help you systematically peer into the future and develop an exponential mindset so you can stay ahead of supertrends along the way:

1. **Establish an interactive information network:** Assess your current information network. Is it at the right size for you? Are you missing any demographics or types of expertise? Do you regularly provide input in addition to soliciting it?

2. **Map your future:** Block off two hours to apply the personal foresight process to your life. Recall the six steps that include framing, scanning, forecasting, envisioning, backcasting, and implementing. Apply divergent and convergent thinking and assess both current trends and the path you want to take. We recommend repeating the personal foresight process at least once a quarter.

3. **Think exponentially:** Immerse yourself to really understand the various trends around you, and push yourself to think through how they might develop in the next one, three, five, and ten years.

4. **Create an early warning signal:** As you think about your most

desired future, pick the critical trends that will influence your future decisions. Determine how you will track them and put a reminder to review them on a regular basis.

5. **Take action:** The future doesn't stand still, and neither should you. We have often noticed that people are more regretful about taking action too late than they are about trying something that didn't work out. In today's world, you can often dabble your toes in the water before changing course completely, so push yourself to try something new on a regular basis, even if it seems scary at first.

Chapter 15

THINKING CLEARLY IN THE BLUR

Obviously, decision-making only gets harder when things are uncertain, not easier. Even with clearly established values, an internal locus of control, and a personal foresight process, thinking clearly and taking the right steps in the blur can be a challenge. Despite the incredible number of decisions we make each day, we are taught little to nothing about the art and science of decision-making. In the future, we will encounter more situations that challenge our beliefs, present us with new facts, and put us in novel situations. Hyper-sociality implies a confusing diversity of opinions and information, whereas AI-driven mass personalization can create information bubbles that cater to our existing beliefs.

Humans are prone to many different biases, which can be mapped so that our behavior becomes "predictably irrational."[1] Unfortunately, many of the biases get worse as the context around us changes. For example, the Dunning-Kruger effect is a cognitive bias where we can be particularly overconfident in situations that we know little about—see Figure 15.1. As we encounter new situations and challenges, we have not yet acquired the meta-cognitive ability to know what we know and what we don't. This can lead to decision-making errors in things like career choices, investment, and social media posts.

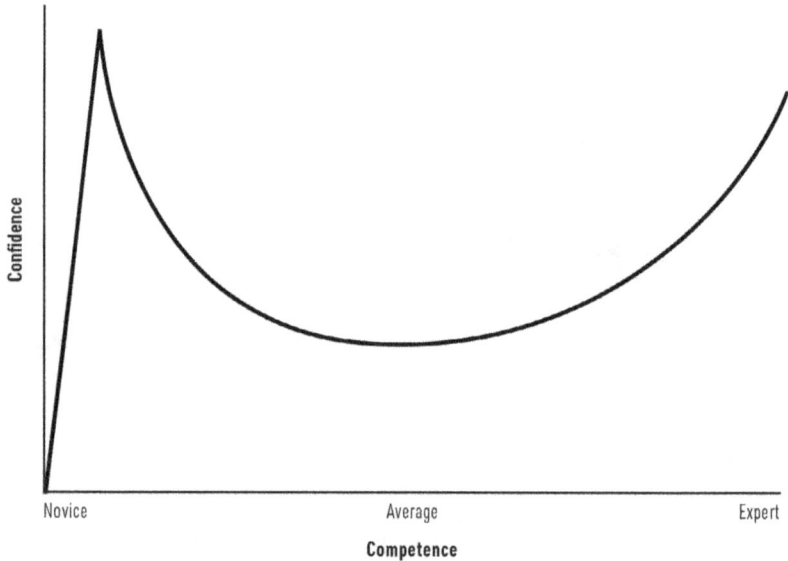

Figure 15.1. The Dunning-Kruger effect.

Other biases that are exacerbated by the blur include **confirmation bias**, which is the tendency to seek out information that aligns with our point of view rather than seeking contradicting evidence; **in-group bias**, which is relying too much on the opinions and points of view of those in our social group; **availability bias**, which is relying on the information we can most easily recall; **recency bias**, which is relying on the most recent information we have; and **confidence bias**, which is being overconfident in our ability to predict future events.

Though humans typically enjoy learning, we are not very good at changing our beliefs when presented with new information. Belief updating is a relatively nascent field of research, but researchers have provided some fascinating insights. One study followed patients who had undergone cardiac surgery. They were prescribed medication and told to change their lifestyles by exercising more, eating more healthily, and avoiding smoking or excessive drinking. They were told they had a high risk of premature death if they did not change. Sounds like a pretty good incentive to start living more healthily, right? What shocked the researchers was that only one in seven at-risk heart patients actually made the suggested lifestyle changes.[2] Other studies have found that we update our beliefs asymmetrically, where we are open to changing beliefs when they further reinforce our existing point of view, but not when they contradict them.

Now, it's not all doom and gloom. There are hacks to make decisions in the blur. But it may require going against your instinct and what feels most natural to you. And most of the time, it requires slowing down ever so slightly in order to then speed back up into the blur.

CHECK YOUR DATA

Future Fitness requires regularly updating your beliefs and worldviews. The key here is to discern what you *know* to be true from what you *believe* to be true. Today, it is incredibly easy to check the validity of almost any claim. "Nuclear power is incredibly dangerous?" Well, not according to statistics.[3] "Global inequality has been rising a lot in recent decades?" No, it has actually been falling a lot.[4] And so forth. Whenever you are in the least doubt about something, check the data from reputable sources and assume that many news sources often don't before they publish their content. If we can't always be the smartest person in the room, at least we may be the best informed.

> There is a great competitive advantage in simply
> checking key data from reputable sources. Most people
> and even mainstream media rarely do that enough.

Especially as you cultivate hyper-sociality, think about cultivating hyper-criticality. More diverse opinions typically lead to more informed choices, but only when those opinions are in fact valid. With disintermediation and democratization of information, there is a risk of lower standards for neutrality and professionalism in terms of new media sources such as websites, blogs, and social media. And we know that AI-assisted news curation itself is fraught with biases. Until we have a solution that effectively limits the spread of narrowly focused and incorrect information online, it means you must work extra hard to weed out fake news and information that simply isn't true.

As such, it is important to remain critical of the data you see and have a structured decision-making process to combat your biases. Elon Musk uses a personal decision-making approach akin to the scientific method when he is coming up with an idea, solving a problem, or deciding to start a business:[5]

1. Ask a question.

2. Gather as much evidence as possible about it.

3. Develop axioms based on the evidence and try to assign a probability of truth to each one.

4. Draw a conclusion based on cogency in order to determine whether these axioms are correct and relevant and whether they necessarily lead to a particular conclusion, and with what probability.

5. Attempt to disprove the conclusion. Seek refutation from others to further help break your conclusion.

6. If nobody can invalidate your conclusion, then you're probably right, but you're not certainly right.

SEEING WITH NEW EYES

One of the most important skills for the future is the ability to unlearn and relearn. This is also called sense-unmaking, which requires an understanding of the origins of your beliefs and an openness to changing them. This starts by acknowledging that our worldviews and how we make sense of supertrends are heavily influenced by our parents, contexts, life experiences, and sense of personal identity, and may not always be fully correct or helpful as the context around us changes. Our beliefs may cause us to dig in and irrationally defend our position due to deep inner motives, rather than be open to change. Recall the six out of seven cardiac surgery patients who failed to make the necessary lifestyle changes despite their lives being on the line.

A large part of Future Fitness has to do with iterative loops. The Creative Loop helps refine concepts and innovations. Pulsating hyper-sociality ensures that new ideas are constantly competing against one another to ensure that only the best and fittest ones survive. Oscillating between divergent and convergent thinking improves decision-making. Similarly, regularly challenging and changing your beliefs and values improves Future Fitness.

One way to do this is to push yourself to ask more questions and to think of a dialogue as one of discovery, rather than one where you must convince the other of something. As part of your growth mindset, think to yourself that you can *always* learn something new. Coupled with this, make a practice of listening and observing more.

Think of a dialogue as one of discovery, rather than one where you must convince the other of something.

One particular practice that we find helpful is **non-judgmental awareness**. Avoid automatically labeling or judging what you see straightaway. With this newfound awareness comes an enhanced ability to make informed and conscious choices, and this is a muscle that gets stronger each time you flex it.

Non-judgmental awareness is also a powerful way to counter biases. It's been proven that we will probably not eliminate all of our biases (i.e., we will still make snap judgments), and the next best thing is to be aware of these judgments as they happen and then take a more appropriate course of action. Just to be clear, there is no way we could navigate through life if we never formed clear opinions about anything. If everything was kept open to consideration, we would become completely unhinged. But when we come across *new* information, we should leave time to initially be curious and humble. This is increasingly important as the world around us changes. In the age of information, ignorance is a choice.

In the age of information, ignorance is a choice.

MINDSET 3: BEGINNER'S MINDSET

It is fascinating watching babies encounter things for the first time, as they treat each moment with utmost awe and openness. They hold no preconceived notions of what things should be like or how to deal with challenges. The opposite of a beginner's mind is an expert mind, where you believe that you've seen it all before and have nothing to learn. While this mindset can be helpful when dealing with familiar situations, it can hold you back from learning when you are exposed to new challenges or ideas.

As we speed into the blur, cultivating a beginner's mind will be a great asset. It will allow you to improve your degree of learning, see challenges as enjoyable learning opportunities, and find more creative solutions.

Core beliefs underpinning a beginner's mindset include the following:

- I can learn something from every situation.
- Everyone has biases—even me.
- There are many possible answers.
- Although my idea is good, there might be a better way.

SLOW DOWN IN ORDER TO SPEED UP

When faced with a new dilemma or situation, we often fall back on existing beliefs instead of being open to diverse points of views and experimenting with new approaches.[6] This can be especially prevalent when we are overloaded with information—which we know can be one troubling consequence of hyper-sociality.

The antidote, perhaps counterintuitively, is to slow down and use all your senses. Deep breathing can calm the body and clear the mind, and using your feelings and gut in addition to your brain can improve decisions. Your gut has about 500 million neurons and is sometimes called the "second brain." Your heart, too, has about 40,000 neurons. Both of these organs are connected to the brain and can send and receive signals in a bidirectional fashion. These signals are not logical thoughts, but they do influence our mental states. As such, as you encounter supertrends and think about the future, and especially when you are triggered, you need both cognitive logic and intuition. Steve Jobs was famous for using his gut on big decisions. So was Einstein, who used hunches to push his theories forward. He once said, "I sometimes feel that I am right. I do not know that I am."[7]

UPGRADE YOUR SITUATIONAL AWARENESS

As we grapple with exponential and converging technologies, cultural changes, new market dynamics, the future of work, and so on, broadening our decision-making tools can be helpful. Complexity science provides some practical approaches. For example, when David J. Snowden and Mary E. Boone developed the conceptual decision-making aid they call the Cynefin framework,[8] they mapped out different situations you will find yourself in and how to think about your response:

1. *Simple* contexts are those where causes and effects are clear, with known knowns. Past patterns are a good predictor of how the future will unfold.

2. *Complicated* contexts have known unknowns. Cause-and-effect relationships are not immediately clear, but discoverable.

3. Some contexts are characterized by unknown unknowns and are labeled *complex*. These contexts do not have stable patterns of behavior, and the future is largely unpredictable.

4. The fourth domain is that of *chaos*. These situations have high degrees of turbulence, tension, and time pressure to act.

The best approach in *simple* contexts is to sense the challenge, categorize it based on your past experiences, and then respond to it. Best practices and standard processes help here. *Complicated* contexts can be solved through analysis and expert insight. Gathering a broad range of inputs, including conflicting advice, can help you make the best decision.

However, more and more of the situations we face today are *complex* or even *chaotic*. The risk is that we try to simply analyze our way out of the situation, or rely on best practices, which by definition are past practices. Instead, in complex situations it is important also to undertake so-called fail-to-safe experiments. These are small-scale experiments approaching an issue from multiple angles, but without overcommitting to one idea or hypothesis. As some experiments non-catastrophically fail and others show partial promise, the investigators gradually begin to understand potential solutions to a problem. The simplest version of this may be to discuss possibilities with many different people until something clicks—a bit like in speed dating. Being hyper-social also helps here. Finally, chaotic situations often require immediate action, and thereafter sensing and responding once the situation has been brought under control.

As you speed into the blur, you will be confronted with a myriad of decisions, many of which will be new and without clear right or wrong answers. It helps to be critical in terms of what you know versus what you believe, to remain open to changing your beliefs, to slow down in order to use both logic and intuition, and to apply the right decision-making approach. Here are some tips to help you develop a beginner's mindset and improve your level of awareness and the quality of your decisions:

1. **Stretch yourself:** Take a personality test to understand how you typically make sense of the world (e.g., detail oriented vs. big picture), and push yourself to practice the approaches that you are least prone to taking.

2. **Challenge your own assumptions:** Push yourself to determine whether your point of view is something you know or something you believe.

3. **Be informed:** Challenge your data sources, especially expert opinion. Is the information shared based on credible and verifiable information?

4. **Broaden your exposure:** Seek different points of view and information outlets. However, be aware of not continuing to seek information just for the sake of it (information bias and analysis paralysis).

5. **Experiment:** When making a decision, put on different "hats," (e.g., Edward de Bono's six thinking hats of creativity, process, caution, optimism, feelings, and facts[9]).

6. **Reset:** Ask yourself, "If I could start over, would I still do things this way?"

7. **Slow down:** Avoid on-the-spot decisions or reactions when you are triggered. If time allows, find a quiet space to think through the facts and tune into your gut and heart before making the final decision.

Chapter 16

LEARNING HOW TO LEARN

As everything gets digitized, globalized, and connected, the rate of knowledge (as measured by data as a proxy) is growing exponentially. It is estimated that in 1900, the speed with which knowledge of all sorts grew would mean that it would take a hundred years for knowledge to double. However, according to one estimate, that number had shrunk to twenty-five years by 1945, twelve to thirteen months in 1982, and as little as one day in 2020.[1] So, while according to Ziman's law scientific activity doubles every fifteen years, the amount of data of all sorts grows infinitely faster. In other words, we must either ignore or deal with more and more information and data, including poor quality data and misinformation. Add to that the fact that people entering the workforce in 2020 will very likely live to be over a hundred years old and perhaps only retire (or semi-retire) in their seventies or eighties, and that they on average will switch jobs every three years or so. So . . . how do you educate yourself for *that*?

GETTING AHEAD OF THE LEARNING CURVE

Let's start with the observation that within knowledge, there are curves. The rate of knowledge acquisition and the ability to do a task often progress in similar ways, which can be approximated by a Sigmoid curve, or an "S-curve," as it is often called. This curve is a mathematical concept that initially shows decreasing returns but thereafter slowly increases and then grows exponentially before slowing growth, plateauing, and declining again. The curve is used in many metaphors in life, such as getting ahead of the curve or getting over a learning curve.

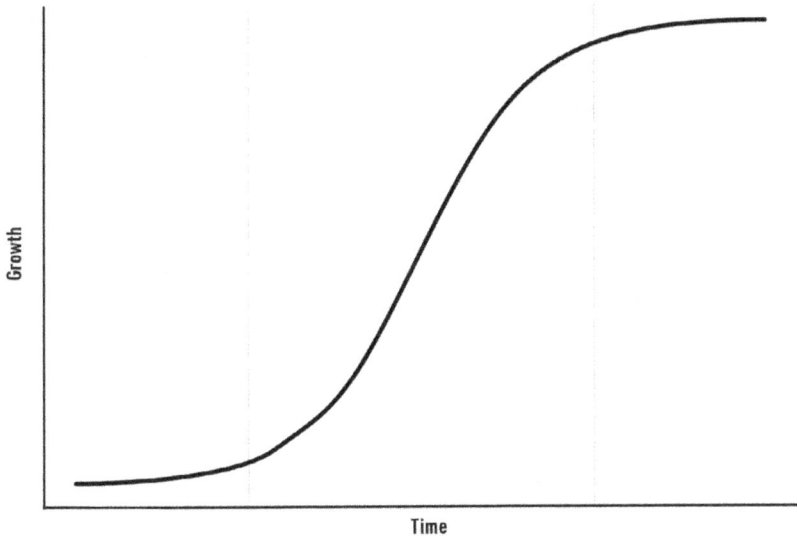

Figure 16.1. The Sigmoid curve (S-curve).

Past civilizations such as the Roman Empire had such curves. Political parties have curves. Companies too. Digital marketing ads have curves. And, yes, skills have them. However, as we speed into the future, we are seeing a general shortening of these curves, meaning that reinvention must happen on a more frequent basis.[2]

In markets for new technologies, the initial growth is often largely driven by core innovation from science. However, as markets take off, the effects of day-to-day fine-tuning kick in and tend to improve efficiency through countless small modifications. Think of a pit stop in Formula 1. On YouTube there is a great video with an F1 pit stop in 1950 versus one in 2013. The first takes sixty-seven seconds and the second takes three seconds. In digital markets, this incremental but relentless progress may be amplified by the effects of increasing returns, where the profits per unit sold rise dramatically for a while as the market grows. Eventually, the market approaches saturation or is replaced with entirely different solutions, and then the fine-tuning effect levels off, and later the related scientific discovery process levels off too. As for these entirely different solutions, Bell's law for the birth and death of computer classes gives an example from this industry.[3] It states the following: "Roughly every decade a new, lower-priced computer class forms based on a new programming platform, network, and interface, resulting in new usage and the establishment of a new industry."

Indeed, and so we went from mainframes to client servers, PCs, browser-based, cloud-based, handhelds, and ubiquitous/IoT.

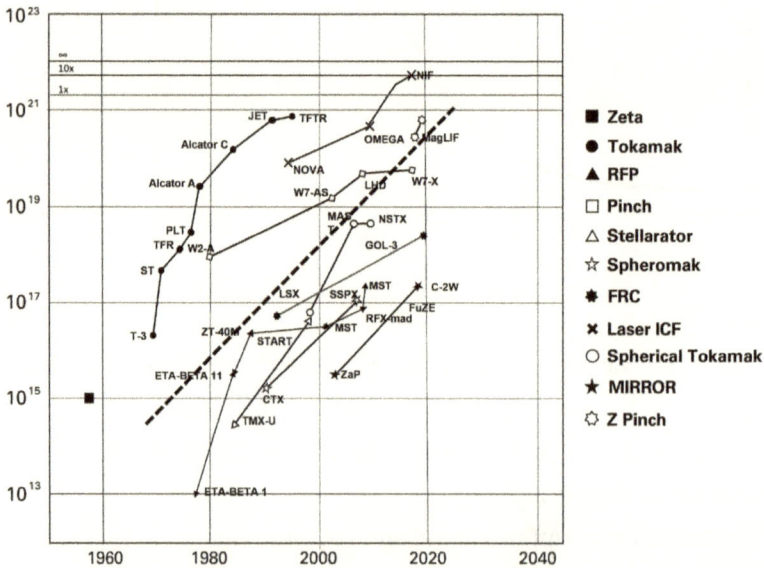

Figure 16.2. The exponential growth of the triple product in nuclear fusion 1950—2021. The vertical axis is exponential and shows triple product.[4]

The tricky part is that you must start the next curve as the first one is still in its ascendancy, which is before it has reached its peak. However, the history of the exponential progress in nuclear fusion illustrates this well. Figure 16.2 shows an overview of how overall this technology since the 1950s has followed an exponential track toward critical triple product. However, the illustration also reveals that this progress has been achieved with a combination of technology approaches along the way, where repeatedly, some have been phased out as others took over.

It's never easy to know when the first curve is about to peak, and humans have a tendency to project future trajectories based on past trends, meaning that in this case we might be overly optimistic. Psychologically it's also very difficult to start the next phase of reinvention when everything is going well currently. However, as individuals we must be keenly aware of when our skills are helping us and when they are at risk of becoming obsolete.

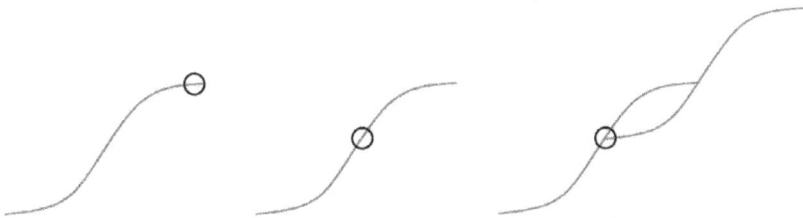

Figure 16.3. Typical transition point, ideal transition point, and implications.

This increasing speed of change means that skills become obsolete much more quickly than before. For example, one study has put the half-life of professional skills at five years, meaning that on the day you graduate from university, what you learned in the first year is only about 50 percent relevant on graduation day.[5] Of course, the degree of skill decay is shorter for many technologies, while other skills such as basic math are more timeless. But even broad competencies such as communication, management, and problem-solving are seeing important changes in terms of nuances. This applies to leading people digitally, working with younger or older generations, interacting cross-culturally, as well as what it means to move into a digital-first world. Also, the risk that you may soon end up working with something that you weren't educated for at all grows. If this happens, some otherwise timeless knowledge that you learned becomes useless to your changing work challenges. There is obviously knowledge and insight that is useful even if it cannot be tied directly to any practical work task, but often the time spent learning some particular skill may have been better spent elsewhere.

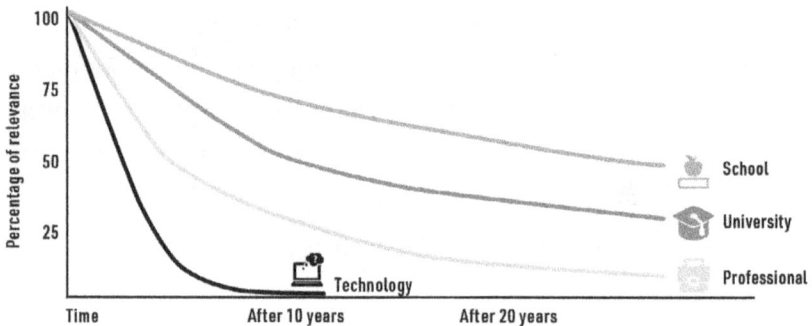

Figure 16.4. How professional skills lose value over time.[6]

One study has put the half-life of skills at five years, meaning that when you graduate from university, what you learned in the first year is only about 50 percent relevant for today. Also, the chance that you end up working outside what you were educated for keeps rising.

Because of these knowledge waves, learning must continue throughout our lives. Think of it like food. It doesn't make sense to eat all the food for your life before you are twenty-five. You need to keep eating smaller amounts every day for your entire life.

Interestingly, we now know that the way we learn not only shapes what we know but also, in some senses, who we become. This is because of **neuroplasticity**, which is the way our brains continue to change even as we get older. This does not only occur during childhood, as scientists previously thought. Unfortunately, education systems in many parts of the world are outdated and have not meaningfully changed in the past hundred years. For example, we still focus heavily on three- or four-year college degrees and perhaps a subsequent one- to two-year master's degree as the basis for a lifelong career. In reality, our learning needs to continue to change throughout our lives. More than ever before, a shorter formal education followed by a lifelong process of intense micro-learning is the better approach.

This means that in the future, more and more learning must be self-directed and happen in real time rather than be guided by educational institutions and employers and delivered in a single, massive trunk.

> **A shorter formal education followed by a lifelong process of intense micro-learning becomes the best approach.**

FROM T- TO M-SHAPED LEARNING

As you think about your career at a macro level, it is helpful to think in terms of letters, "T" and "M" specifically. We can more and more rarely rely on **T-shaped learning**, where you develop deep expertise during university or early apprenticeship years (e.g., in marketing, finance, or operations) and then supplement this with modest on-the-job learning and development and sporadic formal learning courses during your career. Instead, this is increasingly being replaced by **M-shaped knowledge profiles**, where new skills and competencies are developed in earnest every few years.[7] In some cases, this may require you to completely transform your skill sets and career trajectory. Remember that many people are now on average expected to switch jobs every three years or so and change career paths completely every decade. Move over long education. Welcome lifelong learning.

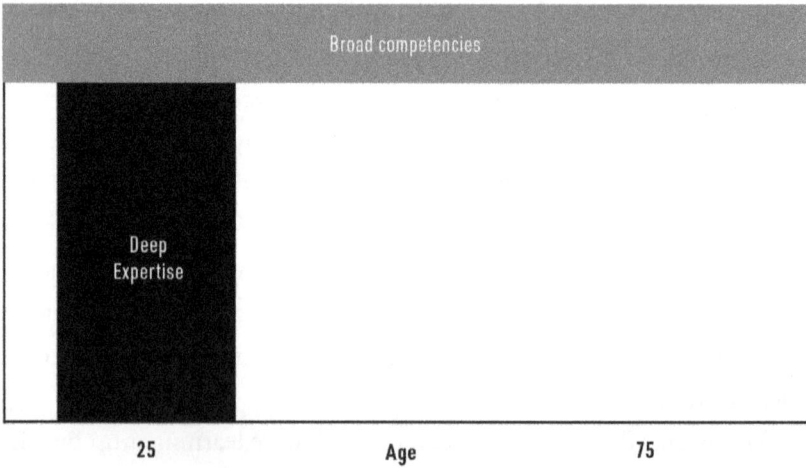

Figure 16.5. Traditional T-profile of knowledge worker.[8]

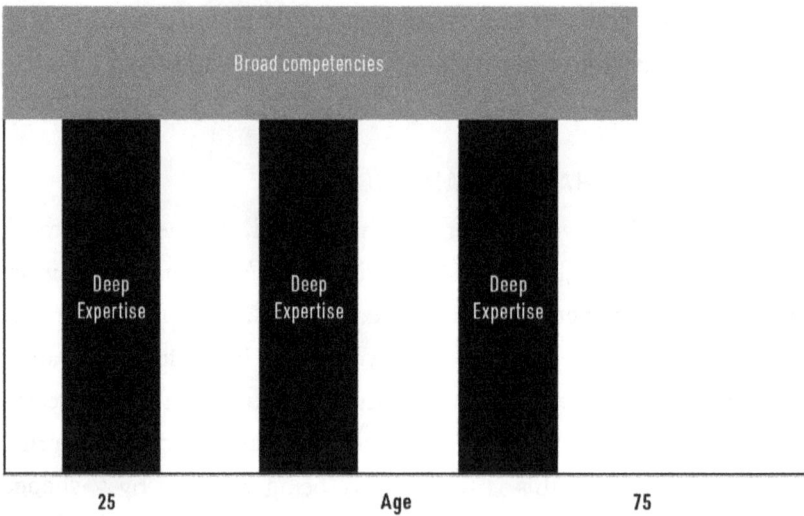

Figure 16.6. M-profile of the modern knowledge worker.[9]

FOUR SKILLS GAINING VALUE

In terms of broad competencies, there will be a decreased demand for skills related to repetitive and simple tasks, as many of these can be partially or fully automated. In particular, there will be an increased demand for skills in four areas:

- *Problem-solving and creativity* (as the problems we face become increasingly abstract and novel)

- *Self-management* (as we need to manage a more fluid world of work with more flexibility and freedom)

- *Working with people* (as complex problems must be addressed with diverse perspectives and profiles)

- *Technology use and development* (we simply must understand how technology works to the extent that we can apply it in our day-to-day work)

The World Economic Forum outlines these skills in detail in a report called "The Future of Jobs Report." This should be required reading for all.[10] Taken from another angle, there will be growth in jobs relating to the precision economy and—increasingly—to the emerging global experience economy.

Many of our job tasks will change meaningfully in the next three years, significantly in the next five years, and will be completely transformed in the next ten years. As for so many sectors and products, learning must move from batch to as-a-service and from aggregated to many more microunits. In other words, a constant flow of targeted learning in small doses.

> **A lot of our job tasks will change meaningfully in the next three years, significantly in the next five years, and transformatively in the next ten years.**

LEARNING AGILITY, MATRIX-STYLE

In the movie *The Matrix*, the protagonist Neo is able to upload new skills into his brain through a computer link. He can learn jiujitsu, kung fu, and a host of other skills while lying in a reclining chair with his eyes closed. In another scene, his compatriot Trinity learns how to fly a helicopter in mere seconds as they flee from the bad guys. That sounds pretty cool, doesn't it?

The crazy part is that for our immediate learning needs, this trend is already happening. Narrow learning needs—often micro-learning needs—are being met immediately, in real time. For example, if you need to learn how to do something on Google docs or a video-editing program, you will immediately search online for a solution. The same goes for cooking a new recipe, filing taxes, or tapping into your personal network and using seek-sense-share loops.

The bad news is that most of us have never been taught efficiently how to learn, and in many cases, we sabotage our own attempts to do so. The good news is that we know so much more today about how to learn effectively. And one of the secrets is rather obvious: we are most motivated to learn something if we need to apply it immediately. And we are far more likely to remember what we learned if we did indeed apply it right away. This is why we need to learn continuously, all the time, while we work. We can call this **just-in-time learning**.

We might not be able to upload new information and skills into our brain directly as in *The Matrix* (at least not just yet), but we can get pretty close.

LEARNING AS A MINDSET

One of the most useful mental distinctions to consider in an ever-changing world dominated by often radical supertrends is whether you have a fixed mindset or a growth mindset. Before we get to what that means, let's just think of the mindset that famously grew out of Silicon Valley. There is hardly any place on Earth more emblematic of the accelerating changes we are facing than Silicon Valley. This is where many of the world's most successful companies are born, so here we might expect to find a prevailing attitude of praising winners and loathing losers to have evolved.

In fact, what has emerged is something else entirely: a mentality with a willingness to risk mistakes and not be shy about it. Here, people are suspicious of those who have not failed, because it means that they have not tried enough and therefore have not learned enough. In Silicon Valley, people are also suspicious of people who do not admit that they have failed, because they may not try hard enough in the future. Fortunately, it is a mentality that has spread since then.

The terms *fixed* and *growth mindsets* were introduced in the instant classic *The New Psychology of Success* (2013), by Stanford psychology professor Carol Dweck. Based on massive research, Dweck noted that "it's not always the people who start out the smartest who end up the smartest," and that this can be explained by significant differences in mentalities.

The less successful would often have a **fixed mindset**, as she calls it. This means that they assume their character, abilities, and other characteristics can't be changed much. Because of this, they're likely to constantly try to prove that they're great and flawless. On the other hand, they won't try very hard to improve their lot, not only because they assume they won't be able to, but also because trying to learn makes you look stupid for a while.

They may also assume that one person's success must necessarily be at the cost of other people—as if the wealth of society also was a given irrespective of incentive structure, and that it is a zero-sum game where every win is matched with a loss and everything is a given.

We probably all know people with predominantly fixed mindsets, and one of their typical traits is to revel in the failure of others—and perhaps more so when otherwise successful and powerful people fail, since this makes them feel better about themselves.

Dweck writes that successful people tend to have a **growth mindset**, which means they assume they can change themselves a lot, and they thrive on challenges, even if that means they sometimes fail and come across as fools. Indeed, to them, occasional failures are useful experiences they can learn from in order to do better next time.

Growth mind-setters take no pleasure in seeing other people fail, but they feel inspired by—and try to learn from—other people's success. This difference is crucial, and as Dweck put it, "The fixed mindset makes you concerned with how you'll be judged; the growth mindset makes you concerned with improving." Fixed mind-setters look for immediate results, whereas growth mind-setters value progress—also in the long term. To fixed mind-setters, a big effort is embarrassing because it shows that you are not smart and talented enough. In contrast, to growth mind-setters, a hard effort is admirable because it *makes you* smart and talented.

The fixed mindset makes you concerned with how you'll be judged; the growth mindset makes you concerned with improving.

THE JOY IN CHANGE

One of the lessons from Dweck is that when evaluating ourselves and others, we shouldn't focus too much on where we are right now, but more on where we are going. In other words, we should focus on how we change—we should not find success only in winning and achieving, but also in learning and improving. In our daily lives, we should be careful with constantly and unconditionally praising coworkers (or children for that matter), because that may stimulate fixed mindsets. Instead, while we should indeed praise what is good, we should point out what could be the next step toward improvement.

A great example of a winner with a true growth mindset is basketball icon Michael Jordan, who famously said, "I've missed more than 9,000 shots in my career. I've lost almost 300 games. Twenty-six times I've been trusted to take the game-winning shot and missed. I've failed over and over and over again in my life." Yes, he failed, but he always grew, and he won far more than he lost. Growth mindset!

Of course, in a world that is constantly and rapidly changing, having a fixed mindset is an even bigger handicap than in a more static society. What will work best in future dynamic environments is a willingness to risk frequent failures and to frequently pivot when things don't work out. In other words, to run your career and private life a bit more as if it were a young growth start-up company with a Silicon Valley mindset.

One way to develop a growth mindset is to consciously consider every day as the start of the rest of your life: "If I wasn't already in this situation, is this then what I would choose today?" If not, then consider a move. In chess, you need to quickly mobilize your officers, who are initially all stuck behind the pawns. Is your life a bit like this? Are there any such obstacles that you can remove to increase your agility? In a dynamic society, you need to be able to move.

Growth mindsets are about always challenging yourself and accepting that failures will be part of your journey but also constructive learning experiences. It is also about viewing the success of others as inspiration, not a provocation.

MINDSET 4: GROWTH MINDSET

People with a growth mindset believe that making an effort and practicing one's skill over time make a meaningful difference. By contrast, people who do not have a growth mindset believe that talent, intelligence, and thus one's professional skills and/or career are innate and unchangeable.

Not having a growth mindset thus contributes to limiting beliefs, while having a growth mindset gives one empowering, "can-do" beliefs. This will only become more important in the future as we are confronted with more and more challenges and situations that we have never seen before.

Core beliefs underpinning a growth mindset include the following:

- Challenges are learning opportunities.

continued

- I appreciate it when I get feedback about my performance, even if that feedback is negative.
- Everyone who is good at some skill has spent a lot of time practicing that skill, regardless of their natural ability.
- It is important to admit my mistakes in order to learn from them.
- Making a mistake does not mean I am incompetent; it means I am learning.

UPDATING OUR APPROACH TO GROWTH

Many of us still harbor outdated definitions of what it means to learn, equating it to formal lessons, memorization, and test taking. This might also lead to a pass/fail view of learning when in reality, progress is much more fluid. You can and should be learning throughout the day when you engage in any task that is challenging. In addition, sometimes you learn when you least expect it, for example by watching a video that is totally outside of your areas of interest, purely to get inspiration and stretch your brain in new ways.

Here are some practical tips to help you cultivate a growth mindset and learn at the speed of the blur:

1. **Create a curriculum:** Identify the skills that you need to achieve your most desired future. Include both broad competencies—for example by reading the World Economic Forum's latest reports on the future of jobs—as well as the area(s) where you need deep expertise. Be very specific about what success would look like for each new skill.

2. **Get specific:** Deconstruct the skills and create your learning journey with a focus on learning by doing and dedicated periods of deliberate learning/practice.

3. **Make it fun:** Use a broad range of resources (e.g., online courses, videos by experts, podcasts, and dedicated classes), and over time narrow them to the ones that are most effective and engaging for you.

4. **Use your network:** Get a mentor or reach out to someone in your network who is an expert in this area.

5. **Get out of your comfort zone:** Once you hit a plateau (when your S-curve starts flattening), find new ways to stretch yourself. This is the only way to keep developing.

6. **Ask for feedback:** Learning happens in iterative cycles, and you need to adjust along the way. Ask for feedback from various sources regularly and also spend time weekly reflecting on your progress.

Chapter 17

THINK BIGGER

If Dubai had been built by less-visionary leaders, it might have turned into the world's most efficient fishing village. We write this with a smile, of course, but the fact is that nothing about Dubai's rise to global prominence was inevitable, despite being a resource-rich city. In fact, similar cities in the region, such as Abu Dhabi, Manama, Kuwait City, and Doha, share similar or substantially more resource-based wealth but have struggled to replicate the same degree of growth and innovation.

Dubai's leaders thought ahead of supertrends and created a vision that leapfrogged current technologies and paradigms, rather than incrementally building on them. For example, Dubai airport has consistently expanded its capacity ahead of demand, as part of a broader vision to grow non-oil sectors such as trade, tourism, retail, and general business activities. In 2020 oil accounted for just 1 percent of Dubai's GDP, compared to over 50 percent in the past. Dubai has also launched a Museum of the Future, where "instead of absorbing the past, you help the future to emerge." Bold thinking indeed.

And this raises an issue: as you craft your most desired future, the unfortunate reality is that there is a high likelihood that you will undershoot and aim too low. Our brain doesn't think exponentially, yet this is exactly how the major trends are evolving.

FROM 10 PERCENT TO 10X

We previously touch on the importance of an exponential mindset. Let us elaborate a bit further here. Decades of research in cognitive psychology illustrate that the human mind prefers simple, linear relationships and struggles with thinking nonlinearly.[1] And certainly it has a difficult time considering exponential development: even as we are well aware of exponential change in the past, we struggle imagining it continuing in the future.

Another one of our many biases is a **linearity bias**, where we assume that a change in one quantity produces a proportionate change in another. When one of these quantities is time, we believe that past trends will continue at the same rate in the future. Okay, perhaps we make the trend grow slightly faster because we know that technology is improving, but this is often in the range of 10–20 percent increase over five to ten years, which can miss the mark drastically. Exponential changes can get to 10–100x increases or more, and as they do, they often create outcomes that are completely different from the present. For instance, a bundle of nerve cells in a worm enables it to move and react to its surroundings. But the much bigger bundle in human brains creates something materially different than just a faster worm. And whereas better battery performance for a while meant longer battery times for our phones, it eventually also meant efficient battery-driven cars, which was a whole new thing.

Linear logic believes that things will be better or worse.
Exponential logic understands that things will be different.

Let's think exponentially for a while. Imagine a world where you can download almost anything in one second (e.g., the three-and-a-half-hour-long movie *The Irishman* in HD). Or where the cost of sequencing a genome is pretty much free and given away as part of a smartwatch or health care subscription. Imagine homes that are 100 percent self-sufficient with energy and where all devices such as phones, smartwatches, music speakers, and TVs can charge wirelessly. Imagine electric cars that charge while they pass magnetic fields on the road. These advances might very well happen commercially in the next decade since they work in theory or in experimental settings now. Just think about the opportunities they would bring.

So, the message is this: linear logic will reinvent the past, only slightly better. Exponential thinking will reimagine the future. When entrepreneurs such as Elon Musk enter new areas, they don't do it with preexisting views of what is possible. Musk was not a technical expert on cars, space travel, or infrastructure engineering, yet these are among the areas where his companies are breaking new ground. Tremendous new ground, in fact. He constantly pushes his colleagues to find creative ways to make things work that often involve exponential thinking.

> **Linear logic will reinvent the past, just slightly better.**
> **Exponential thinking will reimagine the future.**

Rational argumentation and analysis will help you break things down and understand how the world works. This is important and needed. But it will never be enough to create something fantastically different and better. For this you need a possibility-focused mindset, which is bold, aspirational, curious, and asks questions such as *How might we?*, *What if?*, and *Why couldn't we?* In other words, you need a growth mindset.

THINKING BACKWARDS

Here comes a useful hack: allow yourself to dream about what the future might hold, and then work backwards from that to determine what needs to be true to make it happen. This is a diametrically opposite process than starting with what is possible today and then innovating incrementally forward.

Get into the habit of envisioning something fantastically different and better, then thinking backwards to how it may be achieved.

For experts or in areas that you are familiar with, it requires a fair bit of sense un-making, where you challenge your existing beliefs and paradigms. One way to do this is to radically broaden your exposure to different types of information, experiences, and people in search of luck. Monitor your inner voice, and shift from "I already know that" to "I want to learn more."

When you try to think forward, you might get too close to a fixed mindset. Thinking backwards from a future fantasy promotes the growth mindset. And so does what we may call the *abundance mindset*. If you burn a barrel of oil, it's gone. But if you buy a software subscription, nothing is gone. The same can be sold again and again without end. This is one of the many reasons why the world is experiencing more wealth, or what the economist Julian Simon called *abundance*.

Many production processes will begin to have a cost close to 0, in the same way that drinking water feels virtually free in developed countries and data storage is rapidly getting there too. Obviously, choices and trade-offs still remain, but in this future world, there will be many more opportunities for each and every one of us. Harnessing this potential requires breaking away from a scarcity mindset and moving toward one of abundance and possibility.

An abundance mindset is about seeking "A and B" solutions instead of "A or B."

In your own life, you will find more often than not that you can combine your various ambitions into a coherent whole if you dedicate the right time for reflection and visioning. The trade-offs that you believe exist can often be circumvented if you are creative. For example, today it is possible to outsource an increasing number of tasks that take up time. In developed nations, some employees even secretly outsource some of their work tasks to lower-cost labor via crowdsourcing sites so they can use their own time better.

MINDSET 5: ABUNDANCE MINDSET

People with an abundance mindset believe that there are enough resources and successes for everyone to go around. And, as we saw in part 1, this is absolutely the case. Technological progress and innovation are accelerating, and the future will, in general, be far more wealthy, peaceful, and better than the past.

An abundance mindset enables you to think more freely, bigger, and more boldly. Rather than being constrained by fear of running out of resources, your mind is open to new possibilities. People with an abundance mindset also maintain an optimistic, open, and trusting frame of mind and seek out win-win relationships and deals. This is similar in nature to Covey's interdependent stage and can enable hyper-sociality.

Core beliefs underpinning an abundance mindset include the following:

- I believe there is enough success and acknowledgment to go around.
- I often think that the best is yet to come.
- I am happy to share my resources and knowledge with others.
- I believe that the best results are achieved together with others.
- I believe that in the long run, things are not a true "win" if they're not a "win" for everyone involved.

By contrast, people with a scarcity mindset tend to believe that resources and success are finite in quantity, and thus, one person's success is necessarily another person's failure. Consequently, this often hampers their ability to make the most of the opportunities that come their way.

THE FORMULA FOR CREATIVITY

Creative organizations and individuals are also some of the most structured. They combine blue sky thinking with intelligent constraints that both narrow their thinking and ground their aspirations in a practical reality. They use many attempts to get it right, pushing themselves and their teams to come up with and evaluate tens or even hundreds of ideas in short periods of time.

Creativity = blue sky thinking + intelligent constraints

You don't have to be a genius to replicate this process. You just need an understanding of exponential technologies, a growth and abundance mindset of possibility and curiosity, and then you need to come up with lots of ways this might look. In this way, you'll imagine new possibilities. This process can be used for business ideas but also for your life more broadly (e.g., family, health, wealth, and happiness). For example, have you charted different paths toward your most desired future? Force yourself to throw in a wild card option that is totally different from the rest. Then think of three more wild cards.

As you look at the emerging futures and paths, you will begin to see a strategic spectrum and a range of different futures, some that are a better fit for you than others. This is where you move from divergent to convergent thinking. Use a combination of analysis and judgment to narrow down on your most desired options. Here are some tips to help you think bigger and more abundantly as you craft your most desired future:

1. **Think bigger:** Challenge yourself to think radically differently about the future. Take your current aspiration and multiply it by ten, just for fun, and then analyze how you might make that future reality.

2. **Think unreasonably:** Take your long-term future vision (e.g., the one that is twenty years out), and think how you might achieve it in five years instead.

3. **Think outside the box:** Identify constraints in your life that seem like trade-offs. Crowdsource ideas on how to combine them.

4. **Be inspired:** Think about a business leader you admire such as Steve Jobs, Mary Barra, or Jack Ma, and ask yourself what they would do.

5. **Play the numbers game:** For a specific problem area or challenge, write down what you want to have happen, and if there are any constraints (e.g., financial, time limit, or other practicalities). Then set a time for fifteen minutes to come up with as many ideas as possible. Once the fifteen minutes are up, challenge yourself to double the number of ideas.

Chapter 18

CONNECTING THE DOTS FORWARD

In a world of continuous and accelerating change and increasing information, many people experience an unpleasant sense of losing control. It can seem as if the world consists of a completely chaotic swarm of unconnected dots that can neither be predicted nor controlled:

Such a feeling is natural, and feeling a loss of control has been shown to increase rates of depression, stress, burnout, and general health.[1] However, there are proven techniques that not only help you understand and make sense of the swarm of activity around you, but to actually use them to your advantage.

I WAS JUST LUCKY, DUDE

Sir Alex Ferguson is widely regarded as the best football (soccer) manager of all time. He won forty-nine trophies over almost four decades of management—more than any other manager. He won thirty-eight trophies

during twenty-six years at Manchester United, where more than 200 different players played under him.[2] At Manchester United, his teams scored
166 last-minute goals, prompting some to call him lucky. His response?
That the harder his team tried, the luckier they got.[3]

As you spur into a rapidly changing future, it becomes riskier and
riskier to leave things to chance and hope for the best. Turbulence creates lots of opportunities in fast succession but also lots of surprising
dead ends and obsolete skills.

One of the characteristics of great football players is that they are
good at predicting where the ball will go. Great investors can do the
same with financial markets, and great parents can, at the last minute,
prevent their children from making disastrous mistakes. To the outsider, a great footballer or investor may simply seem lucky, but the fact
is that exceptionally skilled people often appear lucky because luck can
be a consequence of how you approach life.

This is where the science of luck comes in. Richard Wiseman is probably the world's foremost scientist in the matter of luck, and one of his
experiments gives us an idea of why some people have far more of it than
others. First, he placed adverts calling for people who thought that they
were either particularly lucky or particularly unlucky. Then he gave both
lucky and unlucky people a newspaper and asked each to look through
it and tell him how many photographs were inside. The result was fascinating because on average, the unlucky people spent about two minutes
counting photographs, whereas the lucky ones spent just a few seconds.
The reason the lucky ones were so much faster was that they noticed a
message in huge letters on page two saying, "Stop counting—There are
43 photographs in this newspaper."

This and many other experiments showed that lucky people generally notice more things than they were specifically asked to investigate.
While lucky people might be able to have a laser focus, they are also
equipped with a radar, so to speak. In contrast, unlucky people have
laser but no radar.

In a world dominated by accelerating change where we need to accept frequent failure and pivot often, the need for luck increases, and it is therefore worth your while to chase. This includes being very observant.

Lucky people might be able to have a laser focus, but they are also equipped with a radar. In other words, their observations and thinking are convergent *and* divergent.

DEVELOPING A BETTER RADAR

How do we develop a better radar to improve our luck? For starters, the less routine your life is, the more good luck and bad luck you are likely to encounter. The thing is, with a little practice, you can typically put good luck to use while minimizing the harm from bad luck. Having a clear vision for where you want to go will increase your chances of building on the luck that can take you there. Your mind will automatically start looking for ways to get you there. Many experiments have shown that if you ask test subjects to focus on a specific element in their environment, such as things that are red, they will be able to recount quite accurately what the red items were, but they will be much less aware of other things in their environment, such as things that are blue. By focusing on red objects, the brain automatically becomes almost oblivious to non-red items.[4] In the same way, by having a sense of the things your brain should be looking for, your radar becomes much more active. In other words, you can train your brain to simply be more observant in general. And according to Wiseman, in addition to generally chasing luck, lucky people also create self-fulfilling prophecies via positive expectations, make lucky decisions by listening to their intuition, and adopt resilient attitudes that transform bad luck into good. We guess the latter is simply yet another example of growth mindset.

EMBRACE UNEXPECTED EXPERIENCES

Another scientist who has studied luck is New York University professor Christian Busch, who in 2020 published the book *The Serendipity*

Mindset: The Art and Science of Creating Good Luck. Busch points out that about half of all scientific breakthroughs are down to luck. So again, luck is important, and if you have a "serendipity mindset," Busch says, you are pursuing "smart, active luck" by connecting dots and by generally expecting the unexpected and hoping to gain from it rather than seeing it as anxiety provoking.

Even though you may work hard and focused, in a complex world with exponential supertrends all around you, things are unlikely to play out as expected—just as in war and football. Exactly because this is so, you should always look out for and expect that you might at times benefit from the unexpected. After all, it is no coincidence that people often say that "crisis breeds opportunity."

Nurture a mindset where you think of the unexpected as unavoidable and as a great source of potential luck and thus opportunities.

> **In general, think of the unexpected as unavoidable and a great source of opportunities.**

DEVELOP HABITS THAT INCREASE YOUR CHANCES OF FINDING LUCK

There are also concrete habits that can help stimulate luck. You can, for instance, try to meet a lot of people, develop a big network on social media, visit many places, read a lot, and try out many things. In addition, if you have a win-win mindset and habitually help others, chances are they will help you back.

> **You can chase luck by, for instance, meeting a lot of people, having a big network on social media, visiting many places, reading a lot, trying out many things, and frequently helping other people.**

Another way of navigating the dots in a complex world is to couple in-the-moment awareness with periods of dedicated reflection time.

This will help you make the unconscious conscious, and you will start to notice new opportunities around you. In practice, you do this by slowing down ever so slightly; stop being on autopilot and start having both hands on the steering wheel.

MINDSET 6: SERENDIPITY MINDSET

People with a serendipity mindset believe that luck can be learned and leveraged just like any other skill. Such people know that they are not simply "luckier" but that the conditions for happy coincidences to arise and be taken advantage of must be cultivated in one's life if one is to succeed. By contrast, people with a jinxed (or even cursed) mindset believe they are generally unlucky in life and that life events are random.

The ability to cultivate luck and connect seemingly disparate technologies, people, and events will become increasingly important as our paths forward become less linear and more frequently resemble cycles of convergence and divergence. A serendipity mindset helps to foster and leverage technological convergence as a driver of innovation and also opens the way to hyper-sociality.

Core beliefs underpinning a growth mindset include the following:

- I like to ask "why" and explore new ways of doing things.
- It is advantageous for me to meet new people and be able to learn from them.
- I set aside time to reflect on my experiences and conversations.
- Unexpected mistakes or deviations are opportunities.
- Sharing my ideas with people from many different walks of life has often proven valuable to me.
- I expect the unexpected and adapt my approach on an ongoing basis.

CONNECTING THE DOTS FORWARD

Luck is often about connecting things in new ways. If someone has exposure to more diverse sets of information, experiences, and people, it is only natural that there will be a higher chance of two seemingly unrelated events coming together in a fortuitous way. Leonardo da Vinci is often associated with iconic paintings such as the *Mona Lisa* and *The Last Supper*. What is perhaps less talked about is that he was an exponential thinker who looked for ways to get A and B, and who frequently imagined the seemingly impossible. He came up with early designs for a helicopter, parachutes, deep water diving suits, armored cars, robots, machine guns, solar power, and a calculator. If we wanted to give an example of someone who was truly Future Fit, Mr. da Vinci would be a prime example.

But here's the thing—da Vinci didn't just come up with ideas out of the blue that weren't grounded in some sort of reality. He was extremely well versed in a broad range of topics, which allowed him to see linkages and opportunities that no one had seen before him. In this way, he frequently took pattern recognition from some areas and applied them in others.

Very few are of his caliber, but we can still use his approach. While Steve Jobs famously said that you can only connect the dots backwards, not forward, it is in your control to increase the number of dots that you are aware of and explore how they might combine in new ways in the future. And of course, it is not really true that you cannot connect future dots. As we have already seen, there are many ways that you can predict and then connect them with reasonable certainty—for instance, by extrapolating exponential trends and looking for coevolution patterns. If you master the fundamentals of that, you might find that you are consistently luckier and better able to take advantage of supertrends than most other people.

DOING PREMORTEMS

There is a so-called *premortem* exercise that involves imagining yourself failing to reach an important future goal. Yes, we know: it's no fun. But take the time to think about your next major milestone six months or a year down the line. Imagine that you have fallen short of your goal, and then outline all the reasons why this might have happened. Push yourself to generate a long list. If you have ten reasons, force yourself to find five more. You will now begin to see major themes emerging, and for each of these, think about ways to mitigate the risk. Imagine future failure, then plan how to avoid it.

Leaving this to chance is a risky strategy in an increasingly volatile world. Even if you do fall short of your goals, you want to maximize your probability of success. It can cause you to lose a sense of agency and autonomy, which can lead to overwhelm and apathy. Leaving things to chance also risks having a future filled with regrets since you might have wasted the greatest asset you have been given, which is time.

Here are some tips to help you think more serendipitously and be better able to navigate and connect the many dots of your life:

1. **Develop both a radar and a laser.** Master both convergent and divergent thinking and practice scanning your environment for signals that may give you clues about what steps to take next.

2. **Embrace unexpected events.** View the unexpected as great sources of potential luck and opportunities.

3. **Chase serendipity.** Develop habits that increase your chances of finding luck, such as meeting a lot of people from a diverse set of spheres, cultivating and interacting with a large social media network, visiting different places, reading, trying out new things, and saying yes to new things.

4. **Be like da Vinci.** Look for patterns in one context that can be applied in another. This can be as simple as taking fifteen minutes on a regular basis to reflect on your experiences and lessons learned in a specific situation and how they might benefit you in other contexts.

5. **Connect the dots forward.** Anticipate future dots by extrapolating exponential trends and try to connect them forward.

6. **Do premortems.** Imagine future failure and then plan how to avoid it. Push yourself to generate a long list of potential failures and roadblocks—even potential "black swan" events that are extremely unlikely but have a massive, negative impact.

Chapter 19

37X BETTER IN A YEAR

I n the previous chapters, we look at values, habits, and mindsets that could help us navigate complexity and become Future Fit. We look at an ownership mindset, exponential mindset, beginner's mindset, growth mindset, abundance mindset, and serendipity mindset, which could all help us understand our surroundings and craft our most desired futures. Now we move to action. In the same way you might train your body to run a marathon or play a sport, you can train your mind to better support you in your day-to-day journey. While real steroids are extremely dangerous and should never be used to enhance physical performance, there are safe and extremely effective metaphorical steroids we can use to become even more future ready and accelerate our progress.

DREAM, THEN DO

When you have mapped out your most desired future, the next step is to take action and maintain momentum. You must step over the line and engage. Lean in. And shape your future rather than letting it shape you.

What often prevents people from achieving their most desired future is a simple lack of discipline.

Of course, when asked, most of us would say we're already doing that. However, in reality, the dreaming stage is often where we get stuck. One trap can be that while reading about the future, learning new things, and crafting a vision are exciting and important, they can also become a form of procrastination for us: we dream and think and plan, but we don't do.

People are especially prone to procrastinating if a task is complex, vague, or seemingly overwhelming or scary. The trouble with that is that as we move into the ever-changing future we describe in part 1, more and more future scenarios will fall into one of those four categories. Indeed, in the future, every year there will be more things that you experience for the first time. And many more things that may disrupt your schedule. Far more experiences that make us think, "Did that just happen?" What we need in this ever-shifting blur is a propensity for quick, consistent, and reflective action. Let's now look at some tools and tips that may help.

COMPOUNDING MINDSET

Imagine if you could get 37x better at something in a year. This is the power of consistent action and compounding. One percent improvement per day for 365 days adds up to 3,778 percent, or more than 37x. Similarly, if you immerse yourself in a topic for thirty minutes a day, and keep deepening your knowledge each day, you will find that you suddenly know a great deal about it after one year (recall the S-curve of learning). In that same period, assuming you wrote just 200 words a day (about two thirds of a page), you can write a book.

We mention this because, as we have seen in the many exponential supertrends, when things compound, they really, really add up over time. The same can happen in personal conduct, if you have a compounding mindset.

In an ever-changing world, a lot more of what you achieve will be up to your own willpower. If you have a growth mindset and train yourself constantly, you will also train your courage and willpower as if they were muscles. In this way, mindsets build character.

**Compounding mindset is about consistency
in the short term for success in the long term.**

MINDSET 7: COMPOUNDING MINDSET

A compounding mindset is the understanding that many little investments (e.g., in time, money, energy) are required, on a continuous basis, in order to achieve disproportionate outcomes in the future. As we've heard many entrepreneurs say, "It took me ten years to become an overnight success."

The importance of hard work and discipline may seem obvious. But there are three main differences today and in the future, however, compared to the past. First, in pretty much every industry, the bar for excellence is rising all the time. This is down to, among other things, rapid information flows, competition, and more precise data (and thereby improvement techniques). Second, it is way easier to get distracted today and more effort is therefore required to stay disciplined and focused. Instant gratification is all around us, and all you need is a smartphone with a few apps to get hooked. Third, we are living longer, which means taking the long-term view of our life becomes even more critical.

Core beliefs underpinning a compounding mindset include the following:

- Discipline is required for me to be excellent in any field.
- What I do (or don't do) today has an impact on who I become tomorrow.
- Small investments over time add up to big results (snowball effect).
- It often takes time to see significant results from my actions (similar to an S-curve).
- There is no such thing as an overnight success.

The opposite of a compounding mindset is a mindset that believes that instant or short-term gratification is better than delayed gratification.

PLAY THE PRUSSIAN HACK

Haven't we all seen movies reenacting warfare from the nineteenth century, where neat lines of soldiers marched against each other on the battlefield accompanied by loud music? And where once the battle breaks loose, there is a flurry of fighting, shouting, and chaos?

That was largely the state of European warfare around the year 1800, where Napoleon was for a time the most victorious military commander. Napoleon succeeded not only because of his enormous forces, but also because he directed them around in very *agile* ways. For instance, in the Battle of Jena–Auerstedt in 1806, Napoleon confronted a Prussian army probably twice the size of his own but nevertheless beat them handsomely through his higher tactical agility.

After this, the Prussians developed the concept of *Auftragstaktik*, which directly translated means *assignment tactics*. Here the military commander gave subordinate leaders

- Clear tactical goals (the objectives)

- A clear purpose (why they must be achieved)

- A clear time frame to achieve them

However, while these three parameters were stated clearly, the subordinate leaders were left wide flexibility in *how* to reach these objectives. They could be agile.

History has demonstrated the hugely superior efficiency of this approach—given that the soldiers involved are trained well enough. During World War II, the Germans fought extremely efficiently using this approach (except when Hitler overruled his commanders to often disastrous effects). Fortunately for democracy, the Allied forces used a similar approach, which they called mission command. More recently, many countries have adopted rules of engagement that outline the circumstances and conditions for which different degrees of force may be utilized. These rules set the limits on what actions are unacceptable.

What these leadership approaches teach is to focus on your broad goals and purposes and on overall strategies and guiding frameworks to get there. You must have a clear view of where you are going and use that direction to inform your daily actions. It is not a coincidence that Dubai consistently built airport capacity ahead of demand. Jeff Bezos of Amazon has likewise said that he is thinking eight quarters ahead, and that the success of the current quarter was laid two years ago. Amazon has a clear vision for the future and principles that guide its day-to-day actions and decisions. Mission-control leadership doesn't plan exactly what will happen, but subordinates do have strong enough boundaries to give them confidence that they will mostly make the right choices along the way. This includes both what they say yes to, and, equally importantly, what they say no to.

As you craft your own most desired future, write down your most desired goals. Perhaps it is that you want to get into the experience economy where you want to focus on visual arts. You can then choose to be flexible on which sort of visual art, like set designer, industrial designer, and art dealer. When it comes to rules of engagement, you might determine, for instance, that you will (1) balance your career, personal development, and personal well-being, (2) work out at least four times a week, (3) take measured risks instead of playing it safe, (4) give as much as you take in relationships, (5) always make criticism constructive, and so on (these are just examples that we both personally happen to like).

Next, write down what the grounding purpose of those goals is. *Why* do you want to be in visual arts, for instance? Or why do you want to have children, or not have children, or be engaged in politics? Linking your activities to strong purposes will help you persevere through challenges, setbacks, and tasks that you may not find particularly exciting. After all, you will likely have to expend real time and energy to move toward your goal, especially in the beginning. Recall the Sigmoid curve!

Through these approaches, you can't make all the decisions up front, but you can decide how you will make the ones that you will face in the future. This will greatly improve your decision-making when things are uncertain and ensure they are consistent with your values and in line with your overall goal.

> Clarity about purpose and rules of engagement can
> stabilize your journey into a turbulent future.

UNREASONABLE DEADLINES, ON REPEAT

For shorter-term planning, lay out milestones and the time frames to achieve them. As we just saw, Amazon has a tactical planning horizon of eight quarters. Modern software developers often use the **scrum sprint** approach. This term, which was first used in a 1986 *Harvard Business Review* paper by Hirotaka Takeuchi and Ikujiro Nonaka, comes from rugby, where a scrum is a formation of players.[1] The term was used because of the fast and precise teamwork needed in that particular game. In modern management, the scrum approach is a series of fixed time boxes during which clear product development milestones must be reached. Normally, these time boxes each are a month or less.

Once you are on such a performance sprint, decide what you may need to give up in order to focus your energy on this new task (this is especially crucial for very ambitious and busy people). And schedule the time in your calendar when you will take action on your goal. Short, daily, or otherwise regular action is often better than infrequent chunks of action. In addition, supplementing daily actions with periods of going super-deep (e.g., blocking a whole day or week to work on a specific goal) can greatly accelerate progress.

Crucially, because the world is changing at an accelerating pace, challenge your milestones to be in weeks rather than months so you can adapt along the way. Think, "What's the minimum I need to do to guide my next decision point?"

Here's a tip if you want to get very far: make the deadlines unreasonable. For example, give yourself a two-week deadline rather than two months to launch a website. Or one week instead of one month to decide whether you want to get into cryptocurrency. Break a longer project, such as a six-month project, into a series of six to twelve of these unreasonable scrum sprints. Let these deadlines determine how you do the work and the quality of the end product you are working toward. Remember, in this day and age with the human cloud and technologies that can assist with virtually anything, it is totally possible to do seemingly large tasks within weeks, if you mobilize an external ecosystem for it. You might want to make your mission command process visual by posting your objectives, purpose, values, and high-level milestones on a whiteboard that you see every day. If, that is, you are very ambitious.

This kind of high-performance mission command execution gives you a clear direction that you want to move toward, but it also gives you enough flexibility to adapt to changing circumstances. It marries intention with emergence, and it allows you to be super-creative in how you tackle each sprint.

> **While working toward your goals at an operational level, divide your tasks into a series of small sprints with aggressive deadlines given to each. And add regular deep dives.**

FAIL FAST-FORWARD

Perhaps you know the expression "The perfect is the enemy of the good." There is a lot of truth to that, as the desire for perfection is one of the biggest obstacles to taking action, especially in today's increasingly chaotic world. We all crave the perfect moment, the perfect environment, or a spark of motivation to finally begin to do the work. Fine.

Except this is a surefire way to constantly feel things are *not* perfect, that you're *not* motivated, and that you're *not* progressing at the right pace.

Often, wanting perfection or nothing comes from expressing a fixed mindset, where you feel that your performance in anything reflects on what you are, not on where you are heading. With a growth mindset, on the other hand, you think of all your short scrum sprints with initially very humble results as mere steps toward a perfection that will be reached at some point down the line. Along the way you will surely encounter obstacles and adjust the course. But that is what failing fast-forward is all about. When what we know about the world changes, we change with it.

> Think to yourself, "What's the most important thing I can do in the next hour to move me closer to my goal?"

COME UP FOR AIR

As we describe, efficient task execution toward a very dynamic future is largely about moving in a series of sprints, where you pivot along the way to changing circumstances. This includes short bursts of activity toward unreasonably short deadlines, enabled by extreme discipline and relentless focus. It's not all gung-ho activity, however. The more quickly you sprint, the more important it is to adapt along the way. Do this by building in rituals that help you come up for air and orient yourself.

For example, you might allocate some time daily, weekly, or monthly to reflect on the following:

- Am I achieving the right goals at the right pace?

- What is working well?

- What do I need to do differently?

- What are my next steps?

Likewise, you should sometimes let go of ambition and just take a walk, an evening, some days, or a long or short holiday where you completely ignore your ambition and just be a completely different you.

Planning to plan is more important in the future, not less.

Here are ten tips to help you take action toward your most desired future and cultivate a compounding approach to your life:

1. **Slay your excuses:** Write a list of all the reasons that you might not do what you have planned to do, then address each and every one of them. Too cold to run outside? Buy winter running gear. No time to work on your side business? Work on your commute or cook dinner in bulk each Sunday for the full week. You don't know how to get started? Speak to three people who have experience in this area to get their advice.

2. **Prime the brain:** Set up a dedicated physical area for the specific task at hand. For example, a dedicated desk for your side hustle. A small home gym. The public library to write your next novel. You can also set a dedicated time each day—for example every day you will work on your project from 8:00–9:00 a.m. This visual and temporal consistency tells the brain that it's time to do the work.

3. **One task, one deadline:** Practice radical focus by cutting everything away except one thing for the next period of time.

4. **Quality not quantity:** Not all action is created equal. Be deliberate and intentional in what you do. Thirty minutes of deep, completely focused work can be miles better than many hours of distracted work. Mute your phone. Log off your browser. Then attack the task.

5. **Reframe challenges:** Challenge is good. Expect periods that will be difficult and where you will be stuck. Build this into your approach and embrace it as a positive. Remember, a growth mindset is built on challenges that we find difficult. For perspective, scientists know of a powerful phenomenon called hormesis,

where a bit of what hurts you makes you stronger. Oftentimes a bit of poison, such as pesticides, is actually healthier than none. A bit of bacterial infections primes the immune system. Tearing your muscle fibers a bit through daily exercise makes them bigger and stronger.

6. **Immerse yourself:** Do occasional very deep dives, where you take your focus on the task to the extremes. Reserve times where you are really in the mood for it and try to see if you can get into what psychologist Mihály Csíkszentmihályi calls a *flow state*. This is the mental state where you become fully immersed in a feeling of energized focus, full involvement, and intense enjoyment of an activity, while you lose sense of time.

7. **Build a team:** Get a mentor or someone who can provide guidance and show you your blind spots and push you outside of your comfort zone. At a minimum, get a peer to act as an accountability buddy. You can even find accountability buddies online where you agree to hold each other mutually accountable to your respective goals.

8. **Make it public:** Declare your goals to your friends and family, or state them publicly.

9. **Sign up for competition/other events:** Even better, sign up to specific events where you will need to showcase progress. For example, a race, a presentation, or a start-up pitch.

10. **Measure progress, not just outcomes:** Early in growth processes, you might be disappointed with your results. Here, a good trick is not to compare yourself with others but with where you were a month, six months, or a year ago.

Chapter 20

RUBBER BALL, NOT GLASS

There is a humorous Mr. Bean video clip where he is shopping for Christmas tree decorations. He enters a store and picks up two glittery round ornaments, one made of glass and one made of rubber. To decide which one he wants, he bounces each one on the floor to test their quality. Obviously the glass ornament shatters, while the rubber ornament bounces back to his hand. Happy with the unanimous results of his test, he picks the rubber ball and walks away smiling. How can we, too, learn how to bounce back rather than shatter under pressure?

Most of us have way more stuff going on today than our parents did in terms of sheer volume of commitments, information, daily decisions, and speed of life. As we move toward more frequent working from home and working from anywhere, the boundaries that can help separate different types of activity are becoming blurred. Many of us are working longer days while taking on numerous activities outside of work as well.

This means we have largely eliminated the short daily bursts of mental downtime that we previously encountered. If we have even thirty seconds with nothing else to do, we check stuff on our phones. And many studies have shown that we are more stressed today than just twenty years ago because, well, "there is so much to do, you know?"[1] Yes, we know, and many of us are also more prone to distractions such as email or social media notifications. It's not unrealistic to imagine the metaverse will only exacerbate this problem, that we'll find ourselves spending a lot—too much, perhaps—time on it, to the detriment of other things.

Living in this world means you must learn to ruthlessly prioritize and take care of yourself in new ways. Accept that you will not be able to keep running faster and faster in perpetuity. It is not a coincidence that minimalism has grown in recent years. Rarely in its most extreme form where you give up the majority of your possessions, but more so as a general philosophy and way of life where you strip back things toward what is truly essential. This includes what you say yes and no to, how you choose to spend your money, and how much of your time and energy you are willing to give away to your smartphone and other devices (digital minimalism).

Living in a 24/7 world does not mean we personally should live on a 24/7 schedule. Many of us feel compelled to do so in order to stay connected to friends, work, social media, or daily news. But study after study shows that this behavior alters our brain structures, and we begin to crave the small bursts of excitement that come with a new notification. Future Fitness requires both leaning into the system to shape it and regularly stepping out of it to moderate our well-being. It is only by ensuring a strong inner core that we can maintain our levels of achievement, personal growth, and well-being in the future.

> **Future Fitness requires both leaning into the system to shape it and regularly stepping out of it to moderate our well-being.**

A RADICAL FOCUS ON WHAT YOU CAN CONTROL

Former McKinsey Senior Expert Kayvan Kian explores this topic in his book, *What Is Water?* In it, he explains that the way to thrive in a rapidly changing future is to have a radical focus on what you can actually control. Which makes sense, since at any given time, there will be millions of things that you cannot control, but also quite a few that you can. Why not focus more on the latter? Here are seven simple, but often surprisingly useful, elements that can make a big difference:

1. Focus on using your strengths and doing things that energize you for the majority of your waking hours. This can be done by outsourcing weaknesses and/or partnering with others.

2. Reduce unnecessary negativity in your life and build up a bank of positive experiences and emotions to get you through hard times.

3. Further boost positive emotions with a daily gratitude practice. Think of whatever does work well in your life and feel gratitude for it.

4. Respond in constructive ways toward others. You cannot control their immediate behavior or what they say, but you can certainly choose your response. If your responses to others are good, then chances are that their behavior will reflect that over time. A good example is how we discuss each other on social media. Is our criticism of those we disagree with constructive or destructive? Are you acting as a coach or as one of Karpman's persecutors?

5. Take the positives from any situation and derive meaning from your day-to-day activities. For example, as a bricklayer, are you laying bricks, building a school, or helping to improve education in society? The choice of perspective is yours.

6. Acknowledge your accomplishments rather than setting the bar too high. Celebrating mini successes breeds motivation, even in daily tasks. And this also means celebrating progress, not just the formal achievement of higher goals.

7. If no one praises you when you think you deserve it, view yourself as if from the outside—and then award yourself that deserved praise.

"MENS SANA IN CORPORE SANO"

"A healthy mind in a healthy body." According to the ancient Romans, this was the foundation of a desirable life, and it still is. Taking care of ourselves is not a "nice to have." It is a critical enabler of your ability to perform at your best and recover from setbacks along the way. The various parts of the body and mind are connected in powerful ways, and they can directly impact each other. The more intense effort you put out, the more important it is to punctuate it with periods of recovery. Just like in sport, overtraining breaks down the body instead of building it up.

Of course, it goes without saying that a good balance includes a foundation of physical strength and well-being through proper sleep, exercise, and nutrition. What you will find here is that they are complementary—eating and sleeping better will make you more motivated to exercise, exercising and sleeping better will help you regulate your cravings, and exercising and eating well will help you sleep better.

The same goes for the brain. The science of meditation and spending time in silence has finally caught up with what ancient traditions have told us for thousands of years—namely that it makes you calmer, happier, more compassionate, and less stressed. Ensure downtime (recovery) from strenuous tasks over an extended period of time and find a practice that allows you to connect with yourself and your thoughts—whether that's through meditation, sport, yoga, or a daily walk. As little as ten minutes a day can do wonders, and studies have shown an increase in the brain's gray matter within as little as eight weeks.[2] It's literally like building a bigger bicep, but for your brain.

Cycling between periods of distraction-free focus with convergent thinking and periods of mental recovery will only become more important in the future as we move toward higher cognitive tasks that require creative thinking and judgment. These types of tasks demand mental clarity, divergent thinking, and an openness to new ideas, which is harder when you are working full speed and down in the weeds.[3] We are incredibly good at keeping ourselves busy and distracted, but high-quality thinking can often unlock completely new ways to do things—remember that the future is exponential and not incremental. In this sense, working professionals must become less like machines and more like artists. Carving out periods of time where you can just think can work wonders. Go to a café with a notebook and a pen and leave your phone at home. It all helps you think better, find your directions, and bounce back from adversity like that rubber ball.

DON'T TAKE THINGS SO PERSONALLY

The future will bring lots of surprises, both at a macro level such as pandemics and other global shocks, and on a day-to-day basis. As you engage with a hyper-connected world, you will find more people who disagree and perhaps even criticize you. And the importance of failing fast-forward means that misses will be inevitable. How you frame setbacks can make or break your success. A fixed mindset sees negative events as permanent, personal, and pervasive. If you lose your job, you might think you will never find another one, that you lost it because you are inadequate, and that it means you are a failure in all aspects of your life. This mindset can lead to depression and a feeling of helplessness.[4]

A healthier and fitter growth mindset instead sees the event as short term, situational, and specific. With this mindset, you view a jobless period as a temporary setback that is due to specific circumstances and not representative of your life in general. With this mindset, you can also make dips less severe and recover from them faster.[5] Although you can't control everything that happens to you, you can control how you view the situation and respond. Instead of seeing the future as concrete, see it as clay. And instead of seeing yourself as a fixed structure, see yourself like a liquid that can adapt to changing contexts. Often, what has happened is less important for our future success than how we view and respond to the situation.

Instead of seeing the future as concrete, see it as clay.

Another tactic that can help you recover from setbacks is to create space for self-connection and state what you are feeling. Thinking and feeling are two different activities, which is why it can be difficult for us to explain how we feel because we can't think of the right words. Or conversely, why stories that trigger strong emotions are so powerful. When you are distressed, the very act of naming negative emotions can help you overcome them. Talking to people about the situation and being open to receiving care from them can help more. You are not your feelings, and decoupling what you feel from how you respond can help you overcome challenges. If your feelings are strong and bad, try not to act on them, but on your values instead.

ZOOM WAY OUT

With all of the change and uncertainty that the future will bring comes lots of choice. Young people probably won't be deciding what specific career direction they want to go in to guide the rest of their lives—instead they'll be reinventing themselves every decade (or every few years), understanding new stuff all the time, and addressing existential questions when they navigate the metaverse or whatever.

As our basic needs are met, we seek to meet higher order needs such as defining and living out our purpose. Basic needs such as food and shelter are tangible and rather easy to comprehend. Higher order needs, on the other hand, need to be defined by each and every individual, which can be confusing as you embark on the journey. We are already seeing a high number of workers quitting the nine-to-five in a search for personal flexibility, freedom, and meaning, but this doesn't mean that the transition will be all smooth sailing. Transitioning from one equilibrium (like a steady job) to another (like a consistent stream of gig work) will bring periods of uncertainty and perhaps make you wonder whether you should just go back to a more stable but less meaningful life.

The antidote is to constantly generate perspective and create and re-create meaning. A personal purpose will help you stay on track, especially when you are faced with things that you might not feel like doing because of an intrinsic lack of motivation. Clarity of the personal purpose will help you through setbacks and periods of uncertainty. The digital metaverse is cool, but does it add significance to your life? Will it make you more fulfilled? Or is it a distraction? How can you use it in intentional ways? The same goes for material things, your career, and so much more. Why do you want it? Or why don't you?

Perhaps the best way to zoom out and generate perspective is to see the world from afar. Carl Sagan, a renowned astronomer, was inspired by a picture named Pale Blue Dot, taken by the Voyager 1 space probe from a record distance of about six billion kilometers. It shows Earth as nothing more than a pixel in the photograph, surrounded by the vastness of space.

Seeing our planet as a tiny speck truly puts our lives into perspective. Things that we take extremely seriously—such as a prestigious job or home—suddenly become less significant. We realize that we are a tiny part of a tiny planet and are here on borrowed time. Living up to societal expectations that don't align with our own values is foolish at best. Zooming out like this will help you make decisions in the face of uncertainty and overcome setbacks. Often nothing is as bad as you initially think it is.

> **"It has been said that astronomy is a humbling and character-building experience. There is perhaps no better demonstration of the folly of human conceits than this distant image of our tiny world."**
>
> **—CARL SAGAN**

These approaches facilitate what we could call a **resilience mindset**. They enable you to cope much better with uncertainty and complexity. If things are blurry or keep changing, you can just think, "Oh well. That is how the world is. I will just adapt with it." Then, when you face dilemmas and contradictions, you can evaluate your values and purpose to decide which response is best for you.

MINDSET 8: RESILIENCE MINDSET

Resilience describes a multilevel personality construct that is used in both clinical and progression psychology. A person is assumed to be resilient if they easily bounce back to their baseline level of functioning after being faced with stress, trauma, adversity, or threat. Resilience can include both the propensity to go beyond one's baseline capacities and the developing of stronger ways of resolving the challenges in one's life as a result of stress exposure.

As we've seen, the future is bringing enhanced opportunities but also curveballs at an increasing rate. Resilient people take care of themselves physically, build emotional support through a strong community, deal with tough situations head-on and avoid amplifying them and making them worse than they are, are guided by a personal purpose or direction, and put in place habits to help them.

In terms of mindsets, the following beliefs help build resilience:

- Negative events and upsets are part of life.
- Nothing lasts forever.
- What happens to me is less important than how I respond to it.
- I have the power to choose how I interpret and move on from a situation.
- I should focus on what I can control instead of on all the things I can't.

The opposite of a resilience mindset is a fragility mindset, where you dwell on your failures and amplify negative situations, which makes it easier to be knocked off course.

DON'T GO AT IT ALONE

In the past, your stable surrounding community acted like a dampener to any shocks that you experienced. Prior to the Industrial Revolution, humans had three main communities—the immediate family, the extended family, and the local community. Most people worked on the family farm or in a business within the local community. These communities formed the backbone of one's life in terms of financial needs, housing needs, education, health care, emotional and social support, and general life guidance based on tradition.

Fast-forward a handful of generations and this has dramatically changed for many of us. We are choosing to move away from home earlier and marry later, to define our own values rather than follow tradition as a given, to live and work globally, and to rely on public or private services for things like health care, banking, safety, and education. This in itself creates new demands on individuals who must become stronger and fend for themselves much more than before.[6]

When we face disruptions, it means less support to help you get through the tough times. These could be things such as losing one's job, divorce or other emotional heartbreak, losing a loved one, or illness. Even a seemingly positive event such as changing jobs or moving to a new country can feel disruptive. When an individual goes through these types of situations, it can trigger stress responses due to the perception of uncertainty and threat, and earlier traumas can resurface. The fact is that there will be a continued eroding of traditions as new generations grow up, experience frequent job and career changes, and have a higher proportion of their marriages end in divorce compared to previous generations.[7] This means you have to find ways to maintain an active support structure amid disruption. Find a tribe that cares for you and reach out to support them as well.

While you cannot control stressful events that happen in your life, you can build a core of inner strength and choose how you react to them. See the journey to crafting your most desired future as one of exploration and take hardship in stride. The occasional fall is inevitable, but there is a lot you can do to ensure you bounce back stronger each time.

See the journey to crafting your most desired future as one of exploration and take hardship in stride.

What follows are six tips to help you strengthen your resilience so you can bounce back from challenges.

1. **Embrace 24/7.** Technology allows us to have fluid boundaries between different commitments, and we are expected to always be on. Instead of fighting the trend, use this to your advantage. For example, if you find yourself working late or replying to emails on the weekend, balance this by taking time during certain workdays for things like family matters or personal hobbies. As long as you are meeting your commitments, it is becoming less important exactly when (and where) they get done.

2. **Have a (radical) focus on what you can control.** This includes doing what you're good at, focusing on positive emotions, how you respond to others, how you derive meaning from situations, and how you view and praise your successes.

3. **Take care of your health.** Now more than ever, it is critical to stay healthy mentally, physically, emotionally, and spiritually. Find out what you enjoy and create a routine that involves friends.

4. **Practice radical self-care.** Taking time to pamper yourself, speaking with others or a coach if you are going through tough times, and giving gratitude daily have all been shown to increase mental health, energy, and optimism about the future.

5. **Be like water.** Often the biggest reasons for frustration or unhappiness is that our expectations about a certain situation are not met. By holding your expectations more lightly, we are knocked less off course if they are not met. This doesn't mean that you should lower your expectations, but rather that you are prepared to adapt if the situation requires it.

6. **Embrace our shared humanity.** We've talked a lot about hypersociality as a pivotal enabler of innovation. It is without a doubt also a critical way to strengthen our collective ability to navigate

the future and handle tough times. Take the time to build deep and meaningful connections with friends from different walks of life, and strengthen family bonds even if it is difficult to do so at first. When we see the picture of Earth from far away in outer space, it illustrates we really are all just one species. We often take ourselves and others too seriously and create separations and conflict because of trivial incidents and slight differences. Life really is too short and too abundant to struggle unnecessarily.

PART 3

TEN SHIFTS FOR FUTURE FIT ORGANIZATIONS

FOR A LARGE PART OF HISTORY, organizational forms were fairly simple and did not change. As there was little change in the external environment (no supertrends, so to speak), groups of people and organizations could be governed by simple rules such as respect for elders, patriarchs and matriarchs, kings and queens or the heads of war bands (regardless of whether the elders were in fact best placed to make decisions), and later anointed chiefs. The tribes or organizations might have been uncertain where to find food, and they may have faced risk of invasion by other tribes, but there was little in the way of rapid technological innovation, real-time communication flows, and developments in higher levels of consciousness around topics such as universal human rights and protecting the environment.

However, just like Earth has broken with the universe's monotony as described by David Deutsch, the same has happened in organizations. Instead of being dominated by large organizations, small entities—and even individuals—can today have a significant impact on their industries and societies. Organizations must adapt and change and at increasing pace to become and remain Future Fit and should foster small, agile units rather than monolithic, slow collectives.

As we look back, there is a clear progression from simple organizations to more complex and expansive forms. New technologies created needs for new organizational forms. And each organizational form brought new innovations and more efficient and effective organizing principles. Yet, each type of organization also reached its limit once the context around it shifted yet again.

Part 3 delves into how recent and expected changes in technologies will impact how we think about organizations. This includes, for instance, microunits of products, services, and data, which become available as-a-service at prices that often fluctuate in real time, and which are often subject to ratings, digital analysis, real-time pricing, and transparent competition. The consumer will have on-tap access to what they need, when and where they need it. Few industries will be spared the necessary transformations.

Workers will continue to migrate from the industrial economy toward the precision and experience economies, just as machines, robots, and computers will continue to take over repetitive and lower-cognitive tasks. Enabled by technology and evolving lifestyle choices, human labor will also shift toward a predominantly on-tap model, with no fixed working hours, no permanent choice between employee, consultant, and freelancer roles, no fixed workplace, no clear holidays, no titles, and no fixed pension age.

By taking the supertrends as our point of departure and working backwards from there, we lay out the key shifts that organizations will need to consider as they navigate the blur. There are ten shifts in total. And while organizations will continue to exist, almost everything about what it takes to be successful will change.

Chapter 21

WHY TEN SHIFTS?

O ver time, the predominant ways that we have organized around work and social structures in general have changed repeatedly. Figure 21.1 shows the evolution of organizations, in broad strokes, as

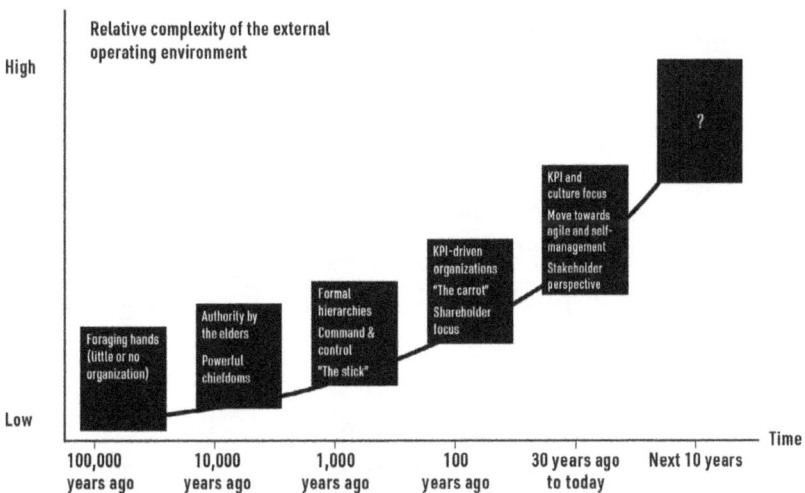

Relative complexity of the external operating environment

High

Foraging hands (little or no organization)	
Authority by the elders / Powerful chiefdoms	
Formal hierarchies / Command & control / "The stick"	
KPI-driven organizations / "The carrot" / Shareholder focus	
KPI and culture focus / Move towards agile and self-management / Stakeholder perspective	
?	

Low

Time

| 100,000 years ago | 10,000 years ago | 1,000 years ago | 100 years ago | 30 years ago to today | Next 10 years |

Figure 21.1. The evolution of organizations.

the level of complexity, the pace, and the scale of supertrends around them increased. As you can see by the image and the scale, the pace of change in organizations has been exponential, and like many super-trends, organizations are now at an inflection point.[1]

The key message here is that each time the operating environment and requirements changed—which was mostly caused by new technologies—the change spawned new organizational innovations, practices, and mindsets. Meanwhile, organizations that failed to adapt often became part of the road instead of part of the journey.

Newer organizational forms built on what worked well in previous organizational forms, just like if you continue to add new features on a system based on an outdated operating platform. The challenge is that many organizations today are still stuck in—or partly based on—outdated modes of operating. They are not fit-for-purpose for today's more complex operating environment, where the pace of change continues to increase based on a multitude of dramatic supertrends. However much you refine an internal combustion engine, it doesn't become a lithium-ion battery. Sometimes you need a paradigm shift.

ORGANIZING FOR THE FUTURE

As a result, we are already seeing new types of organizations emerging. Organizational constructs (or, if you're a cynic, buzzwords) such as *evolutionary organizations, agile, next generation, holacracies, market-oriented ecosystems, team-based, networked, exponential, post-modern, invincible companies, dual organizations, helix, open organizations, humanocracies,* and *deliberately developmental organizations* have emerged. These perspectives all contain valuable ideas. However, too often the proclaimed model is described as the "most correct" model for the future, irrespective of the local situation. We take a different approach—namely a future-backed and trend-backed approach that focuses on the shifts that organizations must consider. Of course, each organization must adapt the approach and make deliberate decisions across each of the shifts (in other words, how much to move and how quickly); there is no single "organization of the future." Many types of organizations can and will exist. But as you will see, there are clear directions worth considering.

Building on part 1, we start from the question "What will the organizational landscape look like in the next ten years?" and then we work backwards from there to define the implications for organizations. We are careful to not only include future of work trends but also all the various supertrends, covering everything from macroeconomic, political, demographic, social, cultural, technological, and consumer angles. We find that this is the most complete way to say something about organizations of the future.

With this future-backed lens, we looked at timeless organizational questions, such as the following:

- Why do we exist?

- What's our strategy?

- How should our products, services, and marketing evolve?

- How should we structure the organization and leverage partnerships?

- How should we carry out the work and make decisions?

- How should we work with technology?

- How do we disrupt before we're disrupted?

- How do we ensure we are learning quickly enough?

- How do we attract, engage, and keep the best talent?

- How do we create a distinctive and healthy culture?

The results of this thinking are ten big organizational shifts we predict for the next ten years.[2] All of them are already happening now, but they are at an inflection point and accelerating.

	From . . .		To . . .
1	Generic purpose statements and tangential CSR (corporate social responsibility) activities	→	Authentic purpose and active activism on topics that matter, that foster meaning to employees and consumers alike
2	Multiyear strategic planning with a strict, KPI-driven (key performance indicators-driven) execution approach	→	Setting direction, not destination, through bold moves and a simultaneous emergent strategy governed by guardrails and values
3	Products/services developed and sold in batches, with limited customer feedback in the process	→	Unbundled, personalized and on-tap products/services that leverage networks and customer ratings
4	Fixed, hierarchical organizational structures that are siloed and slow to adapt	→	Fluid, on-demand organization that taps into the human cloud and deploys talent in a flow-to-work model
5	Sequential, fragmented processes with frequent approvals required from various levels of governance	→	Cross-functional, empowered teams that work in quick, iterative cycles
6	Legacy technology processes and mindset where IT is seen as a support function	→	Technology-first approach where technology is embedded in every area of the organization
7	Innovation separate from business-as-usual activities and limited to a handful of corporate initiatives	→	Innovation as an institutional capability that uses a wide range of approaches to continuously reinvent the organization
8	Just-in-case learning that is typically top down and focused on formal training sessions	→	Just-in-time learning that is embedded into the flow of work through AI, micro-sized learning modules, and peer learning
9	Talent management that focuses on guiding employees through specified careers and development programs	→	Talent enablement platform that supports employees to manage their own careers and development
10	Primary focus on results, with secondary focus on employee experience and fulfillment	→	Results + people focus through a human-centered culture that helps employees perform at their best while thriving in life

In general, organizations that are more evolved and have moved toward the right-hand side of the spectrum on each dimension are higher performing and more sustainable. However, this does not mean that organizations must strive to be all the way to the right on each dimension. The key is to understand your current point of departure and make deliberate decisions about which elements must be improved, and in which order, so you can achieve your organizational objectives. And although their nuances might vary by context, the shifts are applicable across all industries and company sizes. Regardless of your specific role and influence in the organization, you can benefit from understanding the shifts as you plan and carry out your work.

In the following chapters, we outline the core tenets of each shift, including laying out the big idea, what greatness looks like in practice, the underlying supertrends driving the shift, and how you might get started in practice. As you reflect on your priorities, remember that winning in the organizations of the future means making bold moves and focusing on creating the new, rather than fixing the old. This will likely require a dramatic transformation in the next three to five years (and again three to five years after that), many times more quickly and at a greater depth of change than has ever been done before. It also means seeing the journey as one of continuous transformation, rather than a linear and finite change management initiative with defined start and end dates.

In managing organizational transformations, focus mentally on creating the new rather than fixing the old.

Chapter 22

TAKING A STAND ON VALUES

At the UEFA Euro 2020 football (soccer) championship,[1] which for the first time ever was hosted across eleven countries to celebrate UEFA's sixtieth anniversary, the organization got into trouble. In order to be a "politically and religiously neutral organization," UEFA's governing body had long banned advertisements that contained political messages, which seems completely understandable.

For this reason, during the tournament, they struck down a proposal from the Munich City Council to light up its Allianz Arena in rainbow colors during a game between Germany and Hungary. The City Council wanted to show solidarity to the LGBTQ+ community in Hungary, who were becoming increasingly oppressed under the country's autocratic ruler Viktor Orbán.

This resulted not only in a fierce backlash toward UEFA from many, but also a concerted response from UEFA's sponsors, many of whom rapidly voiced their support for the LGBTQ+ community. Heineken tweeted a rainbow image with the words "cheers to all our fans"; Just Eat made a rainbow-colored logo; Volkswagen launched a rainbow-colored mini car with messages such as #WeDriveDiversity; multiple

CEOs called for support of "diversity and tolerance"; and TikTok not only launched a new campaign, #LoveisLove, but also reached out directly to UEFA to encourage the football body to join the company in supporting the LGBTQ+ community. Multiple other organizations followed suit, as well as fans, other football clubs, and national football organizations.[2]

UEFA, for its part, tried to downplay the incident and stated that it was not banning the rainbow symbol but rather the specific request at the Allianz Arena, due to its political undertones.

Defying UEFA's stance on LGBTQ+ advertisements likely required careful consideration, but ultimately the organizations decided that it was the right thing to do, and that a critical mass of consumers would support their actions.

However, the dilemma was clear. It is becoming increasingly difficult even for well-meaning organizations to hide behind the veil of neutrality and nonpolitical messages, especially when it comes to topics that by some are seen as related to fundamental human rights and universal values.

There are countless other episodes that illustrate this point. Simon & Schuster, the publisher, has for many years cited free speech as a reason for going ahead with publications of controversial authors. However, in recent years they have canceled scheduled books because of authors taking what the publishers deemed harmful political stances, including a book from US Senator Josh Hawley.[3] Fun fact, though: in some cases, the canceled books end up getting published by Skyhorse, an independent publisher that is distributed by . . . Simon & Schuster.

Starbucks has long advocated for fair and ethical procurement and supply chains. Ben and Jerry's, the ice cream company, frequently lobbies to improve voting rights and democracy. CVS, a convenience store and pharmacy chain, is actively against tobacco products and related sales. Clif Bar, a health supplement company, has long advocated for student loan reforms.[4] More recently, a number of organizations have mandated that their employees get the COVID-19 vaccine because it is the safest way to combat the pandemic and ensure the collective good. This includes Google, Deloitte, Ford, Citigroup, Goldman Sachs, Netflix, Microsoft, Twitter, Delta Airlines, Facebook, and McDonald's. Organizational purpose and taking a stand on issues that matter are no longer questions of "if" or "why," but rather increasingly questions of "what" and "how."

SERVING A PURPOSE

Whereas any organization can choose to do as UEFA (who arguably have strong reasons to try to stay clear of politics), there is pressure from society for companies and organizations to take a stand. Indeed, having a strong organizational purpose and a well-thought-through CSR scheme have long been widely seen as business imperatives. As perceptions and awareness for issues such as sustainability, local community development, corporate ethics, and employee well-being have grown, consumers and employees have begun voting with their wallets and time, shunning organizations seen to be profiting at the expense of the planet, society, or employees.

Many organizations that have an official policy of not only remaining neutral but also telling their employees to do so (even in these employees' personal capacities) are finding it harder to maintain this line amid dissatisfaction from employees and backlash from consumer groups.

EMPLOYEES AND CONSUMERS CHOOSE MEANING

In the future we can expect a continued reduction in unsustainable business practices that have a negative impact on employees and the environment. And we expect organizations to develop active activism strategies and to regularly take stands on key issues. This may lead to some polarization among employees and consumers and needs to be navigated well, but more and more organizations will begin to draw lines and focus on being on the right side of history, even if it entails difficult short-term choices. What we likely will *not* see, however, is a sudden proliferation of social businesses in place of corporations, or a dramatic shift away from capitalism as the core foundation for most major economies.

WHAT DO ORGANIZATIONAL STANDS LOOK LIKE IN PRACTICE?

We are seeing a number of key shifts in how organizations think about their purpose, fostering meaning among employees, and taking a stand on topics that are deeply rooted in who they are. They start by asking why they exist, what specific solution they are providing, for whom, and how they can do it in a fair and sustainable way. Purposes that are about saving the world in general, as in the rescuer role in Karpman's drama triangle, don't seem to make much sense and can come across as empty marketing blabber. Purpose statements that are so generic that everyone and her dog would sign on to them don't make much sense either.

What can work instead are statements that relate to the specific mission and vision of the organization.[5] Employees increasingly expect cultures and values that include elements such as respect, diversity, teamwork, fairness, and personal growth. The increasing prevalence of culture surveys and real-time employee sentiment tools demonstrate organizations simply cannot ignore this. For example, LEGO, one of the largest toy companies globally, has the following mission and purpose statement: "To inspire and develop the builders of tomorrow." Its values are imagination, fun, creativity, caring, learning, and play, and it measures employee engagement regularly.[6] It has long had a policy not to make military models such as tanks and avoids toy guns to the extent possible. LEGO is very clear on how it is making a positive difference in the world, and its vision, values, and stated promises all align around this.[7]

To be genuine, meaningful, and motivating, stated corporate values must be relevant to the organization's products and/or the daily work of its employees, suppliers, or the like.

CSR activities are also moving from fringe, add-on activities to being embedded into the core way businesses operate. Leaders aren't waiting for a crisis to respond but have preemptively made the choice to shape how they operate in a more sustainable way. Some organizations even embed these activities deeply into their core value proposition, such as Patagonia, which is a certified B Corporation (a business that balances purpose and profit).

Corporate values don't appear genuine if they're introduced as a response to a scandal or a "shitstorm" in media. The better approach is to develop them proactively.

Not all organizations may wish to do that, and don't have to. Starbucks will perhaps never file as a B Corporation, but it's still made noticeable—and welcome—steps to do well while doing good. It's revamped its supply chain and procurement practices to ensure that coffee bean farmers and other suppliers receive fair pay for their work. The key is to ensure consistency between brand, values, and actions. If these elements are not aligned, then the organization may be denounced for greenwashing (i.e., conveying a false or misleading impression of environmentally sound policies), pinkwashing (i.e., attempting to benefit from shows of their support for LGBTQ+ rights), and similar forms of hypocrisy.

Increasingly, leading companies embed some altruistic or socially conscious purpose at the core of what they do, engage in dialogue with their employees, and remain open to listening and learning. At times this can be challenging, but the key is to engage, rather than disengage, with the various topics and issues.[8] Winning organizations see employees as whole individuals who work not only for the money, but who also yearn for social relationships, meaning, and making a difference in the world.

This extends to how organizations view their employees' civic engagement. Instead of banning employees from taking a stance on topics that matter to them, as some organizations do, today's businesses should foster dialogue and create guidelines that balance personal opinion with values such as respect, tolerance, and care.

WHAT SUPERTRENDS ARE DRIVING THESE SHIFTS?

In general, the evolution of humanity has and will continue to be unidirectional, toward increased tolerance, open-mindedness, equality, and cooperation. Although we have a long way to go, we are seeing fewer wars, less racism, less poverty, better health, and better education. Despite some ups and downs and the occasional bigoted despot, the trend is clear. Taking the long-term view, you find that there will only be more people demanding these universal values. As time goes on, our awareness as a species is increasing, we care more, and we move ever closer to universal acceptance.

As our basic needs are met, we are also moving up Maslow's pyramid and increasingly seeking higher-level personal needs like self-actualization and making a positive difference in the world. As more and more people are free from worrying about providing food, security, and shelter for themselves and those around them, they dedicate more of their lives to causes that matter to them. This is accelerated by demographic trends, as the younger generations have been proven to be more concerned with organizational purpose, values, and taking a stand on issues that matter to them.

A McKinsey survey found, for example, that almost 75 percent of employees state that purpose should receive more weight than profits.[9] While profits are of course a prerequisite for a business to continue as a going concern (and the larger the profit, the bigger the development possibilities), employees are rarely motivated by it—they require more to bring their full selves to work and remain loyal to organizations. One study from 2021 found that a 10 percent improvement in employees' connection with the mission or purpose of their organization led to an 8.1 percent decrease in turnover and a 4.4 percent increase in profitability.[10] As job markets become more and more fluid, employees are increasingly able to choose employers whose values and business practices align with their own.

This also extends into investments, where money invested in ESG funds (i.e., funds that aim to promote environmental, social, and governance factors) is growing rapidly. In 2020, ESG funds captured $51.1 billion of net new money from investors, which was more than double the same measure from the year before.[11]

Furthermore, information and noteworthy events spread more quickly online via Facebook, Twitter, Instagram, TikTok, YouTube, and other social media sites. If your behavior doesn't reflect your stated values and purpose, chances are that people will find out. Another trend driving this is formal transparency. In general, organizations are disclosing more about their practices and results—both publicly to build trust and internally to build engagement. Also, we live in a rating economy, and bad ratings because of bad behavior can destroy companies. Finally, we see that our economy is characterized by an increasing diversity of products and services for consumers. With increased choice comes an enhanced ability for consumers to vote with their wallets and be more purposeful in terms of where they spend their money.

> **Well-stated values are not only about building trust but also about building engagement.**

LIVING YOUR PURPOSE AND VALUES

A large number of organizations still treat CSR initiatives as fringe activities that are not core to the business itself. Furthermore, today, only six out of ten organizations have purpose statements, while only four out of ten organizations' purpose statements have any real impact, according to employees.[12]

First, make this a leadership agenda item. There are few elements that truly must be led and championed by the C-suite, but purpose is one of them. This includes both setting the organization's purpose and establishing the way the organization lives it out. Formulating or refining a meaningful purpose and values is a process that can take many months. It requires input from multiple stakeholders and typically many rounds of refinement. It is also important to foster a dialogue with employees during the process to let them know that it is happening and to solicit their input along the way.

Typically, the values an organization lands on will be a mix of universal values—like care or learning—as well as values deeply linked to the organization's unique purpose and particular strategy, like The LEGO Group's creativity and play. Thereafter, it is absolutely critical that the purpose and values are integrated into the core fabric of the organizational culture, into key talent processes (e.g., hiring, feedback, and promotions), and into decision-making at key steps such as choosing suppliers, identifying customers, launching marketing, and managing teams. Values can and should be trained, developed, and measured regularly, and action must be taken if and when lapses occur. Finally, leadership role modeling is pivotal.

At the same time, organizations should formulate internal policies and guidelines for what they stand for and how staff may engage on issues that matter to them. Navigating this shift is tricky for many organizations who are more comfortable remaining neutral and passive, but it is important to find the right balance. Embedding an authentic purpose and moving toward more active activism as an organization is a long-term game, and one which continuously evolves. Few organizations get it right from the beginning, so they must be comfortable with learning along the way.

The following chart can help you assess your current point of departure and where your biggest priorities lie in this area.

From ...		To ...
Generic or no purpose statement	→	Authentic purpose rooted in what the company is
CSR activities are tangential to the core business	→	Conducting business in a way that solves meaningful problems for consumers in a sustainable way
Neutral or passive on issues that matter	→	Taking a stand on issues that matter
Employees discouraged from civic engagement	→	Fostering an open dialogue with employees on values and current topics
Focus on providing employee stability and paycheck	→	Embracing all of Maslow's needs and fostering meaning on a daily basis
Organizational values not existing or lived out, or not linked to who the organization is and what it is trying to achieve	→	Meaningful organizational values that are deeply embedded into the organization's culture and day-to-day decision-making

Chapter 23

SETTING DIRECTION
RATHER THAN DESTINATION

S trategy has for many decades been one of the most prestigious and
in some ways mysterious disciplines. Strategy setting was reserved
to the highest echelon of the organization, and it relied on data and
planning tools that most employees could only dream of seeing. The
typical outcome of a strategy development process was a robust, sce-
nario-based, and analytically sound plan for the future, usually three to
five years out. This would in turn inform yearly budgeting and quarterly execution, with a close monitoring of any deviations and a rigorous
process to alter budgets as operating context changed throughout the
year. Often, it is still like that.

The impact of strategic thinking is hard to overstate. In the same
way that the characters portrayed in *Mad Men* transformed marketing,
the emergence of strategy as a proper discipline has transformed the
way organizations understand what they're doing and what they want
to do in the future.[1] Indeed, strategic planning frameworks and tools
have been one of the most important intellectual contributions to the
world of business in the twenty-first century. They continue to provide

valuable benefits to organizations, and these tools are getting better by the month. The most advanced systems are now leveraging big data analytics and AI.

However, as the world changes, so must organizations. Strategic plans work great . . . until the surrounding context is disrupted. And the problem is that organizations are getting disrupted more and more frequently. The response to this for many organizations has been to double down on planning efforts, attempting to combat the increasing complexity of the external environment with increasingly sophisticated planning tools and an even greater emphasis on attempting to forecast and control the future.

Winning in the future, however, increasingly requires a different approach. It is getting more difficult, if not impossible, to neatly plan your way to success, as the market demands and environment shift too often for that. Strategic planning remains integral but must combine equal measures of data, tools, and analytics with exponential thinking, bold moves, fluid budgeting and target setting, and a more human-centered decentralization approach to the process.

> Accelerating technological change drives strategic planning toward exponential thinking, bold moves, fluid budgeting and target setting, and a more decentralized approach to the process.

BOLD YET FLEXIBLE

In 2021, General Motors announced that it would completely phase out nonelectric vehicles by 2035, with a goal of an all-electric future with zero emissions, zero crashes, and zero congestion. This bold statement was significant for the company, which despite many industry innovations in its over 100-year existence had in recent decades lagged behind competitors in terms of growth, competitiveness, and technology. And it was extremely ambitious, given that at the time of the announcement,

GM had just one electric vehicle in its lineup[2] and electric vehicles accounted for approximately 4 percent of new car sales globally.[3]

But here's the twist: interestingly, GM has said that the all-electric vision is a goal, but not a guarantee, and it is prepared to change course depending on future legislation and demand. According to GM North America chief Steve Carlisle, "We intend to win wherever we're competing and irrespective of propulsion system. At the same time, we're setting ourselves up for this pivot, which is inevitable."[4] Similarly, Executive Vice President of Manufacturing Gerald Johnson has stated that "we've left ourselves some flexibility based on market demand. We're confident in that end point. We're just not sure how the mix will evolve to get to that."[5]

This is one of the key differentiators of strategy setting of the future—namely *setting direction instead of destination*. Although strategic plans remain critical in order to provide clarity and maintain the trust of employees, consumers, and the stock market, it is becoming more and more important to set the direction and provide clarity while also continuing to adjust along the way, given that the world is getting more fluid and harder to predict. For instance, in 2021, GM couldn't know for sure whether fuel cells based on hydrogen would take up some of the demand for clean driving.

"What I've learned in this role is when you put a big goal in front of everybody, there's clarity quickly. Everybody gets aligned, and then they just amaze you with what they're able to do to achieve those objectives," says GM's CEO Mary Barra. An added benefit of an inspiring goal that is both good for the business and good for sustainability is that it can increase the employee value proposition, and GM has already seen applications to the company go up.[6]

Inspiring directions, however, must be accompanied by action. McKinsey research shows that *where* you play is much more important than *how* you play in terms of value created, so organizations must also make bold moves into new industry arenas in order to get ahead and then allow for agility as they pursue those long-term plays. For example, companies that follow an active resource allocation strategy and shift more than 60 percent of their capital spending across businesses over ten years create 50 percent more value than companies that shift capital at a slower cost. Furthermore, capital expenditure that exceeds the industry median rate is also correlated with future success.[7] GM, as an example, is investing more into electric vehicles than gasoline and diesel vehicles in 2021 for the first time ever, and it has announced it will spend $35 billion in electric vehicle and autonomous vehicle product development between 2020 and 2025.[8]

This is a far cry from the linear budgeting and incremental targets deployed in many organizations, which have a patient approach to capital and operate with a scarcity mindset. Instead, bold and transformative moves based on exponential thinking get organizations ahead.

> **A clear target formulated as a stated *destination* removes the ability to be agile and flexible. What is often better is to be very clear about *direction*.**

MOVING THE PLANNING PROCESS FROM BATCH TO FLOW

One of the supertrends we discussed in part 1 was the move from batch to flow in many industries. The same is often desirable in corporate planning and budgeting processes. What is often a linear process that can take many months must be revamped into a continuous planning approach with more fluid budgets. Fortunately, the latest technologies enable real-time views of financial and business data, which allows companies to make more frequent strategic decisions, both at a tactical level but also at a broader company level. Leading companies do not wait until quarterly or annual reviews to make decisions and shift budgets and priorities.

This is important not only for executives, but also for people at all levels. The biggest risk is when a strategy begins to take on a life of its own, when "sticking to the budget" becomes the all-important objective, instead of learning and adapting as you go. Wells Fargo, an American bank, learned this the hard way when salespeople were so pressured to meet the targets set out by the new strategy that they resorted to fabricating sales accounts rather than reporting to senior management what they were actually encountering in the field.[9] Instead of always sticking to your guns, adopt a fail-fast-forward start-up mentality with frequent pivots and create a culture where open discussions and feedback are encouraged rather than penalized. Another way to look at this is through the Five Cs of Innovation—by allowing for some degree of emergence in what and how the strategy gets done, organizations are able to harness a far greater range of creativity and energy.

In products and services, there is a supertrend away from batch delivery and toward delivery as-a-service. This change to an on-tap approach can be useful for corporate planning processes as well.

Note that this more continuous and emergent strategy does not mean that you do not have an overarching goal or metrics. It means that you make strategic choices continuously over time and are fully aware that the strategy you end up pursuing can be totally different from the strategy you thought would be the right one. For the same reason, when a board meeting is held, ideally there is no strong reason to brief the board extensively, since they have been kept in the information loop throughout.

An additional shift and new best practice in the strategy setting process is to recognize the human element in it and actively seek to remove potential biases that have been shown to occur. We've all seen hilarious hockey stick projections, which fail to materialize but are revised upward each year, because "this time it's different"—see Figure 23.1 for a real, disguised company forecast.

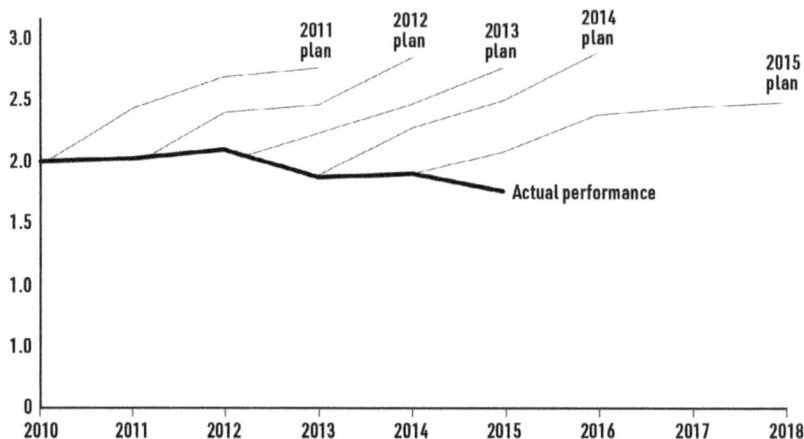

Figure 23.1. EBITDA projects, USD billion, disguised example.[10]

The troubling thing is that we still make these projections and continue to revise them upward. Behavioral psychologists have identified a number of cognitive biases we hold, which lead us to be overly reliant on recent data as we make future projections, more confident in our projections happening than data would otherwise tell us, linear in our thinking even when trends are nonlinear, and generally risk-averse when considering bolder, "never-been-done-before" choices.[11]

Finally, strategy execution is moving from a short-term focus on monthly or quarterly KPIs to a more holistic, transparent, and fluid approach, for example through objectives and key results (OKRs).[12] The key difference is that KPIs typically focus on meeting very specific targets, while OKRs combine the long-term direction of the company with key measures of activity and output that will help organizations reach their overarching priorities. KPIs continue to be an important input into OKRs, but making them the sole focus of execution and performance reviews can in many situations lead to overly short-term and rigid decision-making.

WHY TIMING IS TRICKY

One important driving factor is the impact of the three clouds—computer, things, and human—which have dramatically lowered the barriers for established companies and start-ups to enter new markets. As a result, we are seeing faster cycles of creative destruction and an increasing rate at which large companies are suddenly losing significant market share—and, vice versa, a small company can become a prominent player within just a few years. Furthermore, the rate at which entirely new industries are being conceived and created is increasing.

Another contributing supertrend is that of technological convergence, which makes it extremely difficult to foresee how and when technologies will combine and become mainstream.

Even though you frequently know the direction of trends, the timing is often what surprises us. For example, the Palm Pilot (a personal digital assistant device) was first introduced in 1996 with a promise of reinventing personal productivity and planning. It was one of the first true smart devices for consumers and a precursor to smartphones as we know them today. However, the idea was ahead of its time in terms of technological capabilities, infrastructure, and social acceptance, and after numerous new product changes and releases, it was ultimately discontinued in 2010.

The same goes for products such as electric and autonomous vehicles, internet telephony, and services such as fully automated and machine-led customer service calls. There were in these cases countless premature attempts before someone hit the combination of right product/marketing mix and right timing. Even though we know the direction, we typically don't know exactly when the critical tipping and breakthrough will happen. This only enhances the importance of setting direction but remaining flexible on exactly when and how the future state is reached.

BOLD LEADERSHIP REQUIRED

Like identifying an authentic purpose and what an organization stands for, setting strategy and defining the strategy development process must have a heavy involvement from the executive team. A CEO and leaders around her must embody what the organization aspires to achieve and be ready to lead the charge from the front. This starts with understanding the relevant supertrends that are happening in the actual, adjacent possible, and shadow future. The CEO and company leaders should cultivate exponential and abundance mindsets with a focus on creating the new, rather than fixing the old.

Being able to continuously improve performance and optimize KPIs such as the gross margin remains critical to staying competitive, but they are not sufficient for future wins. At their worst, organizations that do not embrace what is happening around them are like the companies who manufactured horse-drawn carriages in the early 1900s and missed the shift toward automobiles. They focused on making their carriages more and more comfortable, while other companies were inventing an entirely new form of transport, which in the space of around ten years completely shifted the market. In the US the number of horse carriage companies dropped from more than 4,600 in 1914 to approximately 150 by 1925.[13]

Additionally, organizational leaders must acknowledge the necessity and be prepared to lead their organizations through a significant transformation and continuous journey starting today. They need to set a direction for five years in the future when the organization will look fundamentally different, so different that it may be uncomfortable to even think about. But in many sectors, organizations that do not make bold enough moves will very quickly fall behind.

The analytical work then becomes to correctly identify the direction the company needs to go in, and the right moves to take, similar to GM's ambition for electric vehicles. Consider a wide range of potential moves toward the vision, including capital reallocation, large-scale M&A, capital expenditure in new business adjacencies, and even completely new business areas.

In parallel, organizations must revamp the strategy-setting process to make it more continuous, more data powered, and more AI driven.

And to close the loop, they must radically change how they set targets and measure progress. In essence, it is about making bold moves while simultaneously letting go of the road map and daring to learn and adapt along the way. Throughout all of this change, providing continued clarity to employees is absolutely critical so that they can continue to deliver on immediate priorities while navigating the shift toward the new direction and way of working.

The following chart can help you assess your current point of departure and where your biggest priorities lie in this area.

It can be tricky but necessary to make bold moves even when it is difficult to predict what exactly the future will bring.

From . . .		To . . .
Setting destination through a detailed 3–5-year plan, typically with incremental progress	→	Setting a bold direction based on supertrends
Patient approach to capital where budgets are heavily influenced by historical allocations	→	Impatient capital allocation with bold moves into new areas when needed
Strategic planning and budgeting as a yearly process, with limited changes once budgets are set	→	Strategic planning as a continuous, fluid process with real-time dashboards, and frequent pivots as the context changes
Strategy as a purely analytical process, which does not account for human biases, agendas, and motives	→	Strategy seen as an analytical and inherently human process, with relevant safeguards
KPI-driven execution, with a focus on meeting yearly and quarterly targets	→	Strategy as a set of guardrails for execution, with room for innovation and change
Long-term planning but short-term decisions	→	Short-term planning but long-term decisions

Chapter 24

DELIVERING ON-TAP EXPERIENCES FOR A MARKET OF ONE

The industrial economy was characterized by centralization, standardization, and a desire to reach economies of scale through mass production. Goods and services were developed and sold in batches, with significant power in the hands of the supplier. Compared to today, there was limited product choice, and marketing was largely pushed in a mass market way, for example on TV or on billboards. Many industries are still somewhat characterized by this model, including (to various degrees) book publishing, teaching, construction, banking, consumer goods, and retail.

But we have seen that we have entered the precision and experience economies, where information technology allows us to segment the market much more finely and to use enhanced intelligence to meet higher-level complex needs. Future Fit organizations turn their approach to developing and selling products and services on its head. A great and familiar example is the Swedish company Spotify. The music streaming giant boasts hundreds of millions of users, including close to

200 million paying subscribers. Its service has over 70 million songs, all indexed and searchable by artist, album, or genre. Users can also create their own playlists and share these with each other. Spotify exemplifies a lot of the trends we see across many industries.

PUT THE USER FRONT AND CENTER

As technology increasingly fine-tunes insight into consumer preferences and as foundational needs are met with growing abundance, the bar for meeting customer needs—especially higher-level needs—continues to rise. This requires a fundamentally different approach to understanding customers and includes tools such as persona definition, customer journey mapping, empathy mapping, ideating, rapid prototyping, and constant user testing. This design-thinking approach is human-centered rather than focused on root-cause problem-solving, and it is counter to the way a lot of organizations instinctively attack challenges.

Spotify, for example, logs over 100 billion data points per day based on the activities of its 200+ million active users globally. It supplements this with qualitative insights that includes flying user researchers around the globe to visit customers in their homes to conduct in-depth interviews. Based on this, it has created detailed personas to inspire discussions and product enhancements. By understanding user segments in this way and giving them names and identities that are infused into day-to-day discussions, Spotify ensures that customers are front and center of decisions across disparate functions, including brand, product, content, and marketing.[1]

Figure 24.1. The five Spotify personas: Nick, Olivia, Shelley, Travis, and Cameron.

FOCUS ON HIGHER-LEVEL NEEDS AND EXPERIENCES

When Spotify creates empathy maps and identifies the needs of its customers, it goes beyond their core needs. Spotify is not just about providing songs but also about creating enhanced moments by providing the right music at the right time to the right person. Playlists and recommendations can be personalized based on your current tasks (like working out), your current moods or vibes (like chill, focus, etc.), and times of the day, days of the week, and so on. For example, Spotify can serve up a Sunday morning playlist of easy jazz while you have your breakfast and read the news—how amazing is that?

As people meet their basic needs such as housing, food, and safety, they are increasingly able to focus on consuming new products and services that can further enhance their quality of life.

ADOPT INTELLIGENT PERSONALIZATION

IoT, big data, AI, 3D printing, and other technology advances mean we can create ever more precise products and services. And as an increasing share of the economy shifts online, the marginal cost of doing so is radically reduced. This leads to mass customization at very low cost. Some key ways to do this include dividing services and products into micro-objects, offering product variety, targeting segments of one, and enabling users to rate their experiences.

Dividing Services and Products into Micro-Objects: In the olden days, if you wanted your own music, you would buy an album, or LP, which would contain, for instance, fifteen songs. Oftentimes, you really only wanted one or two of those, but it was all or nothing. Then came iTunes, where you could buy songs one at a time. So the products became disaggregated. And you can do the same with Spotify, except that you don't buy the songs.

Building on this, you can now even disaggregate each separate musician and add your own input, or input from an AI. For instance, you can add congas to a song, or replace the trumpet player. The Algoriddim Pro DJ program enables this through its *neural mix capability*, where you can, for example, strip out the bass line of "Seven Nation Army," add in the drums from "We Will Rock You," and then layer in your own vocals on top.

On that note, we should mention Evans's law: "The inflexibilities, incompatibilities, and rigidities of complex and/or monolithically structured technologies could be simplified by the modularization of the technology structures (and processes)."[2] This is named after Bob Overton Evans, who in the early 1960s persuaded IBM's chairman, Thomas J. Watson Jr., to move away from a hodgepodge of incompatible systems and toward a modular approach based on compatible units.

Prior to this era, IBM and other mainframe computer manufacturers produced systems that were unique. Each system had its own distinct operating system, processor, peripherals, and application software. After the purchase of a new IBM computer, customers had to rewrite all their existing code. Evans convinced CEO Watson that a line of computers should be designed to share many of the same instructions and interfaces.

Offering Product Variety: We've seen that product and service diversity has mushroomed in line with technological capabilities and growing abundance. Consider the advent of microbreweries, the rise of designer gin, and the availability of $100 entry-level smartphones. In addition to its free account that contains ads, Spotify offers a premium account tier and has a HiFi tier in the works, which promises to deliver music in lossless audio quality.

Targeting Segments of One: In addition to fine-tuning products and expanding variety, many organizations are expanding into made-to-order offerings that are customized to individual users. For example, we are seeing customized fashion, customized jewelry, customized skin care, customized shoe insoles, customized medical implants, customized vitamins and supplements, and customized food. Subway was an early attempt to allow customers to tailor-make sandwiches, but the latest possibilities go way beyond that, with 3D-printed meals that take into account individual dietary needs, allergies, taste preferences, and weight goals.

Spotify's "Only You" experience acts as a one-stop shop for personalized recommendations and insights. Every user gets daily and weekly lists that are completely customized to their musical preferences, such as Discover Weekly, Release Radar, Daily Mixes, and periodicals like Your Time Capsule or Summer Rewind. It also has fun features like "Your Audio Birth Chart," where the sun is the top artist you listened to over the last six months, rising is your most recent discovery, and the moon is an artist you listen to that shows your emotional side; "Your Dream Dinner Party," where you pick three artists you like for a custom, frequently updated Spotify Mix featuring your favorite songs and fresh picks; and "Your Artist Pairs," which features unique pairings you've listened to recently, including those that span genres. You can dive into personalized insights about how you engage with the music to understand things like the different time periods of music you've enjoyed, your favorite music genres and podcast topics, and how your listening preferences change as the day progresses.[3]

At the end of each year, users receive a personalized annual review called "Wrapped," which highlights the artists, songs, genres, and other aspects of their music listening experience that are important to them. Playlists, Only You, and Wrapped can of course be shared on social media, which increases user interaction and acts as a form of free marketing.

Enabling Users to Rate: Gathering relevant data on users is a critical component of creating personalized experiences. One way is to enable users to like/dislike or rate various components. On Spotify, you can click a heart button to indicate you like a song; you can also follow artists, rate songs, and create custom playlists. The software will notice and adapt your recommendations accordingly.

In the case of products like Spotify or Instagram, where users can like photos or videos, this feature is built into the core product itself. In other products and services, an additional step might be required, such as through pop-up, one-question surveys. Bold companies will go the extra mile and proactively solicit feedback by asking users to rate them on public platforms such as Google Maps or Amazon or directly on their website through built-in plugins such as Trustpilot. We say this is bold because doing so opens a company up for comments and ratings, be they good or bad. But we know the world is moving to a ratings economy, and users are finding ways to rate companies whether companies like it or not, so why not get ahead of the curve?

ON-TAP SUPPLY

Consumers like ease and simplicity, and what is easier than having access to what you want, exactly when you want it, and only paying for the amount that you use? That is the world we are leaning into.

From Vendor-Push to Client-Pull Dynamics: Industries first started shifting away from batch production many decades ago, and the trend has continued from production to the makeup of the products themselves. For example, customized fast fashion is both personalized and produced on demand. The same will likely happen for food, medicine, education, and a host of other industries. With Spotify, while playlists get pushed to every user all the time, it is the action of that user that triggers what each playlist contains. The user becomes an integral part of what the product contains and is in the driver's seat.

From Owning to As-a-Service Models: With Spotify, you don't buy music anymore. You subscribe to an endless flow of music and personalized playlists that you consume on demand. We see similar trends beyond software and digital products, where the trend is toward anything-as-a-service (XaaS). This has profound implications for how organizations are structured, which we cover in more detail in later chapters.

One and You're Done: On-tap solutions are underpinned by extremely intuitive user interfaces and user experiences. User interface (UI) and user experience (UX) systems incorporate design, technology, data science, and psychology. It's not about the product but rather about designing interactions with users based on their behaviors, attitudes, and emotions. Spotify spends serious resources on this and obsesses over the smallest details: button shapes, sizes, what happens when you hover on a button, the unique desktop, tablet, smartphone, and automobile interfaces. Spotify now also has a voice-enabled feature where a user can simply ask it to play a song or playlist, which bypasses the traditional user interface completely.

Incorporating AI in the Provision of Solutions: The algorithms that create general and individualized playlists are generated by artificial intelligence, meaning that if all employees at Spotify took a month off work, users would continue to get personalized playlists and a constant stream of new recommendations. With Spotify's voice feature, users can now simply ask it to play a song they like, and the algorithm will start a curated playlist based on their usage history, profile, and even the time of day and day of the week. We can imagine a future where Spotify knows you so well that you don't even need to ask it to start playing a song—it will know when to do so by itself.

HYPER-SOCIAL BUSINESS MODELS

In an increasingly digital and connected world, scale matters. This not only offers economies of scale and the ability to move from linear to exponential growth but more importantly provides additional consumer data that can be used to create further customization, product enhancements, and value. Consider four moves:

Platform Economics: A platform is "a business model that creates value by facilitating exchanges between two or more interdependent groups, usually consumers and producers."[4] Spotify is an open platform that includes songs from countless labels and artists. Even in a relatively closed ecosystem like Apple's iPhone/iOS platform, there are open standards that allow third-party membership and contribution.

Owning a platform with sufficient scale can be immensely valuable, but digital economies often entail winner-takes-all outcomes, so obviously not everyone can create a market-leading platform. That being said, there are typically existing platforms you can join, and you can consider launching your own. Start small and within a defined niche and grow from there, allow users to rate products and services, and use the data to continuously optimize supply and prices.

Disintermediation: A digital economy means a direct economy. Products are becoming less and less constrained by physical distance, especially with the emergence of more powerful and precise 3D printers. And services can often be completely or partially conducted online—including in banking, health care, education, hospitality, entertainment, marketing, product design and development, and professional services more broadly. Many of these services such as online travel bookings can even be done by an algorithm.

This means that **disintermediation**—or cutting out intermediaries and gatekeepers—is here to stay and sure to expand. Even if you're on a platform—a form of intermediation—you should seek to maintain direct channels with consumers, get access to consumer data, and influence how your product is marketed and sold on the platform. And many platforms are not exclusive, meaning that you can list on different ones at the same time, while also maintaining your own direct-to-consumer sales channel.

Labels still exist on Spotify, but they are cut out of any relationship with the end users. It's the products people want, not the labels. Furthermore, Spotify has also started producing its own original content, which is also the case with platforms such as YouTube, Amazon, Netflix, Tencent, iQIYI, Youku, and Hulu.

Creating Community: Hyper-sociality requires contributing to and cultivating a user community. Not only does community create a direct channel to your consumers, but it has also been shown to improve the customer's experience, increase their loyalty, and spark growth through word-of-mouth marketing. Spotify encourages users to follow other users' playlists and share playlists with one another. It also has a "Blend" feature that uses AI to create playlists based on the preferences of different users, allowing them to share and discover new music in a personalized way. It is certainly not shy about encouraging this sociality. With a simple, in-app guide it prompts users to create Blends, invite friends, and share the Blend results across social media channels.[5]

Spotify even has a feature where users can listen to a song or podcast at exactly the same time, regardless of where they are in the world. Equally, Disney Plus and Netflix have "watch party" features for similar synchronous viewing. Just think about the potential of this in the metaverse coupled with VR wearables and body trackers, which would allow you to host virtual dance parties all night long with people from all corners of the globe.

Network Effects: The more users Spotify has, the better the service gets. First, its increasing power due to the growing user base enables it to do deals for more and more music. Second, the AI that generates playlists gets better the more users there are, since it leans on recommendations based on what people who like what you like are also listening to. And third, the ability to share playlists gets more interesting to each user as more people have such playlists. See the sidebar for additional ideas on how to create network effects.

NETWORK EFFECTS

Just like it is customary to do financial and legal audits, why not consider doing network effect audits where existing networks are examined in considerable detail to determine how it might be possible to create new network effects in a company? Here are ten ways to implement these:

- Early sign-up benefits—Offer benefits for early adoption, such as free trials and discounts.
- Encourage bilateral recruitment—Pay all participants from one side of the network for recruiting people for the other side. For instance, the mobile payment system M-PESA in Kenya paid senders money to recruit receivers.
- Free/paid—Make it free for one side but charge the other. For instance, on a commercial network, charge the sellers, but not the buyers.

- Niche approach—Choose a very small market niche and get it to work there, then expand. As an example, Facebook was initially only available for students at Harvard.
- Piggyback—Launch your network as-a-service within another network that already has critical mass. PayPal got its ignition because it was launched within eBay.
- Pioneer stakes—Attract early adopters and contributors by allowing them to benefit from future upside potential in the business. Tattoodo offered initially some of the best tattoo artists in the world stock options for signing up.
- Scarcity by design—Make it attractive to sign up via selectivity. For instance, "During the first year we will only have the 10 percent best restaurants signed up. Do you want to be included in this exclusive group?"
- Self-supply—Sponsor one side to ensure its presence. For instance, new nightclubs might initially offer happy hour prices before 10:00 p.m. in order to create an atmosphere and increase their chances of attracting more people later. Or when YouTube was launched, the founders posted the first videos.
- Trojan horse—Give potential users a free tool, product, or service, which "happens to" connect them to the network. Once there are enough passive network participants, you try to activate them.
- Two-step—Deliberately focus entirely on one side first and only approach the other when the first is reasonably populated. For instance, OpenTable focused initially entirely on signing up the best restaurants for online booking before then turning to the consumers with targeted advertising.

In quite a lot of companies, the presence of a strong network effect was the one and only difference between massive success and utter failure. And there can be far more than one network effect in any given franchise.

We spend up to a third of our waking hours on our phones and many more hours on top of that interacting with computers, televisions, and other screens around us.[6] Coupled with social networks, user data, big data analytics, and AI, marketing has become intelligent, precise, and supremely user focused. It is now possible to target a segment of one with engaging and experiential content, and the lines between marketing and community engagement are blurring. We furthermore see a boom in mobile marketing and, increasingly, in the metaverse. We highlight three additional prominent shifts.

DEPLOY FLUID, ALWAYS-ON MARKETING

In a world of constant change where consumers want their needs fulfilled in a personalized and on-tap way, marketing must be fluid. Even with a sea of data and an army of data scientists and experts, it is extremely difficult to predict what posts will go viral ahead of time. Recall that in *complex* environments, there are unclear cause-and-effect relationships. Therefore, instead of taking weeks to prepare for a post, modern marketing is fast and iterative—similar to the Creative Loop. Yearly marketing calendars are important but so is adapting them in the space of weeks, days, and even hours.

Another way to look at this is to acknowledge that almost all organizations today are—or should be—media companies, regardless of what industry they're in. It is impossible to ignore the virtual universe, and it's a bad idea to let your online presence take shape without actively shaping it. Consumers are increasingly looking for solutions to their needs online, and the only questions are whether they will find your organization and whether they'll like the content they see when they find it.

> Almost all organizations today are—or should be—
> media companies, regardless of what industry they're in.

Marketing as a Real-Time Conversation: Spotify builds on popular trends as they emerge, and it uses its vast amounts of data to get an "insight into the emotion that people are expressing." For example, it launched a hugely popular "Thanks, 2016. It's been weird" campaign, which included tongue-in-cheek posts like "Dear person in LA who listened to the 'Forever Alone' playlist for 4 hours on Valentine's Day, are you ok?" Another example is when it incorporated the viral "Yanny vs. Laurel" debate in its #2018Wrapped billboards.[7]

Consumers are increasingly looking for solutions to their needs online, and the only questions are whether they will find your organization and whether they'll like the content they see when they find it.

Automating Marketing Processes: There is only one way to combine personalizing product offerings and marketing campaigns to a segment of one and scale: automation. The name of the game is to set up funnels that include lead generation and then automatically send the tailored messages to prospective buyers, depending on their behavior. Soon we will also see AI algorithms that are able to write effective marketing copy themselves.

Embed Marketing in the User Experience: In the growing ratings economy, bold companies will let consumer feedback and ratings speak for themselves. As long as the ratings are real and honest, the products and service that provide the best value will win. This is further enhanced by word-of-mouth and user-generated marketing through platforms, communities, and networks. Spotify benefits greatly from its users sharing songs with others, posting about their personalized insights, and from artists who share their end-of-year streaming statistics.

TWENTY QUESTIONS FOR THE NEW AGE

1. Have we put the use front and center and part of day-to-day decisions?
2. Do we focus on the right higher-level consumer needs (moving up the Maslow hierarchy of needs)?
3. Can we unbundle our products and services?
4. Can we divide our services and products into micro-objects?
5. Can we create a broader product variety?
6. Can we target segments-of-one (mass personalization)?
7. Can we customize our products more? And might we even efficiently customize the product to every single client while remaining efficient?
8. Are there sharing and rating features that we should add to our products?
9. Can we move from vendor-push to client-pull dynamics?
10. Can we deliver our product as-a-service?
11. Can we massively simplify the user experience ("one and you're done")?
12. Can we transform our product so it provides the ultimate client experience?
13. Can we incorporate artificial intelligence in the provision of solutions?
14. Can we use or create open platforms?
15. Can we use disintermediation?
16. Can we enable users to interact with us and each other as a community?
17. Can we create network and viral effects into our business?
18. Can we adapt our marketing in real time?
19. Can we automate the marketing processes?
20. Can we harness user feedback, ratings, and peer-to-peer sharing to market our products and services?

The following chart can help you assess your current point of departure and where your biggest priorities lie in this area.

From ...		To ...
No customer personas, and user experience is not measured or managed	→	Strong customer centricity and understanding that is infused into day-to-day discussions
Focus on meeting foundational customer needs	→	Meeting both foundational and aspirational customer needs
Limited customization of products and services	→	Segment-of-one personalization at scale
Bundled supply, pushed by the vendor	→	On-tap supply that is pulled by the customer as-a-service
Limited potential for network effects and exponential growth	→	Hyper-social business model with strong customer community
Yearly marketing calendar with mass-market approach	→	Personalized, fluid, and automated marketing approach
Customer feedback strictly sought for internal audiences	→	Openness to publicly viewable ratings and customer feedback

Chapter 25

FAST, FLUID, AND FLEXIBLE!

Anyone who has been in business for at least a few years knows that organizations go through cycles of reorganization, first by function, then by product line, then perhaps by customer segment, then with a geographical matrix, and then repeating the process again as new leaders and business strategies take hold. Most bigger organizations aren't standing still, that's for sure, yet typically still feel they are not able to make decisions quickly enough, adapt swiftly enough, or collaborate across silos well enough.

And this problem and its solutions have been discussed for at least sixty years, if not more. Alfred Chandler published *Strategy and Structure* in 1962, which showed how an organization's structure follows strategy and that an organizational restructuring is often part of the strategic implementation itself. McKinsey published "Beyond the Matrix Organization" in 1979; its authors argued that organizations must continually reorganize to stay competitive and manage the inherent tensions that exist between centralization and decentralization. And Peter Drucker posited in his 1988 article "The Coming of the New Organization" that "the typical large business twenty years hence will have fewer than half the levels of management of its counterpart today, and no more than a third the managers."[1]

FAILURE UPON FAILURE

The reality is that the way many organizations are structured today often sets them up for failure, and most attempts to streamline them fail. In fact, as little as 25 percent of organizational redesign efforts succeed.[2] Looking at organizational changes from an elevated perspective shows that there are a handful of reasons why this is so:

1. They continue to rely on strong hierarchies and a chain-of-command execution approach, which rarely works well in today's rapidly changing world.

2. They are linked to a specific strategy (e.g., a new emphasis on products, customer centricity, or geographic expansion). As a result, the structure is by nature rigid and inflexible, and when that strategy changes or new initiatives are launched, new organization changes follow. The result is constant confusion and fatigue among employees and suboptimal execution.

3. They are not optimized for how work actually gets done; they are optimized based on legacy decisions and who should report to whom.

4. They focus on ensuring a logical and controlled execution, rather than explicitly allowing for and expecting changes along the way (deviations to plan/budget and too many organizational changes are often seen as bad, rather than welcomed).

The organizational shifts required, many of which are already adopted by leading companies and fast-growing start-ups, are a far cry from the hierarchical structures typically present to various degrees in organizations today.

For starters, as work in general becomes increasingly granular, short term and fast changing, organizations are being pushed to become fast, fluid, and flexible.

> **Triple-F organizations are fast, fluid, and flexible. This means that they are adaptive and by design optimized for constantly changing priorities.**

Triple-F organizations leave the inflexible origination models and are centered around how value is created in practice and how employees can perform at their best. Organizational levels and departments naturally still exist, but only to the extent that they support the work. They are adaptive and by design optimized for changing priorities, making them flexible enough to handle new strategic needs as they arise.

> **In dynamic environments, make organization structures adaptive and by design optimized for constantly changing priorities.**

SO, WHAT DOES THIS LOOK LIKE IN PRACTICE?

For starters, there is no one-size-fits-all organizational structure or one archetype that is applicable to every business type and size. Agile and leaderless organizations, for example, typically lend themselves best to start-ups and software companies, while large organizations with hundreds of thousands of people require real coordination to derive a competitive advantage in things like knowledge sharing, leveraging scale in procurement and distribution, and sales and marketing due to the fact that they are so big. We are not shunning hierarchy or centralization when they are needed, but there are new and interesting trends emerging.

One of these trends is the **flattening** of organizations, with decisions more frequently pushed to the front line.[3] This is largely because of the increasing complexity of the operating environment. As day-to-day challenges become more multifaceted and novel, decisions require human judgment rather than routine execution. Furthermore, long command chains and rigid hierarchies often prove inflexible and slow moving.

Research also shows that companies that minimize the operational distance between the center and the front line are twice as likely as their peers to become top performers.[4] Other research has shown that leading global organizations typically have as few as six or seven layers, and sometimes even fewer, compared to as many as nine or ten for other organizations.[5] Of course, organizations should not flatten for the sake of it, and pushing decisions to the front line requires a capable and motivated workforce and the right delegation of authority.

Another shift is toward **flow-to-work models**, where employees are assigned to work assignments and projects on a fluid basis as needs change, typically in a cross-functional network of teams that come together for a period of time and then disband again once the project is complete. Here, job descriptions, KPIs, and work assignments should be able to change as needed.

> **Triple-F organizations have flow-to-work models, where tasks attract temporary staff, just like the global market economy but on a smaller and quicker scale.**

This doesn't mean that routine work necessarily goes away—it rarely does—and there will normally continue to be employees who are primarily or exclusively engaged with a relatively stable scope of work.

However, it also doesn't mean that employees should be rigidly categorized exclusively into either fixed or fluid parts of the organization. Leading organizations build flexibility into the very DNA of their structure so that any employee can join new work assignments as they emerge. The job assignments can vary from 10–15 percent of someone's time (as little as an hour a day) to a full-time gig. Some employee groups might have 100 percent fluid and project-based work, while others might have 0 percent, but the same governance mechanism applies to all.

CREATING THE IN-HOUSE GIG ECONOMY

This can be done by creating an internal gig economy or job market with a clear supply of employees whose skills and experience can be called on as needed. These roles are set for a finite period of time and with specific requirements. Everyone can be eligible for gigs, and each gig is staffed based on needs once the employee's manager or coordinator approves. As an example of this, Unilever, a global consumer goods company with over 150,000 employees, launched FLEX in 2019. FLEX is an AI-driven internal marketplace that helps employees work on projects across the organization to varying degrees of their time in order to support fast-moving business goals, plug skill gaps, and increase talent development and retention. Within two years, the platform was already being used by almost half of the workforce, and this in particular helped the company redeploy thousands of employees during the pandemic as consumer demands shifted.[6]

This type of structure also breaks with the remnant practices of hierarchical organizations where a solid reporting line is equated with performance evaluation, employee development, and day-to-day work management (historically with the need for face-to-face interactions to ensure the employee was actually working).

In triple-F organizations, these three practices are typically done by two or three different entities, with new metrics used to govern each one. For example, employees could be organized by functional area (e.g., marketing, product development, consulting) to ensure a strong level of apprenticeship and development.

The gig way means that day-to-day work is managed and executed on projects that are led by different leaders across the organization, depending on need. The work is governed by activity metrics (e.g., utilization, number of accounts, and requests handled), as well as outcome metrics (e.g., project KPIs, deliverables, and manager, peer, and team feedback). Employee feedback and development discussions have historically been done by line managers, but some organizations use a third party, for example within talent management, to manage this performance feedback and development, especially for more senior levels of the organization.

FROM POWER TO PERFORMANCE

Although the most senior levels of the organization are typically relatively stable to ensure overall coordination and alignment on the direction, the subordinate levels can change dramatically based on the work going on. In fact, it is becoming more and more futile to even think about how many people report to a given leader, as this doesn't necessarily have any bearing on how the work is done and how much value that department creates. Layers only exist for coordination and for apprenticeship, not as steps on the career ladder, and generally talent will move sideways much more often. As such, empire building becomes completely irrelevant in a fluid organization.

Power-centric empire building based on number of subordinates becomes completely irrelevant in triple-F organizations. Instead, it is the doing-centric performance that matters.

TAP INTO THE HUMAN CLOUD

In addition to becoming more fluid and flexible, organizations are also becoming more and more on demand by leveraging the external human cloud. Gig workers, who do not work for a single employer but offer their services on a contract-by-contract basis, already make up a significant portion of the workforce, more than 30 percent in some large economies already. And that number is projected to continue growing rapidly—it grew by 33 percent in the US in 2020 alone (albeit largely due to COVID-19, of course).[7] Supertrends experts have predicted that by 2060, over half of the US workforce will be freelancers.

Gig workers can provide new supply to an organization's internal job market and allow the company to fill skill and resource gaps quickly, for the specific amount of time needed. There is even evidence of gigs being successfully used to fill leadership positions. The message is that we can reverse the job funnel: instead of organizations trying to find talent, they can create an internal ecosystem so that internal talent can find tasks. Managers need to understand how to craft effective job (gig) profiles on the internal marketplace that outline the specific skills they need. Internal employees need to encourage candidates to keep their profiles up to date with work history, certifications, and skills. In larger organizations, AI algorithms can then assist in matching gigs to employees.

> **Instead of organizations trying to find talent, create an internal ecosystem so that internal talent can find tasks.**

Although there is a limit between what is theoretically possible and what is operationally feasible with gig working, the proportion of employee hours filled by gig workers (internal and external) will shift dramatically. In line with the consumer trends of wanting on-tap products and services, organizations too will become more and more on tap and on demand.

PRIORITIZE AS-A-SERVICE SOLUTIONS

Building on this, organizations are increasing flexibility by leveraging other clouds and external providers at scale. Software as a service (SaaS) has been around for decades, yet in recent years organizations are embracing anything-as-a-service (XaaS) models as they demand increasing variety and flexibility. A 2021 Deloitte survey found that three quarters of companies are already running more than half of their IT operations as-a-service. And analysts are estimating that the XaaS market will grow by 24 percent per year in the next few years (meaning it will double every three years), reaching more than $340 billion by 2024.[8]

BUILDING ECOSYSTEMS

Finally, there is a growing shift toward plugging into the broader ecosystems and networks of the organization—what some call meta-organizations.[9] This can include XaaS as mentioned earlier, and also things like

- Setting up various advisory boards consisting of young talents, entrepreneurs, futurists, or scientists creating and facilitating online discussion forums

- Using crowdsourcing platforms to find solutions for specific challenges

- Holding innovation jams

- Hosting hackathons that are open to the public

Although some of these elements are not new, they are growing in prevalence. And they all point toward the same shifts in terms of organizational structures and boundaries becoming faster, more fluid, and more flexible, and with significantly more gray areas between what is formally part of the organization and what is not. Tesla, one of the leading car and energy companies, made a bold choice to become open source in 2014, as it believed it was the best way to attract and work with the best engineers globally.[10] Its bet turned out to be a good one, as the company's revenues grew by 10x between 2014 and 2020 and its technology continues to break new boundaries.

We can develop fast, fluid, and flexible organizations by flattening the structures, empowering the front-line workers, introducing flow-to-work models, creating in-house gig economies, prioritizing as-a-service solutions, and working extensively with external ecosystems.

WHICH SUPERTRENDS ARE DRIVING THESE SHIFTS?

Some of the main trends driving this shift is market and consumer needs. As products and services become on demand, so must organizations. The market is dictating more diversity of offerings and more frequent new releases with trends shifting at increasing rates, and consumers want their needs met exactly at their time of choosing (e.g., car-riding services, food delivery, product deliveries, any type of streaming, and even more complex elements such as customized furniture or consulting). They are not waiting for you pushing products; instead, they pull them from you.

Another trend pushing the need for fluid and on-demand organizations is the increasing complexity of typical work tasks.[11] As the challenges we face become more multifaceted and ambiguous, we require more varied sets of expertise and problem-solving approaches to solve them. Long gone are the days when a single person or a set of leaders could routinely make effective top-down choices on behalf of the rest of a large organization. The realities in more and more industries today are simply too vast and complex, so decisions must be pushed to those who are closest to the action, often in cross-functional teams. In other words, the organization fosters a swarm of semiautonomous teams, which each have efficient and flexible Creative Loops.

We've also seen that the half-life of skills is falling drastically. As a result, we are entering a skills-based economy where what you are able to do today is much more important than your prior work experience and degrees. As automation and artificial intelligence grows, the demand for physical and basic cognitive skills will decline and the tasks taken on by humans will require much more creativity, judgment, and social and emotional skills. These tasks are less repetitive and less predictable, and are often best completed in project teams, rather than in business-as-usual processes—further enhancing the need for internal fluidity.[12]

**We are entering a skills-based economy where ability to
continuously acquire new skills is a key currency of value.**

Younger generations increasingly seek a stronger say in their careers
and work tasks, and organizations as a result must adapt or risk losing talent. Specifically, millennials and Generation Z are typically more
likely to want to work remotely or in a hybrid fashion, are keener to
have independence and autonomy at work, want more varied work
projects (e.g., through gigs), and are more open to freelancing and creating their own career ladders as opposed to staying in a handful of jobs
and progressing up pre-organized corporate career ladders. Of course,
there's a flip side to this too: those pre-organized ladders are harder and
harder to find for those who prefer them. That is why they will likely
never disappear completely, even as they become rarer.

COVID-19 has only accelerated this trend. It has been called the
great leveler. As the majority of corporate employees have had to transition to Zoom, Microsoft Teams, and Webex calls from their homes,
colleagues have gotten new, more intimate insights into the daily lives,
families, and pets of those they work with. This has increased the sense
of shared humanity and trust among employees, especially in those
organizations that embraced flatness and treated everyone as equals.
The reverse is also true—those organizations that relied on top-down
decisions, for example regarding work schedules and policies, saw falling levels of trust, resilience, and performance during the pandemic.[13]

Of course, across all this, we should not forget that an on-demand
organization is only desirable if the transaction costs of working with
external partners and gig workers are lower than the transaction costs of
conducting all the work internally with fixed, full-time employees. This
simple yet insightful theory was first put forth in 1937 by Ronald Coase
and continues to hold true to this day.[14] However, technology and
online platforms have decreased the transaction costs of hiring externally massively, even for very short durations or for specific micro-tasks,
and we can expect this trend to further accelerate in the future.[15] On the

other hand, the same transaction cost theory illustrates that there are operational limits to becoming on demand because of the importance of organization-specific cultures and ways of working.[16] There are also potential intellectual property issues. For example, you want full-time people working on your top-secret projects, not just freelancers.

STARTING THE JOURNEY

In our experience, most organizations could do with a comprehensive review of their organizational structure and ways of working. Established companies have typically not made bold enough moves to adapt their organizations to the current context and evolving supertrends (minor evolutions will probably not get you there!), while start-ups and fast-growing companies typically grow organically and would benefit from more deliberate choices in how they work.

An early step is to identify what makes your organization succeed and your direction for the future. But although structure follows strategy, we are, perhaps counter-intuitively, not advocating for a link that is too close, as strategies will continue to change.

Instead, determine your direction and map your structure against that with enough flexibility to adapt to strategies as they emerge. Keep it simple and based on how day-to-day work is managed, how employees will be evaluated, and how employees can best develop. Some roles such as factory or retail roles that require a physical presence might need little flexibility in terms of job scope, and the primary reporting line will be the day-to-day manager. On the other hand, for project-based work carried out in cross-functional teams, the primary reporting line will be the function (e.g., sales, product development, HR) to ensure that the employee has access to sufficient apprenticeship. Push ownership and accountability down as far as possible and remove unnecessary layers. In short, radically simplify.

Determine your direction and map your
organizational structure against that.

In addition to structure, establish the right processes that will allow your organization to be fluid. This includes an internal job market with roles staffed by people with the right skills (demand), a mechanism to capture and certify skills of employees (supply), and the talent processes and culture change requirements to support this shift. Start small (e.g., by allowing employees to specify roles of up to 15 percent of someone else's time), but gradually open up to roles with 100 percent staffing allocation.

In addition to internal fluidity, create external flexibility and linkages. Take a long-term, systems view, and establish trust both for individual gig workers and for other organizations to work with you. This requires a focus on win-win relationships, as well as clearly articulating a shared purpose and ways of working together.

The below chart can help you assess your current point of departure and where your biggest priorities lie in this area.

From . . .		To . . .
Complex, hierarchical, chain-of-command structures with multiple layers and strong silos	→	Simple and flat organization, typically with a network of teams, with distributed authority and front-line empowerment
Solid line reporting relationships synonymous with delegated work and KPIs	→	Fluid, flow-to-work model where employees work on impermanent gigs and projects as needs arise
The vast majority of work is carried out by full-time employees or long-term contractors	→	Flexible, on-demand organization that uses external gig workers to adopt to fast-changing needs
Strong preference for in-house development and vertical or horizontal integrations	→	Partnership-first approach that uses anything-as-a-service to its full potential
Fixed organizational boundaries that do not change over time	→	Networked organizations with fluid boundaries in terms of innovation, collaboration, and knowledge sharing

Chapter 26

MANAGEMENT, AT THE SPEED AND RICHNESS OF LIFE

H ere is one thing we have never seen: a football (soccer) player running around in a game with a "how to play football" manual in their hands. That wouldn't work, obviously. Instead, every player has to constantly make decisions on their feet, and even in the best of times, the winning team makes loads of mistakes on its way to victory. This doesn't mean that football doesn't have rules (yellow and red cards, you know) and management. But during the actual game, at least 99 percent of the decisions are made on the fly by the individual players.

The point about this is that decision-making in organizations often needs to become a lot more like football, since the rate of change in the world is speeding up, largely because of supertrends involving technology. Machines and robots are continuing to take over lower-cognitive tasks at work, meaning that humans increasingly focus on higher-cognitive, unpredictable, and creative tasks, which are more often project-based, short term, and fluid.

Humans will increasingly focus on higher-cognitive, unpredictable, and creative tasks, which are more often project-based, short term, and fluid.

Technology has also dramatically lowered the barriers to entry in industries, as start-ups can now attack incumbent companies on the cheap by leveraging the instant low-cost offerings from the digital cloud, human cloud, XaaS offerings, and digital marketing. This means that the rate of creative innovation—and destruction!—keeps rising.

LOSS OF SUPREME MANAGEMENT CONTROL

Technology is also rendering organizational hierarchies obsolete, as new information flows can bypass formal structures and lead to more efficient collaboration in real time. Perhaps the junior employee now knows a lot about some technologies affecting a business that the CEO doesn't. Perhaps she found it on the internet yesterday, whereas the boss didn't.

Knowledge is no longer centered at the top. Because of the internet, it's everywhere. And this speaks for decentralization.

The ratings economy is also making inroads in organizations, where people can provide feedback and even rate colleagues they have worked with on various projects. Performance management is thus becoming an ongoing and fully transparent dialogue, rather than a secretive event. Yes, the boss can still rate the employee behind closed doors, but the employee can also rate the boss on the internet through services such as Glassdoor!

This opens up the floodgates for unleashing people's full potential in less centrally controlled ways, as they are incentivized to deliver quality work as they build their reputations. What they do can be seen by the world, including online talent scouts, not just by their bosses.

THE SPEED YOU NEED

COVID-19 accelerated some of these trends. For the first time in history, most working professionals went home and were forced to adapt and collaborate virtually. They mostly realized that it actually worked, and many enjoyed the change. During the COVID-19 lock-downs, in the course of just a few weeks, for millions of people the world over, "work from X" ceased being a possibility and became a necessity. Here, many discovered the potential for distributed teams to collaborate well despite sitting in different parts of an organization and perhaps thousands of miles away from each other. And businesses were forced to adapt, many of which adopted radically new ways of working—implemented within weeks, instead of years. Even one of the most regulated industries—pharmaceuticals—showed that it is pos-sible to develop and launch an effective vaccine in approximately a year instead of the five to ten years it has historically taken if the right people come together and challenge existing processes to work in new ways.

It's all about speed. When the COVID-19 virus RNA sequence was released, it took pharma company Moderna just forty-eight hours to computer design an RNA vaccine. For decades, business schools across the globe have taught students about the four Ps of marketing, which are product, price, place, and promotion. These describe the marketing mix, but today, it makes sense to add a fifth P to this: pace.

> The new marketing mix is product, price, place,
> promotion . . . and pace.

FROM OPTIMIZING ROUTINE TO OPTIMIZING INNOVATION

The time it takes to complete a repetitive task generally drops each time you do it, due to learning. The drop is rapid at first, and thereafter has diminishing returns. It can be applied to dropping units of time, but also to things like optimizing resource usage and quality.

Practice curve of typing
Illustrating an eliminative curve of time

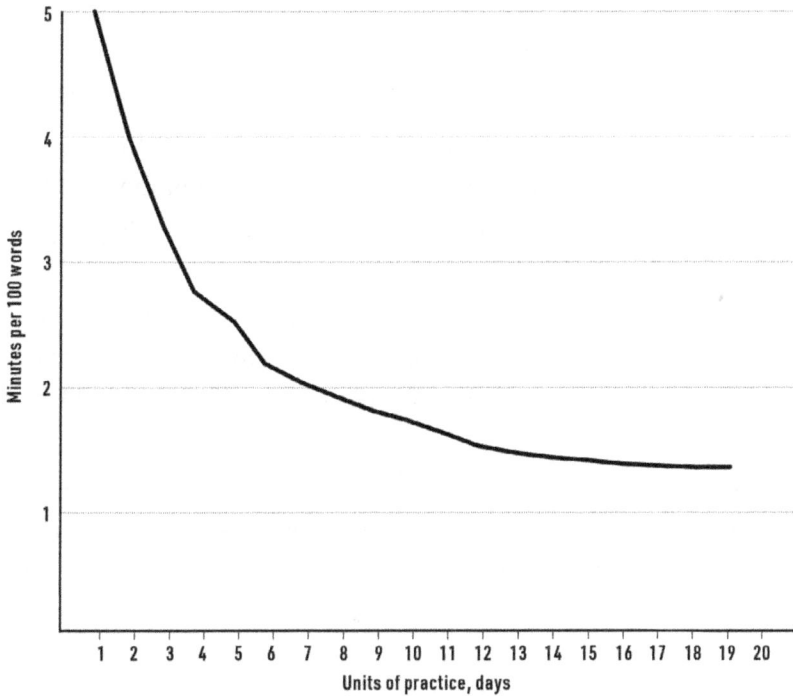

Figure 26.1. Typing performance over time, illustrative of a clear learning curve.[1]

Such optimization is great for repeatable tasks and has been crucial since the beginning of the industrial economy around 1800. They require strong processes and stringent controls. They are typically manual and have historically benefited from strong oversight. For example, workers in factories have generally not been paid very well and were often not particularly intrinsically motivated in their tasks. The stick, rather than the carrot, was therefore allowed to reign supreme.

Between the 1950s and 1970s, additional management innovations were created that focused on making processes even faster, with fewer errors, and done with fewer resources. Toyota's Lean system and Deming's Plan-Do-Check-Act (PDCA) are prime examples.

More recently, other approaches have emerged, typically in fast-moving environments such as the Observe-Orient-Decide-Act (OODA) approach in the US Army and the Lean approach and its Build-Measure-Learn (BML) loop for start-ups.

The problem is that more and more repeatable tasks are getting automated and because of the pace of change, we are confronted with new stuff all the time. Typical challenges facing organizations include optimizing every area with big data and machine learning (e.g., operations, marketing, HR), revamping talent processes to enable the future of work, and undergoing comprehensive transformation programs, including M&A, all while managing external supply and demand volatility. This means that standard processes such as PDCA, OODA, and BML are only so useful, and that it is impossible to define clearly up front what needs to be done. Leaders who try to manage things top down may quickly learn that they do not know enough about what is happening at the edges to do so effectively. Instead, they must increasingly enable their employees to take charge.

WHAT *NOT* TO DO . . .

Let's think the opposite for a second. How do you delay, degrade, and add cost to an execution process?

Keep people in functional silos.

Ensure that they do not work together synchronously but rather sequentially by handing tasks back and forth.

Avoid sharing information so no one on the team really has the full picture.

Include frequent process checks with various governance bodies (who are busy and difficult to get time with) to make decisions to move forward.

This what-not-to-do scenario is unfortunately all too familiar in many organizations.

WHAT TO DO INSTEAD . . .

What about, instead, doing the following:

- Get all the key stakeholders involved for a period of—let's say—two weeks, to problem-solve, brainstorm, make decisions, and create outputs.

- Thereafter test the outputs with end users, get feedback, set priorities for the next two weeks, and go again.

This is the essence of the agile approach, which was originally designed for software development, and which was popularized in the 2001 Agile Manifesto[2] published online. However, if an organization does this with many teams, it starts operating according to the Creative Loop processes among the city-states that triggered the creative explosion in the West—and which even possibly played a key role in developing humans as competitive species in the first place.

Granted, the majority of us are not creating software day to day, and for many of us this approach in its purest form will not work in our organizations. But we can learn a lot from some of the principles, the key ones listed below:

- Work in short sprints to continuously test and learn.

- Bring the required stakeholders together at the same time, instead of having constant handoffs.

- Focus on outputs as the measure of progress instead of activity.

- Have fewer priorities with shorter deadlines instead of many priorities with long ones.

- Welcome changing requirements, even late in the process, if they improve the end output.

- At regular intervals, reflect on the process and how the team can work together even better. Be open to completely reimagining the process.

Obviously, this is not to say that planning and tried and tested methodologies are not needed, but these must be second to the overarching objective and the openness to adapt along the way.

Barnes & Noble, a major bookseller with over 600 retail stores, has given store managers more local autonomy regarding the books they stock and how to display them in order to build stronger connections with local customers and increase the engagement among staff. Interestingly, the strategy includes an acknowledgment that there will be a significant learning curve in doing this: "As you let the stores diverge, a quarter will be brilliant and a quarter will be absolutely terrible. A significant number of your stores will become worse, not better. Then you teach and encourage them, and, in time, everybody becomes better."[3]

Even companies such as Starbucks, Walmart, or Marriott hotels, which for good reasons rely on strong routine processes, could benefit from combining their standard operating procedures with variations of front-line experimentation and customer feedback, as they seek to continuously improve what they do. What if Starbucks baristas were able to experiment with music, in-store layouts, and merchandise placements in order to increase customer satisfaction and sales? What if front-line hotel staff could experiment with customer check-in and check-out procedures to continually improve how they work?

In terms of outputs, working in iterative sprints requires constant testing and learning and getting feedback from customers along the way. This is sometimes called "failing fast" or "failing forward," but the word *failure* has a negative connotation and can push people toward trying anything in the spirit of experimentation, and then sprinting toward trying something completely new again. This is not efficient. It is important to be open to failure, yes, but the real goal is not to fail but rather to iterate, test, and learn in accelerated Creative Loops.

Iterate, test, and learn in accelerated cycles/short sprints, where information processing is parallel, not sequential.

Software development is probably the easiest example of how to do this, and companies like Apple and Google regularly release software in beta version because it is the best way to truly get customer feedback, uncover bugs, and identify required improvements. In addition to sharing beta versions of products, many tech companies also share beta ideas in the form of their overarching development road maps with customers and prospects to continuously get input and develop, with stakeholder input front and center.

Continuously test beta ideas and beta products with the market.

However, non-software companies can apply these principles as well. For example, Zappos, an online shoes and clothing retailer, was launched as an e-commerce site in 1999 with *pictures* of shoes, rather than the

- We work in high-performing teams
- We empower teams
- We care about talent and craftmanship
- We continously learn from customers and apply learning to improve
- We set priorities with the big picture in mind
- We are consistent in our organizational design and way of working
- We organize for simplicity
- We re-use instead of reinvent

Figure 26.2. The ING one way of working principles.[4]

inventory itself, to test whether consumers would indeed be willing to buy shoes online.[5] In case someone actually ordered the shoes (a lot did), they had a deal to buy them from a retail shop at a discount.

Procter & Gamble, a global consumer packaged goods company, has applied "test and learn" principles to its marketing efforts.[5] And ING, a Dutch multinational bank, has also embraced many of these principles in how it develops new offerings and serves its customers.

FROM EMAIL TO SOCIAL COLLABORATION TOOLS

All of the above is underpinned by a new paradigm of collaboration and information:

- New rituals such as quick daily check-ins and intense problem-solving meetings where tangible outputs are created are the order of the day.

- General "status update" meetings are kept to an absolute minimum.

- Email is supplemented with more fluid and real-time channels such as Slack, Google Chat, Discord, Yammer, WhatsApp, and WeChat.

The same goes for how team leaders interact with their team members. Instead of waiting for a weekly one-on-one or an email reply to discuss specific topics, they can be handled in real time. Of course, in this environment it becomes increasingly important to block off time without distraction for deep work and perhaps only check the various messaging platforms a few times a day. But even with this approach, replies move from taking a few days to taking a few hours, if not minutes.

Information sharing is then moved to the cloud to ensure a single source of truth and transparency in terms of tasks and deliverables. Gone are the days where individuals stored files on their hard drives and shared them via email. Meetings refer to online documents that are updated in real time and are typically recorded and shared so that members who are not able to attend can follow the progress. In this way, everyone is on the same page, and that page is updated in real time.

We know hyper-sociality is critical for individuals as we speed into the blur, and the same goes for organizations. The new fast, fluid, and flexible organizational structures and management paradigms we are describing require more collaboration, not less. It's been shown that informal networks are often a key way that large organizations create value,[7] and encouraging hyper-sociality through collaboration tools, transparency of information, and empowerment is critical. The latest technologies can even map social networks, which further supports hyper-sociality in practice.

Keep key information in shared files that are updated in real time.

GOVERNANCE-AS-A-SERVICE

As teams come together from various parts of the organization, they must be empowered to fulfill the objectives based on their expertise, and they must allow for (and even welcome) changes along the way, if these can speed up or improve delivery. This requires true delegated authority, not just on paper and in theory (where the team still feels like it must go to senior executives to make decisions) but in practice too. This entails a shift from hard policies (defining specific methods) to judgment-based guidelines (defining values, goals, and a few nonnegotiable rules of engagement), and specifying what decision types can be made by the team and where it must seek input from others. As a consequence, the team gets freedom to experiment, and it is fully acknowledged that they are best placed to take the majority of daily decisions, as they are closer to the action and typically have more expertise in specific topics than senior leaders. We call this "governance-as-a-service" or "governance-on-demand": the team is entrusted and expected to move things forward, only occasionally pulling in senior stakeholders.

It's also important to revamp *how* decisions are made.[8] Typically organizations have many decision-makers (e.g., a specific committee) and a few people presenting their analyses and recommendations (e.g., a team leader who has been preparing the presentation for weeks). What works best in triple-F environments is instead the inverse—one or two decision-makers (e.g., the team lead) and a wide range of people who provide inputs and discuss the issue at hand (e.g., leaders and subject matter experts), but who are not ultimately responsible for making the decision or implementing it. This shifts the dialogue completely, from one where people are trying to convince each other about their point of view to one where the facts are discussed openly and then left to the accountable individuals to decide and act.

> Move from many decision-makers but few idea presenters
> to many idea presenters but few decision-makers.

BUT HOW DO YOU GET IT DONE?

Overall, much of what we have described above is about—

- Changing long-term planning to a series of short sprints

- Moving management processes from sequential to parallel

- Moving information from email and local storage to shared social media apps, where it is updated in real time

- Testing early and constantly

- Reversing the decision processes

Within this context, there is also a general move of management from a batch approach to an as-a-service approach, which is a complete parallel to what is happening to many products and services. If anything, this approach can help break David Deutsch's laws of monotony and the hierarchy rule and thus stimulate recursive intelligence in the organization.

For some organizations, moving toward empowered teams working in an iterative way is a bigger shift than it is for others. Many start-ups and newer organizations are born agile, while companies that have been around longer probably struggle in this area, even when the concepts make perfect sense. For both young and old companies, however, it is a journey of continuous adaptation, and few organizations truly master this model—*at scale!*

There's no quick fix, and it often requires not just a technical change but even more importantly a cultural change and real skill building. People easily fall back to what they are used to and what they know, especially during turbulent times. So, this shift requires top-down leadership role modeling and integrated actions to change the full organizational system.

Moving toward more agile ways of working should be done in an agile way. You can start in a specific area of the organization, like a specific department. You likely already have cross-cutting initiatives in place, but you must start being more deliberate about staffing and creating transparency around people's capacity and work durations. For example, as discussed in the previous chapter, you could formalize processes that allow for more flexible work allocations, even if it is as little as allowing up to one hour a day (10–15 percent) of flexibility to support other projects. Thereafter, expand the flexibility to more employees and to more varied types of projects. Nail it before you scale it.

> **Moving toward more agile ways of working
> should be done in an agile way.**

It's critical to define, communicate, and then recommunicate the organizational and departmental objectives so there is absolute clarity on what needs to get done and why. Define the guidelines and boundaries that employees should work within (e.g., business areas, decision rights, budgets). Keep them simple but with enough clarity so that teams can feel empowered to experiment within them.

Working in this way is enabled by the flow-to-the-work model described in the previous chapter. It is crucial to create transparency around work supply (employee capacity and their skill sets) and demand (project needs and skills required), as well as a mechanism to transparently assign people to shifting projects. Technology providers already offer solutions for these internal job markets. Combine them with best-of-breed technology platforms for cloud file sharing, intelligent information curation, and virtual collaboration.

Don't worry about structure for now. Worry instead about how work gets done. When the work gets done the right way, you can then tweak the structure. But chances are, if you're doing it right, few will notice that the structure has changed in any case.

Netflix, the digital media company, is a great example of an organization that has adapted and reinvented itself many times to become and remain market leading. Remember, Netflix started in 1997 as a low-tech, mail-based DVD rental business, and it only started offering streaming services in 2007. Since then, it has expanded into original programming and local content and is present in 190 countries. In 2009, Netflix published a 125-page "culture deck" online[9] and continues to stress the importance of "freedom and responsibility," "context not control," and ensuring teams are "highly aligned, loosely coupled."[10] These principles mirror the key elements in the Five Cs of Innovation. In an organizational context, ensuring compact units, healthy competition, common standards, cooperative networks, and change agents are present will do a great deal in terms of both innovation and overall employee engagement and effectiveness.

There are countless other examples, many from non-tech companies. For example, Barclays, a bank founded in 1896, which now operates almost 5,000 branches in more than 55 countries and has more than 80,000 employees, has adopted agile principles to empower teams and encourage flexibility to produce "better, faster, safer, happier" outcomes.

It has even applied the principles to areas such as audit, where auditors have decreased the average time it takes to complete an audit by one-third by limiting work in progress and empowering teams to do their best work.[11]

The following chart can help you assess your current point of departure and where your biggest priorities lie in this area.

From . . .		To . . .
Process-heavy and sequential execution with input/activity focus	→	Iterative and adaptive sprints with output/delivery focus
Wait until it's perfect	→	Continuous experimentation, customer testing, and feedback
Governance-heavy, typically with many decision-makers	→	Governance-as-a-service with true delegated authority and freedom to experiment
Collaboration based on email and many meetings	→	Multifaceted collaboration technologies
Significant resources spent on coordination	→	Real-time coordination and decision-making
Information on local drives that is shared when needed	→	Information stored in the cloud with full transparency on work tasks and status of deliverables
Hoarding of information	→	Sharing of information

Chapter 27

BECOME A TECHNOLOGY COMPANY

W e recently time-traveled back to the year 2010 and got into a Fiat Panda. Not literally, of course, but close. It was fascinating to see the technology in the vehicle—or lack thereof. Limited onboard diagnostics, no USB ports, no Bluetooth integration, no cruise control, no reverse camera when backing, no parking sensors, no digital screen, and only five gears. Stepping into a similar price point/marketing position car just ten years later has all of these features, plus more than five gears. And let's not even get started on cars such as Tesla or NIO, who are leading the way for electric, autonomous vehicles that are closer to full-fledged intelligent robots than mere transportation apparatuses.

Technology is slowly but surely creeping into every nook and cranny of life. However, when we look at technology day to day, it often seems to move slowly. Apple releases a new iOS system. Yawn. Microsoft releases a slightly thinner and faster laptop. Yawn again. TikTok launches new video-editing tools. Who really cares?

But it adds up. Relentlessly and exponentially, in fact. For instance, wearable technology can now measure your blood oxygen levels and alert you if they drop below a certain level. And you can now view IKEA furniture directly in your home with the help of augmented reality. The point is that when living through it, we typically see evolution rather than revolution. But this misses the forest for the trees, because when we look at as little as five years, the accumulated shifts often become dramatic.

Count on this supertrend: everything that can be digitized will be—it's just a matter of time. And when something becomes digitized (or partly digitized), it enters exponential growth. Rather than debating the specifics of what's coming, organizations in every industry must go all in on technology and continue to maintain a keen grasp on what's happening. For some companies who are already behind, this means going through a significant technological transformation, starting now.

Everything that can be digitized will be.

THE DIGITIZED HUMAN

Every industry is now changing at a pace never seen before, and we can safely say that all industries will face multiple disruptions over the next ten years. Within this process, more and more of us will become centaurs—or computer-supported people. For example, professional service sectors are increasingly using big data, algorithms, and automation to conduct analyses and even make preliminary recommendations. Strategy consulting firms are also increasingly deploying digital tools and assets—together with their experts—to help clients. These tools can, for example, measure employee engagement, assess organizational effectiveness, and forecast future industry developments—and also make suggestions for improvement. Lawyers are also using technology and AI to carry out essential tasks, including analyzing thousands or millions of pages with natural language processing and more that would typically take a paralegal years to go through. However, it is possible that primarily outsiders will develop robo-lawyers and robo-doctors, just as it was the outsider Apple that developed the smartphone. And as this happens, we don't talk of centaurs but of transference, whereby technology shifts activity from workers to consumers.

Furthermore, there is an increasing amount of automation involved, especially for repeat purchases. For example, the Tmall Genie Smart Speaker from Alibaba was introduced back in 2017 and helps consumers stream music, surf the web, control their home, and make purchases. It's as simple as saying, "Tmall Genie, I want to buy some milk," after which the speaker and integrated software will provide different options for you to choose from. Amazon has a similar offering with its Alexa-enabled speakers, which also integrate with your smartphone and subscription services. Even the Amazon Dash (a physical button that allowed for immediate reordering of fast-moving consumer goods such as laundry detergent and toilet paper), which was pioneering and cutting edge when it launched in 2014, has been replaced by smartphone and voice-activated controls instead.

Industries typically considered low tech will also go through a renaissance. For example, as we have seen, farming is moving from being labor-intensive, manual work to being high tech, AI-, and robot-enabled. New climate innovations will happen; we will cultivate edible and tasty meat in labs with stem cells that are cheaper, less polluting to produce, and do not harm animals in the process. There will be mass disintermediation, digitization, automation, and AI-enablement across service industries like education, health care, and financial services, and anything to do with people and physical hardware, including the transportation, hotel, and manufacturing industries, will become automated and self-governing, such as self-driving cars. Other examples include a radical shift to digital currencies and digital data storage such as blockchain. The days of handwritten and printed medical records, bank ledgers, or real estate certificates will cease. Again, virtually all industries will be dramatically different ten years from now, and many will be unrecognizable.

There will be mass disintermediation, digitization, automation, and AI-enablement across virtually all service industries.

FASTER CYCLES OF CREATIVE DISRUPTION
THROUGH TECH-FIRST START-UPS

Creative disruption has and always will be an important part of any well-functioning and innovative capitalist system. Only about 10 percent of Fortune 500 companies from 1955 are on the Fortune 500 list today.[1] The remaining 450 or so companies have either gone bankrupt, been acquired, or contracted, often due to a significant loss of competitiveness relative to other companies.

What is different today is that the rate of change and disruption is speeding up. The average lifetime of an S&P 500 company in 1935 was ninety years, while in 2010 that number had fallen to eighteen. More recent studies show that the number has continued to fall; for example, one study from 2015 found that the typical company lasts about ten years before it is bought out, merges, or gets liquidated. Corporate disruption is speeding up, and statistically the risk of failing is among the highest it's ever been. Again, the forces of creative destruction are increasing, and the trend will likely continue.

Average company lifespan on S&P 500 index (in years)

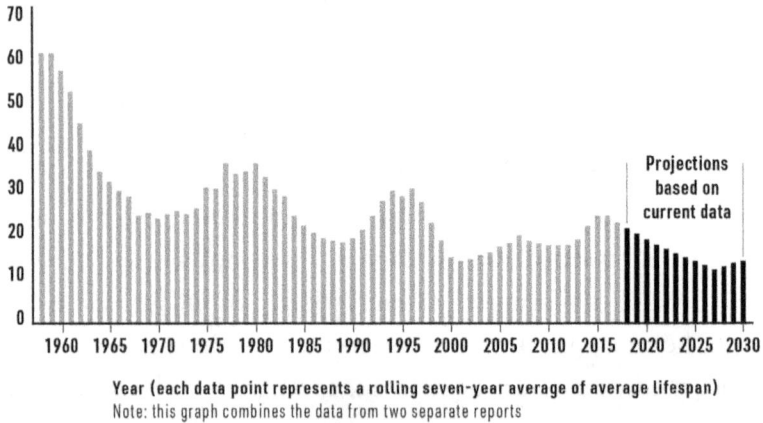

Year (each data point represents a rolling seven-year average of average lifespan)
Note: this graph combines the data from two separate reports

Figure 27.1. Average company life span on the S&P 500 Index.[2]

A big driver of this disruption is technology, and specifically tech-first start-ups, and the speed at which these nascent organizations are displacing established players is rising. The ten most valuable companies in the world are now predominantly data companies, instead of the previous list with oil companies, automakers, retailers, and industrial manufacturing companies. Or, to put it in other words, previously the biggest business was mainly from the industrial economy. Now it's mainly from the precision economy.

We are also seeing growing amounts of investment capital diverted to venture capital and start-ups and an increasing share of the economy composed of relatively young organizations. In other words, creative disruption has increased in the past, and as technology trends continue to speed up the general pace of business, the scale and pace of creative destruction will increase.

An increasing number of so-called tech-first start-ups will emerge. This is the phenomenon where a start-up enters a sector where incumbents use some technologies but don't have these as its key competitive feature. When a tech-first start-up enters such a sector, it prioritizes cutting-edge technologies and thereby eats into the profit pool available in the sector.

Increasingly, incumbents in sectors with big profit pools are attacked by young tech-first start-ups.

Traditional companies fighting back may end up looking very different and disrupting themselves to survive and thrive. In fact, we posit that most organizations will have to go through a profound technological revolution in the next three to five years (consisting of everything from their products and services, ways of working, and capabilities and culture), or risk being left behind.

Most growth start-ups today are *born* digitally across the spectrum. They have the benefit of not having legacy products or old ways of working. Nor do they have any customers to start with, which on the surface definitely looks like a disadvantage. However, this enables them to approach the markets in entirely new ways. These start-ups are mostly radically different, and, yes, tech-first.

Another interesting duality is that start-ups and new entrants are at times completely redrawing industry boundaries, while at other times they are narrowing the focus and specificity of products. For example, Apple started as a computer company but has now branched into personal finance, health care, TV, video games, news, books, and education. It simply attacks these huge legacy profit pools with a smart tech-first approach.

The same holds true for other large technology players, which started out with specific products but have expanded significantly beyond their traditional industry boundaries. Incumbent companies must therefore increasingly include "nontraditional" companies as their competitors. Take health care, for example, which now includes Apple, Facebook, Google, Amazon, Baidu, and Walmart as established players across various parts of the value chain. The same goes for finance, education, media, journalism, and a host of other industries. Tech-first giants are attacking from all sides, eating from the cake.

Incumbent companies must now increasingly include "nontraditional" competitors.

This is what giants do, but at the other extreme, we see start-ups targeting very specific products or services. For example, while traditional banks often offer a broad range of products, new players have emerged that focus exclusively on corporate credit cards, personal investing, or digital payments. The same goes for manufacturing, where you have tech-first niche players within almost all areas—even those where large companies typically dominate—such as skin care, clothing, jewelry, and liquors.

Starting up is getting cheaper all the time. A major reason is that start-ups today can rent/lease industrial equipment, including advanced robotics and 3D printers. They can also pay for software on a monthly software-as-a-service basis, rent digital storage space in the cloud, and outsource virtually all tasks through freelance marketplaces. As such, their start-up costs can often be kept extremely low compared to the past, with few fixed costs and initial investments required. It also gives them easier access to venture money.

This allows them to enter the market with relatively little risk, focus on just one product, and then attack at high speed. In competitive strategy, this is called a salami tactic (akin to how you slice a salami), where smaller tech-first players chip away at incumbents one piece at a time. Each individual move is too small to warrant a major countermove, but over time there can be a dramatic shift in market share.

Start-ups are often biting at the profit pools controlled by legacy companies one piece at a time. They enjoy that the costs of running start-ups are constantly going down while funding opportunities go up.

Of course, one benefit that established companies have is that they typically have stronger balance sheets and existing bases of loyal customers, which makes them more resilient to economic shocks and downturns—such as those experienced by many industries during COVID-19. Established companies will also typically have larger budgets for things such as capability building, investments, and hiring.

However, the trend is quite clear. The advantages of size and depth are often not sufficient for established organizations to survive. They too must think tech-first (which typically means digital tech) and disrupt themselves before they are disrupted by others. However, those who view technology as an opportunity rather than a threat will prosper and more easily reap the rewards of their efforts. Those who don't will fall behind the competition.

> **As the rate of innovation goes up, so does the rate of creative destruction, while the average life span of companies goes down. An obvious countermeasure for legacy companies is to try to disrupt themselves.**

In the 1980s and 1990s, a digital transformation meant embracing computers and everything that entailed for people who had previously done everything in an analogue way. As it became possible, this included using the world wide web for information gathering, file sharing, and email, and creating websites to begin to reach consumers online. And for some lucky individuals, it meant getting access to a pager, a Palm Pilot PDA, or even a mobile phone. For most, these changes were profound.

In the 2000s, digital transformation meant a presence on new social media platforms such as Facebook, YouTube, and Twitter, as well as building online sales channels and even digital business models. The most forward-leaning companies started to accept digital payments. After 2010, organizations began in earnest to get into social media marketing and leverage consumer data. For most organizations, all these changes were profound.

However, it's only really since 2015 or later that for most organizations, a digital transformation truly has meant far more powerful and profound technologies such as the cloud, big data analytics, artificial intelligence, digitization, and automation. And it is also very recent that some have begun dabbling in areas such as VR and AR, IoT, wearable tech, and 3D printing. For many organizations, such changes continue to be profound.

UNINTENTIONAL TECH COMPANIES

Unfortunately, many companies still view tech as a peripheral feature where it should be part of their core. Technologies are converging and reaching a scale at which they will completely and inevitably transform the business landscape. Rather than continuing to play catch-up, why not acknowledge that almost every company must become a tech company if it is to be viable in the future, whether it likes it or not? And if indeed the shift to becoming a tech company is unintentional and somewhat forced, the more quickly organizations make it intentional, the better.

> Almost every company is now a tech company,
> whether they like it or not.

Digital had already snuck into every industry before the start of the pandemic in 2020.[3] However, during 2020 and 2021, digital adoption grew significantly in most industries, including entertainment, utilities, public sector services, banking, education, health care, and retail. Interestingly, developing countries such as Brazil, India, China, and Mexico have had *faster* growth rates in digital adoption in this period, meaning they are catching up to countries in the EU and the US, partly by bypassing legacy technologies.[4]

HOW DOES TECH-FIRST HAPPEN IN PRACTICE?

Becoming a tech company starts with people and culture. Leaders and employees across departments must be radically upskilled and ways of working must change. Perhaps oddly, even technology leaders like Microsoft struggled to adapt to the new digital revolution, and one of the first things Natya Sadella did upon becoming CEO in 2014 was hit reset and undertake a comprehensive transformation of the organization's culture and collaboration approach. "Innovation was being replaced by bureaucracy. Teamwork was being replaced by internal politics. We were falling behind," he says. "But what upset me more was that our own people just accepted it."

If it's not easy for Microsoft, it's not easy. However, Sadella started by giving all senior leaders a book that was required reading. The book was *Nonviolent Communication* by Marshall B. Rosenberg, which focuses on the critical skill of empathy.[5] Sadella knew that if Microsoft was to fulfill its potential, he would need to break down silos and have different areas of the business collaborate on new and market-leading ideas. He also sought to create a learning culture, which is typically harder to do the more successful a company is. But he wanted to move from a know-it-all culture to a learn-it-all culture.

> Move from a know-it-all culture to a learn-it-all culture.

Why did Sadella focus so much on empathy, by the way? Because empathy is critical not just for internal collaboration but also for innovation. Sadella knew that without empathy, Microsoft would never truly understand customer needs, let alone meet them.[6] Customer centricity is one of the most important hallmarks of successful start-up tech companies, and it requires a fundamentally different way of solving problems anchored in design thinking and human-centeredness.

What about handling the actual technologies? In our experience, most employees in organizations have heard of blockchain, big data analytics, machine learning, and perhaps IoT, but few can truly explain the concepts, let alone apply them to improve their daily work. Your culture and starting point might be very different from Microsoft's, but chances are that some degree of technology-related upskilling and new hiring is required, and fast.

Thereafter comes application and experimentation of the technologies. Execution is moving toward an iterative test-and-learn approach, typically done in cross-functional teams. Many organizations get stuck here, and it shows. For example, as we write this, few of what we would call relevant standard technologies are actually deployed well enough—if at all—in the mainstream financial industry. Just see for yourself in Figure 27.2.

Financial institution readiness to leverage digital technologies

Please indicate the level of readiness of your organization to leverage these technologies to deliver expected business outcomes (Scale of 1-5, where 1 is very low and 5 is very high)

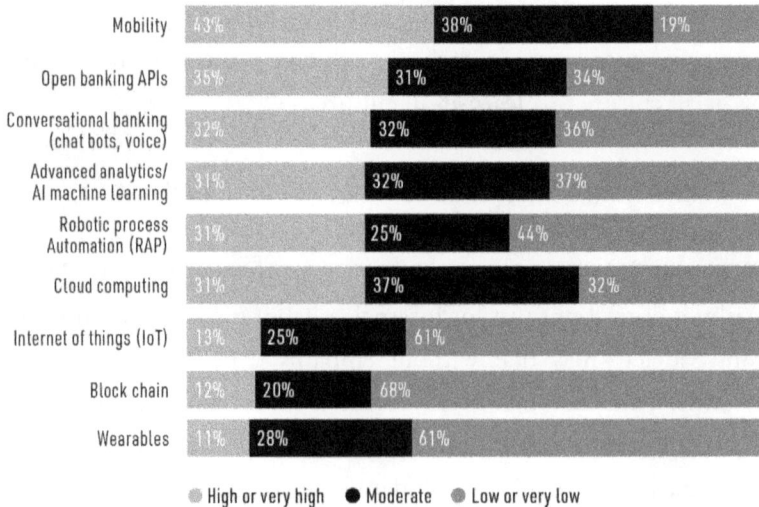

Figure 27.2. Financial institution readiness to leverage digital technologies (indicated readiness to leverage these technologies to deliver expected business outcomes).[7]

ENTERING THE WINNER-TAKES-ALL GAME

In practice, organizations must use customer journey maps and an understanding of converging technologies to completely redefine the way they create value through their products and services. This can often mean disrupting yourself and your core business models. The importance of setting direction and making bold moves continues to hold true when it comes to digital transformation.

Markets are often winner-takes-all due to primarily three phenomena:

- Network effects (the service becomes more attractive for any user the more users there are)

- Switching costs (it's too complex for clients to change suppliers)

- Big data (the biggest players have the best knowledge)

This is why for many tech companies bold first-mover moves have often paid off. However, fast follower strategies and efficient execution can also generate significant value when it comes to entering new tech markets.[8] But this also means that if you have considered your company non-tech and are turning it into tech, these are the new rules to play by.

Sadella pushed hard into cloud computing and made bold decisions around moving from a license to a subscription mode, giving Windows away for free, offering Xbox games as-a-service, dropping the Nokia phone project, and revamping the user experience.[9] He was not scared to kill ventures that weren't deemed successful and saw cannibalization in a very different way than many others do. "The move to the cloud is actually not cannibalistic. There may be time frames where our business models are shifting. But in terms of total addressable market for us and our ability to add more value to our customers, it's a massive total addressable market expansion."[10]

SERVE YOUR CLIENTS WITH TECH

The frequent need for bold decisions also applies to internal processes and ways of working. All employees have a customer—these might just be internal ones—and must be constantly looking for ways to redesign what they do through technology. For example, big data analytics, AI, and robotic process automation can be applied widely already today. Start with the data you already have, just to get started. Most functions could benefit from some type of voice-assisted support, and managers should have bots under them to support repetitive tasks—indeed, why not make the number of bots a metric of corporate success, rather than the number of humans you are managing?

All employees have customers—internal or external. And all must constantly think how these can be served better with technology.

When it comes to using data, leading companies are smart and make decisions based on real-time data flows. Many of these decisions are automated and predictive. For example, algorithms influence around one-third of the decisions consumers make on Amazon and more than 80 percent on Netflix.[11] Stories abound about how accurately Netflix can predict the success of shows based on a host of factors before it buys the rights or invests time to produce it.[12] They have also had surprise hits such as *Squid Game*, but then their algorithms learn from those as well.

Obviously, the exponential growth and convergence of technologies are at the core of why all growth companies must become tech companies. In addition, we see the rapidly falling costs of many start-up activities, which means that new competitors can disrupt markets more quickly. Start-ups are typically born digital and have an inherent advantage in this sense compared to established companies.

Furthermore, the newer generations have grown up with smartphones at their fingertips, and they expect fast, online, and typically self-service solutions to their needs. They have been spoiled when it comes to the user experience on leading social media platforms and expect the same smoothness on other websites and apps. Just like young companies can be born digital, so can new generations of clients.

> **As well as young companies are often born digital,
> so are young generations of clients.**

NAVIGATING A DIGITAL REBIRTH

A digital transformation is a multiyear journey that must touch on all areas of the business and should center on *becoming* digital, rather than doing the bare minimum. It touches on strategy, systems, capabilities and culture, processes, and data. It requires taking a broad view, and rather than focusing on specific technologies, building and hiring a true digital workforce that can navigate and apply a wide range of cutting-edge technologies.

Setting a digital strategy requires solving for both the near term so you don't miss the bus on what's happening in front of you and making requisite bets on the medium and long term. It will likely require significant investments, even in areas that are often too early to become profitable for at least five years. It's critical to start getting ahead of the curve and building the right capabilities and experience that can only be gained by *doing* and experimenting over and over again. You will likely have to transform a broad range of areas, including your capabilities and culture, core technology stack, data and analytics, and core processes.[13] Again, if it was not easy for Microsoft, it is not easy.

For capabilities and culture, clarify which roles need to know what, and invest heavily in capability building. Furthermore, plug capability gaps by hiring top technical talent—leapfrogging rather than playing catch-up will pay off many times in the future. Changing the culture requires changing a full system, including the incentives and talent management systems, on-the-job mentoring leadership, role modeling, and communication. Here are four good questions to check if things are going right:

- Are people incentivized to prioritize digital?

- Do people know what great looks like?

- Are leaders asking the right questions?

- Do employees understand the urgency and what they are expected to do?

Measure progress regularly. For example, measure the percentage of your workforce with digital skills and specializations, employee understanding of various technologies, and ongoing employee sentiments regarding the digital transformation.

For processes, put the customer at the center of everything you do, both internally and externally. Make creation of customer personas, journey maps, empathy maps, and other design thinking tools required competencies. Instead of improving processes, reimagine them. Measure customer satisfaction as a standard metric, as well as net promoter score. This also applies to internal customers.

In terms of data, train or hire enough data scientists who can build and analyze your data architecture, as well as individuals who can straddle both the business and data worlds with sufficient breadth. And consider using data science as-a-service companies. Data is already the new oil, and the most valuable companies in the world are already those who can harness the best data.

An extra word of caution regarding cybersecurity. We do not have space to dwell on this topic here, but we will suffice with a quote by former FBI director Robert S. Mueller III: "There are only two types of companies: those that have been hacked and those that will be hacked." Some will argue that a third kind of company exists—those that have been hacked but don't know it. That wasn't meant as a joke, so take this warning seriously and over-invest in this area.

Overall, it is critical to have an ecosystem perspective and make bold moves. The risk with cloud and XaaS is that providers will be spread too thin, and integration thereafter will become a nightmare. There will be migrations, yes, and they will be timely, but choosing the easy option of staying on legacy systems just a little longer means you are missing out on future efficiencies.

There are practical ways to accelerate your digital rebirth. You could take your ten most important processes and challenge the process owners to reimagine them with the use of new technology. At some organizations, there's a step even before this: identifying the process owners in the first place. Chances are, you can do the processes faster and with higher quality if you apply bold ideas and dare to reimagine them. Similarly, you could take your five most important recurring decisions, whether that means hiring, promotions, new business investment, or purchasing, and ask how these might be radically improved with the use of big data and AI.

The following chart can help you assess your current point of departure and where your biggest priorities lie.

From . . .		To . . .
Analog company where technology is an add-on or an afterthought	→	Digital-first company where technology is the DNA of the company
Technology strategy is in support of the overall business strategy	→	Technology and digitalization are core components of the strategy itself
Employees do not fully understand the latest technologies and how they can be applied in their daily work	→	Employees are technology leaders who constantly push the boundaries of what's possible with available technologies
Cumbersome internal processes and legacy systems, with limited incentives to improve	→	Reimagined, automated, and simple internal processes that measure internal customer satisfaction
Decisions typically made with little or no real-time data available	→	Data-driven decision-making based on big data analytics and predictive insights

Chapter 28

NO TIME TO DIE

The theater can be a wonderful pastime and offers an exciting get-away from our daily life. Seeing the gripping James Bond saga *No Time to Die* on a big-screen IMAX theater with immersive surround sound is really something else, and you can't help but get swept away by the action.

Unfortunately, organizations often approach innovation as a flurry of initiatives and activities that are separate from business-as-usual activities and limited to a handful of corporate initiatives. These keep everyone involved busy and, on the surface, look like progress. But in essence nothing truly changes, as the underlying structure, culture, and business models in the organization do not change. This has been dubbed "innovation theater"—lots of action and entertainment, but only ever a short-term escape from reality. Like the handsome cowboy who is all hat but no cattle.[1] By the way, it is not only within corporations that useless innovation theater occurs. It is also quite common when the public sector wants to spend money stimulating innovation.

HOW ORGANIZATIONS LOSE THEIR FITNESS AND DIE

Try to imagine an organization as a human body. They age. This is because they develop rigidities, at both the individual and organizational level. Raw human brain capabilities also peak at embarrassingly young ages—mostly midteens to midthirties, depending on task. We therefore work with rules of thumb, habits, and biases to solve problems we face regularly. These mental models can be efficient as they help us act quickly, but they can also impede creativity and innovation. "I do this because that is what I have always done."

Organizations, too, develop rigidities in terms of structure, processes, performance, and reward systems, which again are helpful in terms of coordination and swift execution—but detrimental when it comes to reinvention.[2] However, Future Fit organizations do not allow themselves to get too rigid or comfortable. Instead, they continuously disrupt themselves rather than waiting for others to do so.

The natural tendency for organizations is to lose fitness over time— just like it naturally happens to human bodies.

When you study the root causes of organizational failures, you will find that the vast majority of cases are due to the organization failing to adapt to a changing external environment. In essence, there is a mismatch between the external context and the internal strategies and operating model of the organization. Rather than being a victim of "bad luck," the organization has typically failed to act or acted too late. In fact, in sessions with leaders where we have probed to uncover the real root causes of their failures and missteps, there are often only a handful of reasons. They almost always come back to how the company is organized, how it makes decisions, its leadership, and its culture.

Invincibility bias and excessive positivity: The belief that the current strategy and operating model is a guaranteed recipe for future success, because it has worked in the past.

Decision-making biases: Being influenced by available information, even if it is irrelevant (anchoring bias), assigning greater probability to recent events or events we can recall (recency and availability biases), and looking for confirming rather than disconfirming evidence (confirmation bias).

Fear of taking risks: Choosing the "safer bet" rather than the unknown or high-risk/high-reward option (loss-aversion bias). This applies to all types of decisions, from speaking up in meetings to broad-ranging strategic choices.

Short-term focus: Focusing on short-term rewards rather than waiting for a larger future reward (present bias). This is often compounded by financial and nonfinancial incentives that reinforce near-term actions, including stock option–related bonuses and quarterly and yearly outcome KPIs. Short-term thinking can also occur when leaders are on the verge of retiring or looking to change jobs, causing them to delay or avoid launching multiyear initiatives.

Linearity bias: Assuming that a change in one quantity produces a proportional change in another. The human mind prefers to think linearly and often assumes that a change in one quantity produces a proportional change in another. This completely misses exponential trends and technological convergence and can be fatal at a strategic level.

This list is backed up by more comprehensive studies, which find that corporate decline is largely self-inflicted and follows a predictable pattern. The good news, though, is that these mistakes are not inevitable, and organizations can maintain the power to turn things around and reinvent themselves.

UNLEASHING CREATIVITY

When *Squid Game* was launched on Netflix toward the end of 2021, it became the network's most watched show in less than four weeks. In the series, 456 debt-ridden contestants accept an invitation to play a series of children's games in the hope of winning the grand prize. But the catch is that if they lose a game, they die. Intrigued yet?

One of the games has to do with carving out a preset shape from a round honeycomb candy about ten centimeters in diameter. The shape has been loosely pressed into the candy so that it is thinner and more fragile where the pattern is marked. The participants only receive a needle and are told they have ten minutes. If they break the shape or run out of time, they die.

You can imagine the adrenaline running through the participants' veins, especially as they begin to hear gunshots and see fellow participants drop to the floor because of broken honeycombs. Their hands are literally shaking, and they are sweating while trying to concentrate on the task at hand. Needless to say, this environment makes it much more challenging to take risks than one where there is not such a high cost of trying new things. Stressful situations trigger the sympathetic nervous system, which makes us more alert and ready to take action but also less aware of our surroundings, less empathetic, and less open to new ideas.

Why then are so many organizations more fear-based and rules-driven rather than trusting and supportive? To truly unleash innovation, organizations must frame the challenges and opportunities they face in positive ways and help employees perform at their best. This means creating a positive, strength-based, and supporting environment that rewards innovation and new thinking. This doesn't mean giving entirely free rein, however. Creativity works best under some degree of constraints, which ensures that the organization is moving in the same direction.[3]

A STRUCTURE TO THE MADNESS

It can be tempting to view innovation as an activity centered on moments of brilliance by lone geniuses who suddenly transform products and industries. And it is definitely a combination of art, craft, and even science. But the most innovative companies are very structured in how they decipher supertrends and approach innovation. They are very clear about what type of innovation they are looking for (e.g., incremental, disruptive, radical). They also have a stringent innovation process[4] that typically includes the following steps:

- Having an inspirational purpose that frames the customer opportunity in a way that resonates with all departments and levels

- Discovery, customer engagement, and ideation

- Idea evaluation (e.g., desirability, viability, feasibility)

- Customer testing and validation (e.g., proof of concept, minimum viable product, alpha release, beta release, split testing)

- Launch-ready product release

- Execution and scale

This type of innovation funnel starts with a large number of ideas that then must pass through a number of gates or checkpoints to ensure certain criteria are met. It is definitely a numbers game, as it is very hard—if not impossible—to pick a winner up front. One piece of research found that out of every hundred venture capital investments into start-ups, 64.8 percent will fail, 33.7 percent will find some degree of success (between 1–20x returns), 1.1 percent will achieve 20–50x returns, while only 0.4 percent, or 4 out of 1,000 investments, will make returns 50x or more of the invested capital.[5]

The higher the return you expect, the more projects you will need to invest small sums in. One way to minimize risks is to use metered funding, where new ideas or ventures are only given a portion of the required budget after passing each of the four or five gates in the process, rather than approving the budget up front, which is typically how organizations work with their yearly planning cycles.

One approach to innovation in larger organizations is to start many projects but use metered funding, where new ideas or ventures are only given a portion of the required budget after passing each of the four or five gates in the process.

IS THAT A *DRAGONS' DEN*?

Because the speed of change is increasing so quickly and the nature of problems is becoming so interconnected, it is impossible to plan everything from the top. Sometimes the best ideas are sparked serendipitously and without the intention of creating something new. As such, execution, as well as idea generation and innovation, must be enabled across the organization. Employees who are closest to the relevant action and actually carry out the work often have unique customer and business insights that can unleash a host of innovative ideas. However, they must be supported.

> **Idea generation and innovation must be enabled across the organization.**

Leading organizations use a wide range of approaches to help individuals and teams identify and act on opportunities they see. We've already discussed the importance of creating platforms where self-forming and empowered teams can come together in fluid ways.

Another no-regret move is to build core innovation capabilities at scale through digital and in-person modules such as design thinking, customer empathy mapping, customer journey mapping, ideation and creativity (yes, it can be learned), business model mapping (to document key assumptions and idea viability), and rapid prototyping. This is on top of the no-regret call to enhance technological fluency and data literacy in your organization.

It is also helpful to ensure adequate resources for these types of ideas, whether that is money, time (e.g., allowing employees a percentage of their time to work on side projects), or other assets such as shared VR/AR headsets, 3D printers, or "micro-factories" where employees can experiment with bringing an idea to life. Other ideas include the following:

- Intrapreneurship programs that provide a programmatic apprenticeship of theory and practice for select individuals (like Ericsson has done)[6]

- Inspiration budgets that individuals or teams can use on inviting speakers and doing events to get them out of their comfort zones and daily routine and inspire new ways of thinking

- Revamping the physical office space to foster more collaboration and creativity

- Appointing innovation evangelists

One organization we worked with provided digital and physical idea boxes throughout the company and *guaranteed* that the ideas would be reviewed and responded to within forty-eight hours.

We've also seen numerous organizations use innovation campaigns and awards, as well as hosting *Dragons' Den/Shark Tank*–type competitions (these are shows where entrepreneurs present their projects to potential investors). This can also be extended to external participants. Hilton, for example, has used the *Dragons' Den* method with suppliers with the goal of saving money and reducing the environmental footprint.[7]

INNOVATION AS AN INSTITUTIONAL PRIORITY

In addition to enabling individuals to innovate, organizations must also make decisions that galvanize a broader set of resources in a unified direction. For example, innovation jams or hackathons that bring together employees for a finite period of time to solve a specific goal are widely used by organizations like IBM, Facebook, and NASA. When they're in person, people sometimes bring sleeping bags and compete over twenty-four to forty-eight hours nonstop. Online hackathons have the advantage of being able to tap into a global audience, and they can sometimes include tens of thousands of people.

Some organizations set up "red teams," which are established with the sole objective of figuring out ways to disrupt the main organization. Skunkworks projects are another strategy commonly used, which typically entails a small group of individuals who research and develop a project with the goal of doing something radical. The advantage of skunkworks projects is that the team can operate separately from and unhindered by existing organizational processes and paradigms. Sometimes, these projects are secret and only ever revealed after launch. The term *skunkworks* was coined by Lockheed Martin, an American aerospace and defense company, which used the approach during World War II and continues to use it to this day. Often, skunkworks are housed in a different building from the main office, and teams are given higher degrees of autonomy than usual. Once proven successful, the projects are then scaled and integrated into the core business. Some organizations, however, seek to create new ventures as a business model in itself. For them, success is not reintegration but rather serial spin-offs.

There are also a number of organizational levers you can pull. For example, Johnson & Johnson uses a decentralized approach to spark innovation and train corporate leaders.[8] Some organizations use large-scale hiring to rapidly upskill their workforce and spark new thinking. For example, they may hire hundreds of data scientists, design thinkers, and innovation experts in one go, or hire experts in a specific industry that the company wants to enter into (e.g., a car company hiring power technology and battery engineers). This can be formalized by setting up new centers of excellence or horizontal organizational units (that innovate across entities), respectively. Creating a more diverse and inclusive organization is another way to enhance creativity and innovation.

HAVE MONEY, SHOW ME THE IDEA

A discussion about innovation wouldn't be complete without considering the ecosystem level. Accessing the best talent, ideas, and execution capabilities requires tapping into the meta-organization (e.g., expert, youth, and customer advisory boards), crowdsourcing ideas, and even establishing corporate venture funds and accelerators that invest in and support start-ups. Acquisitions are a wholesale way to get access to new technologies, IP, and talent, and alliances have also been increasing in recent years, including among big players such as Amazon, Berkshire Hathaway, and JP Morgan.[9]

Other ecosystem tactics include setting up app stores (e.g., Apple and Google), orchestrating or participating in platforms (e.g., Microsoft and Alibaba), going open source (e.g., Tesla) or open architecture (e.g., Credit Suisse), and developing business hubs (e.g., the free zones in the UAE and China).

THIRTY-FIVE WAYS TO STAY ALIVE

If your organization is not entirely young anymore, and if you think it nevertheless is not time to die right now, here are thirty-five ways to institutionalize corporate innovation at the individual/team level, organizational level, and ecosystem level.

Individual/team level	Organizational level	Ecosystem level
Self-forming and empowered teams	Serial spin-offs	Meta-organization
Building core innovation capabilities at scale	Skunkworks	Crowdsourcing
Intrapreneurship program	Decentralization	Corporate venture fund
Inspiration budget	Horizontal units	Corporate accelerators and incubators
Innovation awards	New centers of excellence and digital factories	Acquisitions
Internal *Dragons' Dens*	Business model cloning and quickly copying others' success	Alliance
Percentage of time dedicated for own projects	Innovation jams	Open source
Access to resources	Online hackathon	Open architecture
Digital ideas box with guaranteed action	Participation in external start-up accelerators	App stores
Revamping the virtual and physical office space	Transparent innovation dashboard	Hub development
Appointing innovation evangelists	Disruptive and radical organization-wide events	Orchestrating and participating across ecosystems
	Building a diverse workforce	
	Establishing red teams	

As you can see, predictable and democratized innovation requires an integrated and coordinated approach rather than a few one-off innovation theater initiatives. It is linked heavily to other parts of the organization and builds off having an inspirational purpose, setting direction rather than destination with bold moves, enabling self-forming and empowered teams, becoming a tech company, and tapping into your broader ecosystem.

All of this presupposes that the organization continues to manage the core business competitively, without losing focus. Future Fit organizations manage for both the immediate term and for the future *in parallel*, and they manage budgets and talent accordingly. It is typically not advised to put all your top talent either on failing ventures to turn them around (as large conglomerates have been prone to do in the past) or to throw them all into the shiny new ventures that are not yet proven. Instead, take a holistic approach that considers both immediate and future needs, as well as the specific skill profiles of your top resources compared to the skill profiles of the various positions in demand.

The following chart can help you assess your current point of departure and where your biggest priorities lie in this area.

From ...		To ...
Financial targets and fear-driven and risk-averse organization	→	Positively framed opportunity and a culture of courage and possibility
Innovation as one-hit wonders with limited governance or process	→	Structured and steady flow of innovation; managed portfolio
Primarily top-down innovation	→	Adequate resources, support and incentives that enable innovation to happen anywhere
No tolerance for change or disrupting the status quo	→	Bold moves at the organizational level across a wide range of levers (e.g., skunkworks, hackathons, and new centers of excellence)
Closed innovation approach with a "not invented here" mindset	→	Ecosystem approach with a collaborative and open mindset (e.g., through alliances, crowdsourcing, and corporate venture funds)

Chapter 29

WHAT YOUTUBE CAN TEACH US ABOUT CORPORATE LEARNING PROCESSES

What if we gave you $1,000 per person in your organization and asked you to invest it with a flat or even negative return on investment (ROI)? What if we even asked employees to take time away from their day-to-day work to use the money, leaving them more stressed and frustrated afterward? Does this sound like a recipe for madness? What if we asked you to repeat this process year after year after year?

What we just described is not entirely dissimilar from how learning and development (L&D) takes place in many organizations. We're exaggerating, admittedly, but just a little. Historically, learning and knowledge management has always been one step behind and in many cases seen as an unnecessary cost center. Identifying skill gaps relied on yearly or biyearly performance reviews, and these skill gaps were thereafter plugged by L&D programs that relied on in-person teaching methods. These processes were far removed from the speed of business and how modern work increasingly gets done.

Globally, organizations spend nearly $400 billion on training and development each year, yet few can truly show how their learning efforts provide bottom line impact and a positive return on investment. Consider that 75 percent of managers in one survey were dissatisfied with their company's L&D function. Or that 70 percent of employees report that they don't have mastery of the skills needed to do their jobs. Or that only 12 percent of employees apply new skills learned in L&D programs to their jobs.[1]

And it's not like the external environment is standing still. We know that industries are being disrupted faster than ever, and job and skill requirements in five years will be very different from what they are now. The World Economic Forum predicts that 50 percent of employees will need to be significantly reskilled between 2020 and 2025.[2]

The reasons? As technology continues to automate repetitive and simple tasks, humans must take on more creative and abstract tasks requiring more emotional intelligence, conceptual problem-solving, and systems thinking.

Now we're not trying to pin all responsibility on HR or L&D departments, because success also requires a shift in the broader corporate culture and for each individual to take responsibility as well. However, the facts speak for themselves: as the world around us speeds up, a new paradigm of learning is needed.

TEACHING FOR REAL CHANGE

Let's start with the learning strategy. Most organizations have poor governance for learning, often delegating it down many layers in the organization, and they take a reactive approach to it. Like many other budgets, they are often set yearly and are far removed from actual job needs. During business transformations, learning is often an afterthought.

This approach completely misses strategic learning needs. At worst, budgets are used by employees on what they find enjoyable, because they have the money to spend. This is not necessarily bad in terms of employee engagement and motivation, but it should not be confused with job-related skill building.

Instead, organizations should couple L&D to the very transformations and objectives they are trying to achieve and use L&D as a direct enabler of the strategy. In other words, don't just teach how to do what you already do—just a tad better. Instead, go to the core of what you actually want to achieve, then teach for this.

For example, a bank call center strategy might simultaneously aim to reduce costs by automating repetitive and simple calls to improve customer service and to grow share of wallet per customer. Many goals, yes, but a realistic situation. Working backwards from these goals, the organization can then identify the specific behaviors and skills required for the call center agent of the future. For example, with new call routing technology and AI-enabled internet bots, call center agents no longer have to answer calls about simple tasks such as address changes or billing statements but instead must focus on more complex issues such as payment disputes, fraud, and even sales of new, differentiated products. Once the skills are defined, the organization can look at current skills levels of call center agents today and then design learning interventions to bridge those gaps. Super-targeted and totally linked to the business strategy.

With this also comes a shift in how learning impact is measured. A typical framework like Kirkpatrick's model has four levels of L&D impact measurement:

- Participant reaction to the training

- Degree of learning

- Behavioral change on the job

- Contribution of L&D to business results

Today, most organizations measure L&D impact in the wrong order. They focus predominantly on measuring participants' reactions to learning (Was the training engaging? Was it a good use of your time? How was the facilitator?) and, to some extent, degree of learning through things like short multiple-choice assessments before and after the training. The two latter levels, which are about the practical consequences of the training, are rarely measured in practice.[3]

Future Fit organizations must flip the measurement framework on its head and work backwards to create the learning strategy. This starts by defining the business objectives that L&D is trying to enable—for example, improving first call resolution from 73 percent to 75 percent and improving customer Net Promoter Score (NPS) from 20 to 35 for a bank's call center. Thereafter determine the skills and behaviors needed on the job for a given population group (e.g., knowledge of credit card products, dispute resolution skills, and empathy). Assess current proficiency across key skills and prioritize the skill gaps to focus on, and then develop learning required to bridge the gap (including both formal and on-the-job training).

> **Train for specific business objectives, not just for the sake of skill acquisition itself.**

The result is a learning strategy that clearly maps out how many people need to know which skills, to what degree they need to know them, and by when. Budgets are then set depending on priorities and what it will take to close the gap. Closing the skill gap is not just seen as the remit of the internal L&D function but is a shared KPI between L&D and the business. L&D is treated as a partner to the business rather than as a service provider, and return on investment can more clearly be connected to value at stake from improving OKRs (objectives and key results).

ADAPTING THE WHAT, WHEN, WHERE, AND HOW

Before the pandemic, classrooms in many schools and organizations still resembled those of long ago: instructors had virtually no information about who was in the room in terms of skills and experiences; it was a one-size-fits-all delivery approach; learning took place far removed from the actual application itself; and it occurred way ahead of when it was needed.

L&D is often still designed for an in-person world where jobs, tasks, and employees are stable and in which the pace of execution and decision-making is slow. This fundamentally doesn't work in today's world, where tasks are becoming more and more project-based, undertaken by impermanent teams, staffed with more and more contingent (freelance) workers, and where things need to get done ever faster. Technology has shifted not only *what* we need to learn, but also *when*, *where*, and *how* we learn. If L&D is to effectively support organizations to transform, L&D itself must be transformed.[4]

Thankfully, this is happening. Indeed, we are now seeing a shift from just-in-case to just-in-time learning. This means that instead of learning being removed from work (for example, in a classroom), it is happening within the flow of work.

It is also much more targeted in terms of skill needs. Instead of having to sit through many hours of an in-person lecture, you can learn in short bursts (sometimes as little as a few minutes). This is enabled by digital micro-courses that focus on one specific skill or subskill. This type of micro-learning has been shown to be vastly more effective than traditional learning in bulk, as it is more tailored to the individual, is more accessible, happens when it is most needed, and caters to the way the majority of us, and especially the younger generations, like to consume media (on the go, through videos, and in short bursts).[5]

We are seeing a shift from just-in-case to just-in-time learning: instead of learning being removed from work (for example, in a classroom), it is happening in the flow of work.

MICRO-LEARNING AS-A-SERVICE

This also has the advantage of moving away from a one-size-fits-all batch delivery approach and toward a personalized on-tap approach. Intesa Sanpaolo, an Italian bank, is an example of this. It realized that its reliance on formal, traditional classroom and e-learning methods were disconnected from the needs of the business, as it was slow, not scalable, and offered limited measurements and analytics. Instead, it was inspired by companies such as Netflix and YouTube and created a cloud-based learning platform that housed redesigned, micro-sized learning content on a wide range of skills. Learners are now provided personalized recommendations and suggestions based on their current needs and preferences, like YouTube does when it offers recommendations and content related to what you have watched and liked in the past. And employees can easily search for additional content they wish to take. In other words, learning is not pushed to them in batches. Instead, they pull it as required.

This sounds a lot like YouTube, and the result has been a dramatic reduction in the time it takes to onboard new employees, perform reskilling, and handle changes of all sorts.[6] You can imagine that a call center agent at Intesa Sanpaolo has a much easier time to develop new product knowledge or learn new skills such as complex dispute resolution in the flow of work with the help of such a learning-as-a-service platform.

> Learning can be more inspired by how YouTube creates individualized playlists than by the classroom one-size-fits-all approach. This also moves from batch to on-tap learning and from a push to a pull approach.

GET TECHY WITH "PHYGITAL" LEARNING

Even for in-person or live virtual sessions, which continue to be important for things such as leadership development or where greater interaction is needed, technology can help provide much more tailored support for the participants present, depending on their needs and real-time feedback. For example, simulations with avatars on VR headsets or iPads feed real-time data back to the facilitator, who can then see how participants are doing. This approach has been dubbed "phygital" and continues to make inroads.

New tech is here, stretching the realm of what's possible, including immersive VR experiences (frequently used in manufacturing or retail environments), AI-enabled simulations with avatars, and fully gamified scenarios that the participant must navigate, which is useful to test skills like conceptual problem-solving. We are even seeing virtual coaches emerge that provide real-time feedback to leaders depending on what they're saying, how they're saying it, and how much they're talking in each conversation or meeting. These "coaches" integrate wearable technology, natural language processing, and big data analytics and can help leaders practice behaviors such as pausing before speaking, listening more in meetings, or varying their tone of voice to be more inspirational while giving presentations. There even exists a version of this called fitness mirrors, where companies such as Tonal, Mirror, Echelon, and Tempo provide mirrors that can transform into screens where life-size fitness instructors do private sessions. These services also offer prerecorded standard training programs, plus the ability to automatically monitor and correct how the client performs the exercises.

One note of caution—technology choices must be driven by the learning strategy (who needs to learn what skills and when). Start with the learning strategy and then determine what method is best suited to close the skill gap.

INSIGHTS AT YOUR FINGERTIPS

Much of what we just said can be summed up with a simple analogy: what happened to the music markets over the last ten years. In the olden days, you bought music on an LP, or you turned on the radio and listened to whatever a radio host fancied to give you. Nowadays, it is much more on tap—much more situational and much smarter.

With mobile devices, you can easily choose when and where you want to watch YouTube videos, including saving them for offline viewing. This is at-your-fingertips availability of personalized, adaptive, pull-based, as-a-service solution to content. It is the same that we must achieve in learning and development in organizations.

To do so, learning must be segmented and chopped up into micro-modules to be delivered on tap.

Ideally, these will also be driven by AI. Adaptive learning predicts what learning modules will work best for a given employee, suggests the module to the right person at the right time and through the right channel, and then collects feedback to continuously improve the results. AI pushes the modules that are most likely to help each team member, but it decides based on the actions of each person, which makes this apparent push actually a pull process.

Ideally, learning is at your fingertips, personalized, adaptive, pull-based, and delivered as-a-service like YouTube.

FEEDBACK BETWEEN PERFORMANCE AND LEARNING

This is enabled by a real-time integration between performance measurement and learning so that on-the-job performance triggers suggested or required learning modules when an employee needs it.

Consider our call center agent. Call centers can now segment calls based on a few cues from the caller, to figure out the type of query (e.g., a specific product, unrecognized charges, or travel insurance advice for an upcoming trip). Natural language processing can determine whether the call query was solved or not, who did most of the talking (customer vs. agent), who had what emotions (anger, frustration, happiness). You can measure how long the call took. Based on all this information, it is relatively easy to see which agents are good at what types of calls, and where they struggle, allowing an adaptive learning algorithm to suggest a micromodule in a targeted way.

Such a machine continues to learn by looking at the performance of agents who did or did not take various modules, as well as by collecting data from agents through micro-assessments or other feedback tools. It can furthermore analyze the effectiveness of modules depending on their length, content format (e.g., video vs. multiple-choice questions vs. drag-and-drop boxes), facilitator, and a host of other factors to continually optimize the learning modules themselves, too. The net result is personalized and predictive learning modules that continuously learn based on real-time data. And then the AI and the agent have morphed into a centaur.

ALL THE KNOWLEDGE IN THE WORLD

"If Siemens knew what it knows, it would be a rich company."[7] So goes an old saying in business.

Okay, it is a rich company, but it could always become even richer. Siemens is a German industrial technology and manufacturing company founded in 1847. In 2022, it has around 300,000 employees spread across about 200 countries.[8] With the breadth and pace of its business activities, no wonder it is difficult for L&D to keep up with the new skill requirements on a constant basis.

There is another way to look at this, however. AI-driven adaptive learning may appear to be a push approach to learning, where learners are fed or mandated to take required learning content. However, it is really a pull approach where employees themselves train the computer and where they are able to find the content they need, exactly when they need it. This will arguably become even more important in the future, when we must increasingly know how to learn and where to get specific information, rather than memorize specific topics. As a result, L&D should ask itself how Siemens might know not only what Siemens knows and thinks, but also what the whole world knows and thinks. This is what YouTube does, when it comes to video (and now audio) content. It knows what its 2 billion active users and 50 million subscribers feel about more than 37 million channels and 800 million videos.

Learning platforms of the future will look much more like YouTube, Netflix, Alibaba, or Amazon than closed knowledge portals. Traditional knowledge management will be replaced by intelligent knowledge curation. The content will be both L&D generated and user generated and will also include links to external sources. Intesa Sanpaolo, the bank example mentioned earlier, has over 1.3 million hours of content in total on its platform. This is 445 years' worth of content, assuming you took eight hours of courses a day, five days a week. It would be impossible for the bank to create anything close to that amount of content per year by itself.

Traditional knowledge management will be replaced by intelligent knowledge curation, where AI constantly guides each person to the most useful snippets of insights.

The role of L&D will thus move toward facilitating knowledge development and acquisition, putting in guardrails for how content is produced and how it is tagged (to make it searchable), measuring the effectiveness of content, and continuously weeding out out-of-date material. Best practices continue to be important, but in line with the more rapidly changing work environment, their lifetime value continues to shorten as well.

Some organizations, such as the military, are taking this even further and are experimenting with brain-machine interfaces (like a real-life *Terminator*) that help their employees extend their cognitive abilities by utilizing the cloud. This allows them to tap into a global pool of knowledge, as well as extend their memory, and even provides them with a more powerful intelligence.

One final word of advice—all of this has to be enabled by a systematic integration with broader organizational processes, culture, and ways of working. Technology alone will not solve the learning imperative but rather underpin a new organizational learning culture. Leaders must role-model a growth and learning mindset and make it clear that the strategies and skills that made the organization successful in the past will not be wholly sufficient to reach its future goals.

LEARNING AT PACE AND SCALE

We believe that the winning organizations of the future will not necessarily be those that know the most today, but those who are best able to learn, unlearn, and relearn at pace and scale.

The below chart can help you assess your current point of departure and where your biggest priorities lie in this area.

From . . .		To . . .
Ad-hoc and reactive learning that is decoupled from strategic objectives	→	Learning strategy and budget closely integrated with the business strategy, with a focus on the skills that matter most
Just-in-case, in-person, and one-size-fits-all learning approach	→	The right content, to the right person, at the right time, enabled by digitized micro-learning modules
Limited feedback loops and measurement of the impact of learning	→	Adaptive learning that gets smarter the more it is used
Knowledge management in a closed ecosystem	→	Intelligent knowledge curation that taps into global knowledge sources
Reliant on best practices and what worked in the past	→	Growth and lifelong learning culture that is able to learn, unlearn, and relearn effectively

Chapter 30

FROM TALENT MANAGEMENT TO TALENT ENABLEMENT

In organizations operating in fast, fluid, and flexible environments, it is problematic to maintain talent management models optimized for the industrial economy but not for the precision and experience economies. Why?

Because the best talent may go out the door. A record number of employees are either actively seeking new job opportunities (more than 50 percent of people by some accounts), and for those who aren't actively seeking, a large share of them would seriously consider switching if approached by a prospective employer.[1] And this will only continue, as more than 60 percent of the global workforce is already made up of millennials and Generation Z, who are projected to have as many as eighteen jobs and six different careers. Employees are more and more looking for jobs that are meaningful, provide opportunities to learn, grow, and advance, and provide flexibility. And of course, compensation remains important.[2]

In fact, a study from 2021 found that more than half of employees globally would consider quitting their jobs if more flexibility was not provided post-pandemic, with millennials more than twice as likely to quit as baby boomers.[3] Employees are more likely than before to see themselves as driving their careers than leaving it up to the organization and are prepared to take action if needed.

> One study showed that 83 percent of employees wanted a hybrid work environment combining in-person interaction with flexibility for remote work.

Coupled with the growth of the gig economy, human cloud, internal job markets, and organizations that must be fast, fluid, and flexible, there is a shift toward a skills economy, where your know-who and know-what are becoming less important than your know-how. Work tasks are increasingly being staffed by internal and external candidates who have the precise skills that the role requires, regardless of their age, education, prior experience, or location.

What this all means is that how organizations manage talent often must change. In fact, the new world of work requires less talent management and more talent enablement, with the goal of empowering individuals with the tools and resources they need to perform in their current role, explore new roles to constantly learn and reinvent themselves, and to truly own their career development.

> The new world of work requires less talent management and more talent enablement.

This has profound implications across the full talent cycle, including filling job openings, performance management, career pathing, L&D, and retention. Just as employees are competing in transparent markets for great jobs, companies are competing in transparent markets for great employees.

> Just as employees are competing in transparent
> markets for great jobs, companies are competing in
> transparent markets for great employees.

CREATING THEIR OWN LADDERS

Talent managers often try to shepherd employees through certain career paths, with a special focus on top talent. They craft detailed workforce strategies to pinpoint exactly how many people they'll need for which roles and by when for the next three to five years. However, as strategic planning has shifted from setting destination toward setting direction based on bold moves, so must strategic workforce planning change. Workforce plans will be approximate, at best, because of the fluidity of business and the market. Instead, talent enablers should focus on creating gig markets in real time and based on skills, not seniority. Of course, cross-cutting organization initiatives and talent investments must still be managed, but they should be supplemented with this fluid approach.

> In talent enablement, the focus is on creating
> ecosystems where talent can find tasks and where they
> can create their own career ladders.

This gives everyone a fair chance to see what is required and reinvent themselves accordingly, regardless of their history. Furthermore, some organizations are even experimenting with matching supply and demand of employees within their wider organizational ecosystem, effectively "renting out" talent if they have a temporary surplus. You can imagine a future where job opportunities and employee skill profiles across the majority of organizations are certified and maintained in one cloud database, making the whole world of work a transparent and competitive market for talent.

LESS EVALUATION AND MORE COACHING

A key pillar of traditional talent management is performance management. Companies have gotten very good at setting KPIs, evaluating and ranking employees against these KPIs, and then providing feedback on an annual or semiannual basis. We would be the first to say that a strong performance orientation is absolutely vital for an organization to be successful. The most successful and admired organizations such as McKinsey, Google, Amazon, Apple, and Netflix would not be where they are today without a solid foundation of performance.

However, rather than managing performance through fear (what you want to avoid), it is better to enable performance through trust and support (what you can achieve). The previously mentioned organizations are some of the best in terms of providing clear guidelines for what it will take to be successful, fostering a culture of continuous and strengths-based feedback, "feedforward" (focusing on what you need to do and how you must perform in the context of the forthcoming objectives, rather than focusing on past performance) and coaching, and offering strong apprenticeship and support along the way. In other words, employees are made very well aware of what is required to succeed, starting during the interview process, and are then supported relentlessly to get there.

The same principles hold true for other organizations. If you believe people want to do well if you show them how, the vast majority will prove you right. Be clear about job expectations and simultaneously provide a proper chance to meet those expectations through apprenticeship, development opportunities, and continuous feedback. Using data and analytics can further support individuals and help them to understand where they are and how they can continue to improve. As they discover this themselves through the data made available to them, they are actually being coached rather than evaluated.

As performance data and educational micromodules are made available to employees, their experience can change from being less evaluated toward being more coached.

HANDING OVER THE KEYS OF DEVELOPMENT

Empowering individuals with their learning requires access to a YouTube-like ecosystem of educational micromodules. Learners can then shape their learning journeys. The reward is the development opportunities, access to jobs, and the work itself. Thankfully, various cloud-based skills taxonomies now exist to help categorize learning modules and certify the proficiency of learners.

It's not total anarchy though. In the same way that workforce planning still needs strategic analyses and direction setting, organizations still need to develop specific competencies that are part of their unique culture and way of working. Figure 30.1 outlines these differences.

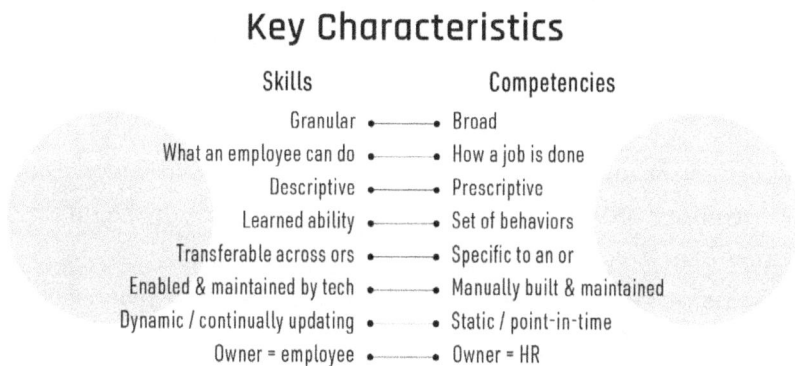

Key Characteristics

Skills	Competencies
Granular	Broad
What an employee can do	How a job is done
Descriptive	Prescriptive
Learned ability	Set of behaviors
Transferable across ors	Specific to an or
Enabled & maintained by tech	Manually built & maintained
Dynamic / continually updating	Static / point-in-time
Owner = employee	Owner = HR

Figure 30.1. Skills vs. competencies.[4]

SHAPE THE FUTURE OF WORK

Finally, enabling talent to perform at their best while growing and maintaining personal balance requires flexibility. The pandemic showed us that flexibility in terms of location can work—even when implemented at lightning speed. The next shift will be flexibility in terms of time. In fact, radical flexibility in terms of where, when, and how much to work has actually been shown to improve productivity by more than

50 percent in some instances, and employees are happier.[5] Enabling performance, growth, and well-being go hand in hand and are complementary and synergistic—these are not trade-offs.

> **A study showed that radical flexibility in terms of where, when, and how much to work improved productivity by more than 50 percent in some instances.**

All of this points toward new employment deals between many employers and employees. Of course, this new model is not perfect—no model is. Remote or hybrid working models can negatively affect employee growth, especially for younger generations, as there is less access to on-the-job coaching and apprenticeship.[6] Maintaining a shared sense of purpose and culture, and cultivating connectivity and informal networks can also be more challenging. So, for sure, opening up the door for a global talent pool represents all kinds of opportunities and pitfalls to navigate. And work-from-X models put new requirements on managers and leaders as well. But the future of work is here to stay.

The most successful organizations will often be those that take bold moves to experiment, learn, and adapt the model along the way, as they learn what does and does not work for *them*. Rather than be stuck in a model they inherited that is based on the industrial economy, each shapes their future in their own way. In such processes, they must listen to employees and let employees be a part of shaping the future organization. Over 50 percent of employees have stated that their organizations are not effective or only somewhat effective at empowering people to manage their own careers.[7] Fostering an active employee voice and using the insights to drive strategic and day-to-day decisions is no longer a nice-to-have, but critical to winning in the future.

The following chart can help you assess your current point of departure and where your biggest priorities lie in this area.

From . . .		To . . .
Talent management that aims to funnel employees through fixed career ladders	→	Talent enablement that supports employees creating their own ladders
Backward-looking performance evaluations against KPIs, every six or twelve months	→	Continuous, forward-looking performance coaching to help employees fulfill their potential
Fixed learning journeys depending on your career progression	→	Employee-led skills development that empowers them to continuously reinvent themselves
In the office from nine to five, five days a week	→	Flexibility in terms of when, where, and how much you work
Employees have a limited say on how work gets done and how the organization evolves	→	Active employee voice that helps shape the future of work model and culture

Chapter 31

MASLOW ON THE JOB

The year 2021 saw the birth of the Great Resignation, when workers started quitting their jobs at unprecedented rates. In the US alone, nearly 20 million workers left their jobs between April and August 2021, which is 60 percent higher than during the same period the previous year and equals about one-third of the US workforce on an annualized rate.[1] Other studies from the same period have shown that around 40 percent of workers said they were likely to quit their jobs within the next three to six months.[2]

SEEKING THE QUALITY LIFE

Some of the most important reasons why people are quitting have to do with them not feeling valued by their workplaces, not feeling valued by their managers, not feeling a sense of belonging, and not being able to achieve a balance between their work and personal lives.[3] During COVID-19, many employees discovered the simple yet priceless pleasures of cooking at home, kissing their kids good night, and pursuing hobbies they had put off for way too long. During 2020, for example, there was a marked increase in employee focus on mental well-being;

diversity, equity, and inclusion (DE&I); continued personal growth; and work flexibility.[4] Over two-thirds of salaried employees want to ditch the requirement to work five days a week in the office, and many are moving into freelance work.[5]

Perceptions around these topics have likely shifted for good, and organizations ignore them at their own risk. Sometimes it takes a crisis for an unsustainable situation to course-correct or even reset, and we are seeing a power shift from employers to employees, who are now more and more becoming consumers of jobs, rather than just providers.

Employees are increasingly becoming consumers of jobs, rather than just providers. This means that the job needs to be sold to them.

MACHINE-LIKE CULTURES
PRODUCE MACHINE-LIKE OUTPUTS

Literally any CEO can be heard saying, "Our people are our most valuable asset," but their cultures and daily practices often tell a different story. Legacy mindsets from early organizational forms often continue to prevail. We still see many leaders who view their organizations just as machines that can be configured and optimized, where each employee is just a cog in the wheel rather than as collections of individuals who bring with them each their own values, aspirations, and challenges. According to legacy mindsets, cultures and systems are designed to be rational, unsentimental, and productivity driven. Employees are assumed to be untrustworthy, are controlled through strong policies, and are granted limited decision-making rights. They are assumed to be driven primarily by their own financial self-interest, and they are primarily incentivized by things such as bonuses (which are also quickly taken away if targets aren't met).[6]

We're not saying that you shouldn't focus on business results or that aspects of these legacy mindsets aren't sometimes necessary, but the way to achieve results in a sustainable way has changed. Machine-like systems optimized for productivity rarely work in today's world.

There are many reasons for this. At its most basic, for humans to flourish, the answer is *not* to be in the same location for eight hours a day, doing repetitive work. Furthermore, the execution speed and variety of work tasks employees face each day are increasing. To compete in this environment, employees generally need greater trust and empowerment.

The contract between companies and employees has also changed. Long gone are the days where companies could offer lifetime employment and retirement packages in return for loyal service. Today, companies can and do fire employees much more frequently than before, and employees can and do change jobs much more frequently. Increasingly, loyalty demands more than a steady paycheck—it requires bringing humanity back to the center of operations.

So, the job market is getting faster, more fluid, and more flexible, and the world is moving from an industrial economy toward a precision and experience economy, where consumers, including job consumers, seek new, differentiated experiences that often meet higher-level needs than before. We might even call it a human economy to further differentiate it from the physical and knowledge-based work of the past.[7] This requires employees with more empathy, creativity, and judgment to work, plus behaviors that are underpinned by a human-centered culture.

As we move toward the experience economy, the demand for employees with more empathy, creativity, and judgment increases. This must be stimulated by the way organizations are managed.

One of the best examples of this is from Southwest Airlines, one of the leading airlines in North America. A passenger, Mark Dickinson, had bought a last-minute ticket because his grandson had tragically passed away. Although he reached LAX airport two hours before the flight, the length of the lines meant that he was sure he would miss his flight. He tried everything to skip the security lines, but to no avail. He arrived at the gate twelve minutes past gate closure and was devastated. To his surprise, the captain of the flight was waiting for him at the gate. Somehow, Mark's wife had gotten hold of a Southwest customer service representative by phone to tell them about the situation. The pilot, who made the decision based on compassion and a sense of shared humanity, said to Mark, "They can't go anywhere without me, and I wasn't going anywhere without you. Now relax. We'll get you there. And again, I'm so sorry [for your loss]."[8]

Can you imagine what this scenario might have looked like if a corresponding airline did not have the same compassionate and empowered culture as Southwest?

DESIGNING SYSTEMS FOR HUMANS TO FLOURISH

Human-centered organizations start with the belief that people want to perform well, they care about their customers, and they will do the right thing when given the chance. Clear goals and a strong performance orientation remain critical, but these organizations also understand that a more holistic approach is needed to unleash their employees' full potential. This holistic approach is often captured well in employee engagement models. They show the importance of things like

- Having the right equipment

- A conducive work environment

- Peers whom you like and trust

- Autonomy

- Flexibility

- Growth opportunities

- Clear goals

- A manager who supports, recognizes, and coaches you

- A manageable workload

- The ability to state your point of view without risk of retribution

- The alignment between your values and the organization's values

- Meaningful work[9]

MASLOW ON THE JOB

Think of it this way: we previously saw that generally, once the lower rungs of Maslow's pyramid had been filled, marginal consumption moved toward the higher levels. The same happens when organizations shift from seeing themselves as providers of jobs to marketing tasks to consumers of jobs. Meeting these elements of engagement will impact not only employee job satisfaction and loyalty but also important talent and business KPIs such as attrition, manager effectiveness, sales, innovation, productivity, and transformation success.

Some organizations believe that the choice between performance and engagement is a trade-off and a zero-sum game or that you can paper over the engagement cracks by offering isolated initiatives such as mental wellness webinars (cringe). For sure, there are instances where you might squeeze out more performance at the expense of an employee's well-being and engagement. This holds especially true in high-pressure businesses like start-ups, health care, and high finance. But these results are short-lived and may hurt the business in other ways. They may cause employees to burn out; they may crash long-term efficacy; they may perpetuate a poor employee value proposition; and they may drive top talent to competitors.

The reality is that human-centered cultures are win-win when done correctly. When organizations measure employee engagement and foster an active employee voice, they can remove roadblocks to employee well-being and performance at *the same time*.

EMBRACE THE WHOLE HUMAN

Employees often feel that they must act "professionally" and leave any personal issues at the door when they get to work. Managers, on their part, might believe it's better not to ask about anything personal and use their ignorance to their advantage. This is perhaps best summed up by the quote from the movie *The Godfather*: "It's not personal, Sonny. It's strictly business." This justification is often used when organizations make decisions that will have a negative impact on employees.

Human-centeredness starts by acknowledging that people are not just their nine-to-five selves. When you hire someone, you hire the whole person. They have real challenges that you cannot just pretend do not exist. An employer may not be responsible for fixing any obligations or challenges that employees have—such as family commitments or personal matters—but they are responsible for taking them into consideration. As such, organizations must shift from managing employee experience to managing employee life experience. This is not only the right thing to do, but it also has been shown to have a positive impact on the mental and physical well-being of employees, on employee loyalty and performance, and on the ability to attract top talent.[10]

> Organizations must shift from managing employee experience to employee *life* experience.

Moving to managing employee life experience requires a mindset shift across the organization, plus manager training, new people/HR policies, and actually treating employees as their most valuable assets. This can be measured through engagement surveys, which ideally are given and acted upon on a weekly basis.

Coupled with this is the concept of *wholeness*. If you want people to bring their whole selves to work and go above and beyond what is required, help them *be* their whole selves at work. This requires creating environments where people feel comfortable being who they are, warts and all. There is no shortage of research that shows that people and teams perform best where there is trust, acceptance, and psychological safety.[11]

One of the best descriptions of wholeness comes from ex-McKinsey consultant Frédéric Laloux and his pioneering work on reinventing organizations. Here, he refers to wholesome cultures as "practices that invite us to reclaim our inner wholeness and bring all of who we are to work, instead of with a narrow 'professional' self." These practices include the following:

- Fostering safe and supportive team environments

- Creating ground rules for healthy collaboration and defining acceptable and unaccepted practices

- Offering quiet spaces for reflection

- Cultivating meetings that allow people to express their full range of ideas, thoughts, and feelings

- Addressing any conflicts that arise[12]

Embedding these practices in reality often requires true culture shifts. This can be done by establishing people-centered values and embedding them into all aspects of the talent system (recruiting, feedback, learning and development, internal mobility choices), and ensuring leader behaviors, communication, and other organization systems all reinforce the desired behaviors. Culture change is never a quick fix and can be a multiyear journey—the key is to ensure the culture is moving in the same direction as the trends around you.

DIVERSITY, EQUITY, AND INCLUSION

We are also seeing an enhanced focus on diversity, equity, and inclusion. Chances are you've heard about the importance of DE&I, and the facts certainly don't lie. More diverse and inclusive organizations typically have higher financial performance, as well as healthier organizational cultures compared to their less diverse counterparts. In fact, this performance gap has been widening in recent years.[13]

The fact is that many organizations struggle to truly be diverse, equitable, and inclusive, and progress has been slow. For example, according to the World Economic Forum's Global Gender Gap report of 2020, it will take a hundred years to reach gender equality based on current trajectories. McKinsey has found that most organizations' efforts have stalled.[14] Of course, there can be statistical differences in what type of work the average man or woman prefers, but there should not be statistical obstacles against participation from one gender.

However, such obstacles can exist, and so can obstacles against hiring people from other cultures and races. This is troubling for many reasons, particularly because workforces are getting increasingly diverse and will continue to do so rapidly—after all, people are relocating more than before, and remote work opens up the possibility for companies to hire people from literally any part of the globe.

Addressing this challenge requires a systematic approach. Attention and reporting at the board and executive levels is critical, as are organization-wide priorities, revamped talent processes, and robust training on things such as biases and fostering inclusion and trust. DE&I can be measured, and leading organizations are taking a pulse on their efforts on a monthly or even weekly basis. Avoid a one-size-fits-all approach or ad-hoc initiatives or arbitrary KPIs that might incentivize the wrong behavior. Furthermore, remember that DE&I is very different depending on geography. For example, in the US there are stronger racial tensions than in many other parts of the world, while other countries in their own turns are grappling with class gaps, caste systems, or discrimination based on gender or nationality. Focusing, for instance, on racism in environments where it doesn't really exist can be counterproductive.

In many ways, the changed working habits during the COVID-19 pandemic brought attention to real human issues that for decades had been bubbling under the surface yet silenced when it really mattered. As tragic as the pandemic has been, it was also the catalyst for billions of people globally to reflect on what truly matters to them and begin to take a stronger stand. We've reached a tipping point where winning organizations of the future predominantly will be those that are people-forward and human-centered.

The following chart can help you assess your current point of departure and where your biggest priorities lie in this area.

From ...		To ...
Work processes optimized for an industrial or knowledge economy	→	Work processes optimized for an experience (or human) economy
Organization sees employees as a cog in a machine, incentivized by financial self-interest	→	Organization designed for human flourishing by meeting both basic and higher-level human needs
Focus on employee experience	→	Focus on employee life experience
Professional mask, 9-5 persona	→	Embracing whole person, warts and all
One-size-fits-all or ad-hoc DE&I approach	→	Systematic DE&I strategy that mobilizes and transforms the full organization

CONCLUSION

P hew! We've covered a lot of ground about how the world is evolving and what the underlying forces driving these changes are. We've seen that the Five Cs of Innovation—when present together—can unleash innovations of all sorts. These include exponential supertrends, which can trigger radical changes in technologies, markets, lifestyles, organization forms, and more. These supertrends need to be understood by anyone hoping to master the future.

Such changes have created huge opportunities in the past. And as the speed of such change is accelerating, the same applies going forward, just faster and faster. This is all great.

However, in order to keep up with these changes, we must continuously adapt. Going forward, we must become faster, more fluid, and more flexible in how we think and act and build new levels of awareness of ourselves and others.

At the *individual* level, we discussed a number of approaches that can assist us through the accelerating blur. These include hacks for self-motivating, learning, and adapting—all the time. As the external environment around you evolves, so must your ability to understand yourself and your surroundings.

We outlined eight Future Fit mindsets centered on personal accountability and ownership, exponentiality, a beginner's mind, personal growth, abundance, serendipity, compounding, and resilience.

We believe these mindsets reinforce each other, and that once you've reset your thinking to incorporate them, becoming Future Fit won't be nearly as daunting as it may sound.

At the *organizational* level, we discussed ten key shifts that every organization should consider. Of course, every organization has its own circumstances, so *consider* is as far as we will go, but we find that the shifts are typical for organizations that outperform in modern, dynamic environments. These shifts are about values, strategic direction, market approaches, speed, flexibility, technology implementation, innovation, talent, culture, leadership, and more.

The way we see it, there is overwhelming indication that the future will—mostly—be far better than the present, just as the present—mostly—is far better than the past. However, understanding how and why the world changes takes some effort. And learning to contribute well to it—and to thrive in it—requires insight, reflection, and determination. We hope this book has helped you on this journey. We learned a lot as we wrote it, and we are grateful that we got this opportunity.

ENDNOTES

You can find endnotes to each chapter, self-tests for future readiness, inspirational material, and much more here:

www.frommalthustomars.com

ACKNOWLEDGMENTS

No book is created in a vacuum. Indeed, *From Malthus to Mars* is the result of significant hyper-sociality, including many conversations with some of the most interesting people around. We want to thank everyone who was a part of this journey, contributed insights, and challenged us along the way. A special thank you to—

- All the futurists, management coaches, and colleagues at Supertrends—your wisdom and experience sharpened the book and made it a much better product

- The 160+ experts who contributed to the Supertrends timelines and continue to refine our map of the future

- Greenleaf Book Publishing and Fast Company Press, who have been true partners throughout the process

- Samira and Lærke for your input and support throughout the writing process—including your dedication and patience every time we want to "quickly shoot a video about the book to post online!"

And finally, a special thank you to you, the reader, for taking the time to explore this book. Please do connect with us online so we can continue the conversation and connect the dots forward as we jointly speed into the blur.

ABOUT THE AUTHORS

LARS TVEDE (B. 1957) is an investor, award-winning serial entrepreneur, and futurist. He has founded/cofounded thirteen companies, including the top-performing venture fund Nordic Eye and the forecasting company Supertrends AG, which uses AI and crowdsourcing to outline and visualize innovation and supertrends. He is the winner of numerous awards, including Red Herring Global 100 Award, IMD Top Swiss Start-up Award, Bully Award, and Adam Smith Award. Lars is the author of eighteen other books, including *The Psychology of Finance, The Creative Society, Entrepreneur*, and *Supertrends*.

NICOLAI CHEN NIELSEN (B. 1987) is an entrepreneur, educator, and adviser on the topics of leadership development, personal growth, and organizations of the future. He is a partner at Supertrends AG and previously an associate partner at McKinsey & Company, where he was responsible for McKinsey's latest research on leadership at scale. He has designed and delivered development programs that have reached more than one million employees globally. Nicolai has coauthored the books *Leadership at Scale* and *Return on Ambition*, the latter which was shortlisted by GetAbstract as one of the five best books among 10,000 books in 2021 and won the gold medal in the American Benjamin Franklin Book Award in 2022.